EIGHTH ARMY'S GREATEST VICTORIES

Eighth Army's Greatest Victories

Alam Halfa to Tunis 1942–43

by

ADRIAN STEWART

LEO COOPER

First published in Great Britain in 1999 by
Leo Cooper
an imprint of
Pen & Sword Books Ltd
47 Church Street
Barnsley
South Yorkshire
S70 2AS

ISBN 0 85052 6663

Typeset in 10/12.5pt Plantin by
Phoenix Typesetting, Ilkley, West Yorkshire

Printed by
Redwood Books Limited,
Trowbridge, Wiltshire

To the officers and men
of the Eighth Army
who shared their experiences with me.

CONTENTS

ILLUSTRATIONS

MAPS

ACKNOWLEDGEMENTS

The author is grateful for having been allowed to quote extracts from the following works:

Operation Victory
> Reproduced by kind permission of the estate of the late Major General Sir Francis de Guingand and of Hodder & Stoughton Limited.

Monty: The Making of a General 1887–1942
> Reproduced by kind permission of Nigel Hamilton and of Penguin Books Limited.

A Full Life
> Reproduced by kind permission of the estate of the late Lieutenant General Sir Brian Horrocks and of HarperCollins Limited.

The North African Campaign 1940–43
> Reproduced by kind permission of the estate of the late General Sir William Jackson and of B.T. Batsford Limited.

The Life and Death of the Afrika Korps
> Reproduced by kind permission of the estate of the late Ronald Lewin and of B.T. Batsford Limited.

The Rommel Papers
> Reproduced by kind permission of the estate of the late B.H. Liddell Hart and of HarperCollins Limited.

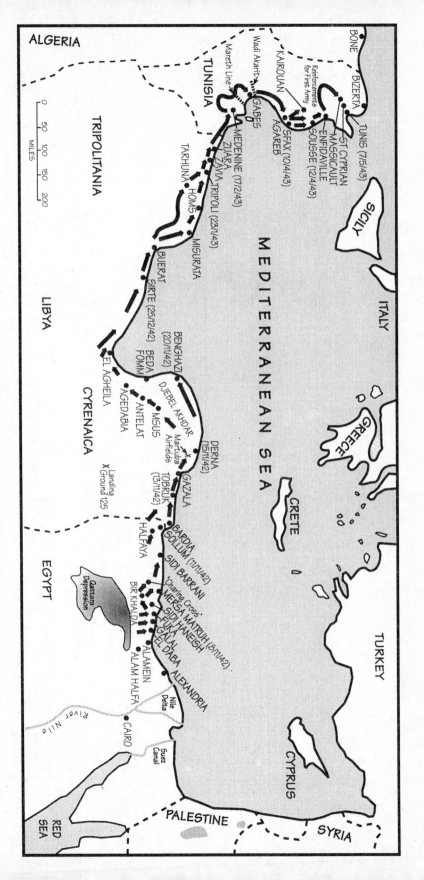

MAP 1: EIGHTH ARMY'S GREATEST VICTORIES: ALAM HALFA TO TUNIS 1942–43.
The dates after place-names indicate when they were reached by men from Eighth Army

ALGERIA

TUNISIA

BONE

BIZERTA

TUNIS (7/5/43)

ST CYPRIAN

MASSICAULT

ENFIDAVILLE

SOUSSE (12/4/43)

SFAX (10/4/43)

AGAREB

Reinforcements for First Army

KAIROUAN

GABES

MEDENINE (17/2/43)

Mareth Line

Wadi Akarit

ZUARA

ZAVIA

TRIPOLI (23/1/43)

TARHUNA

HOMS

MISURATA

BUERAT

SIRTE (25/12/42)

TRIPOLITANIA

LIBYA

SICILY

ITALY

M E D I T E R R A N E A N   S E A

GREECE

CRETE

TURKEY

BENGHAZI (20/11/42)

BEDA FOMM

EL AGHEILA

AGEDABIA

ANTELAT

MSUS

DJEBEL AKHDAR

Martuba Airfields

DERNA (15/11/42)

GAZALA

TOBRUK (13/11/42)

Landing X Ground 125

CYRENAICA

HALFAYA

BARDIA

SOLLUM (11/11/42)

SIDI BARRANI

'Charing Cross'

MERSA MATRUH (8/11/42)

SIDI HANEISH

FUKA

GALAL

EL DABA

ALEXANDRIA

BIR KHALDA

ALAMEIN

ALAM HALFA

Qattara Depression

EGYPT

Nile Delta

River Nile

CAIRO

Suez Canal

CYPRUS

PALESTINE

SYRIA

RED SEA

```
0   50   100   150   200
        MILES
```

So now to these campaigns – to these golden pages
of the history of British arms.

Major General Sir Francis de Guingand,
Chief of Staff, Eighth Army in *Operation Victory*,
referring to Eighth Army's victories in North Africa.

Introduction

THE FORGOTTEN VICTORIES

By mid-April 1943, the Second World War had raged for over three-and-a-half years and although even the most pessimistic could feel that the tide of Axis conquest had at last begun to ebb, the prospects for the future still appeared bleak in the extreme. The Allied powers had now to liberate the occupied territories, then strike at the heart of the enemy homelands. It was a task which many feared would prove endless.

There was ample excuse for this belief. In North Africa, an Anglo-American army had for four months been striving in vain to break through the Axis defences on the western border of Tunisia. In Russia, the Germans, recovering with remarkable resilience from the disasters of the previous winter, had begun a new offensive. In North-West Europe, France, the Low Countries, Denmark and Norway were still in enemy hands; in South-East Asia, so were Burma and Malaya. In the Pacific, the Americans had captured the strategically vital island of Guadalcanal in February 1943, but this had taken them six months and even then the Japanese had successfully evacuated the remains of their garrison.

There had, however, been one Allied triumph which provided a dramatic contrast to the slow progress made elsewhere – an achievement to delight and justify the resolute, to astonish and hearten the gloomy. In less than six months, the British Eighth Army had conquered the enemy-occupied part of Egypt, the whole of Cyrenaica, eastern province of Italy's North African colony of Libya, the whole of its western province, Tripolitania, and a good three-quarters of Tunisia. It had also, as would shortly transpire, ensured that the remains of the two Axis armies in North Africa could not be evacuated.

No wonder then that de Guingand refers to these campaigns as 'golden pages'. No wonder that General Sir David Fraser in his history of the British Army in the Second World War, *And We Shall Shock Them*, declares that

1

Eighth Army's 'succession of victories, its triumphant march from one end of North Africa to the other' had already become 'renowned and will remain immortal'. Yet in practice most later accounts of the fighting in North Africa, let alone those of the Second World War in general, have tended to dismiss Eighth Army's conquests after the great Battle of El Alamein with only the briefest of descriptions.

El Alamein admittedly is normally described in some detail – and rightly so – but even here justice is rarely done to Eighth Army as a whole. De Guingand for instance reviews the battle by reference to what he calls 'the stepping stones to victory'. All of these are High Command decisions. Vital though these undeniably were, the emphasis placed upon them tends to hide the ultimate reason why victory was achieved. As Brigadier C.E. Lucas Phillips, an artillery officer in Eighth Army at the time, points out in his *Alamein*: 'Under the direction of a commander of the first order, it was very much a "soldier's battle".'

Moreover it has frequently been overlooked that the mutual trust between the commander and his soldiers which, Field Marshal Montgomery tells us in his *Memoirs*, 'was to make Alamein possible', had been forged in the earlier battle of Alam Halfa. And Alam Halfa also, as de Guingand sadly remarks, 'is hardly ever spoken of nowadays and comparatively few knew it took place. It deserves study and a prominent position in our military history.'

This is doubly the case because prior to Alam Halfa there had been a long period during which the Allied forces in North Africa had endured continuous disappointments. It was not that they had known only defeat. There had been advances, but these had always seemed to be followed by retreats. There had been successes, but these had never seemed to bring any lasting benefits. Hopes had been raised, but they had been dashed again so often that there were few indeed who had not begun to wonder whether final victory would ever be achieved.

Perhaps because they left such lasting scars, these ordeals have by contrast received much subsequent attention. Nonetheless it seems right to relate them in outline once more, for they provide the sombre background against which the forgotten victories of Eighth Army shine all the more brightly.

Chapter 1

THE DJEBEL STAKES

The war in North Africa had begun as long ago as 10 June 1940, when the Italian dictator Benito Mussolini had declared war on a Britain he believed was doomed, though it was only on 13 September that his troops, under Marshal Rudolfo Graziani, finally invaded Egypt. Four days later they had captured a few white mud-brick buildings, a mosque and a landing ground which the Italian communiqués elevated to the status of the 'town' of Sidi Barrani. Exhausted by this achievement, they then halted, to begin building a chain of forts stretching off to the south-west.

The battleground over which the rival armies were to fight was the Western Desert, extending southward from the Mediterranean, westward from the River Nile, to cover most of Egypt and Libya. Not here the golden sand dunes of romantic imagination. Indeed the 'sand' was really gritty dust, providing a normally shallow carpet over a rock base that frequently emerged to form low ridges. There were also cliffs, or escarpments as they were called, where the land climbed from the coastal plain to the inland plateau. The largest of these, near the Egyptian frontier-town of Sollum, rose to a height of 600 feet.

Nor was the 'sand' golden. Over most of the area it was a tawny brownish-yellow, becoming grey towards the coast where the underlying rock was limestone, though the Mediterranean beaches were a pure, dazzling white. And in the Djebel Akhdar, the 3,000 feet high Green Mountains in the Cyrenaican 'Bulge' between Benghazi and Derna, there were fertile valleys with a reddish soil that reminded many an Englishman of Devonshire.

In this harsh wasteland, where the days were usually stiflingly hot, with the winds driving the dust before them to permeate everywhere and into every-thing, where the nights were often bitterly cold, where the armies had to be supplied not only with petrol and ammunition, but with food and water, communications were vital. Yet in the whole of the Desert there were just two metalled roads: the Via Balbia in Libya, which hugged the Mediterranean coast all the way from Tripoli to the Egyptian frontier, and the less well constructed coastal highway in Egypt, originally running from Alexandria to Sidi Barrani but later extended to the frontier. Both were singularly inadequate as well as being exceptionally vulnerable to air attack.

Moreover the distances involved were immense. Hence the paradox that the more successful an army might be, the weaker it became, because the farther it advanced, the less easily it could be supplied. Major General J.F.C. Fuller in his book *The Decisive Battles of the Western World*, compares each side's line of communications to 'a piece of elastic' which could only 'be stretched with comparative safety to between 300 and 400 miles from its base – Tripoli on the one hand and Alexandria on the other'. If it were stretched further, it would snap. Yet by the coastal road, Tripoli and Alexandria were almost 1,400 miles apart.

Nor were difficulties limited to supply-lines in the Desert; supply-lines *to* the Desert had also to be considered. In theory the Axis powers had much the easier task here because they dominated the Mediterranean, thereby compelling the British to send their convoys some 14,000 miles round the Cape of Good Hope. By contrast, the distance from the port of Messina in the north of Sicily to Tripoli was only 350 miles.

Fortunately for the Allied cause, 60 miles south of Sicily, right in the path of the supply routes, lay the island-fortress of Malta, from which surface warships, submarines and aircraft could decimate convoys to North Africa. Thus by a strange twist of fate the most important focal point of the Desert War lay outside the Desert. As Rommel would later point out: 'With Malta in our hands, the British would have had little chance of exercising any further control over convoy traffic in the central Mediterranean . . . It has the lives of many thousands of German and Italian soldiers on its conscience.'[1] The Italian Official History sadly remarks: 'Malta was the rock upon which our hopes in the Mediterranean foundered.'

Because Malta was vital, one of the crucial prizes in the Desert was the airfield complex at Martuba, just south of the town of Derna in the north-east of the Cyrenaican 'Bulge'. From here British fighters could cover convoys bound for Malta. It was not for nothing that when such protection was not afforded the seas between Cyrenaica and Crete became known as 'Bomb Alley'.

The logistic problems also emphasized the value of two other prizes: Benghazi in the north-west of the 'Bulge' and Tobruk which lies to the south-east of Derna. These were the only sheltered harbours between Tripoli and Alexandria which could accommodate sizeable ships. If they could be brought into use, they would shorten the distances which the 'piece of elastic' would be asked to stretch.

Finally, mention should be made of the most important 'bottlenecks' on the supply lines. One was at El Agheila on the western border of Cyrenaica, where the coastal plain was hemmed in by deep sand, formidable 'wadis' (dry watercourses) and salt marshes which approached very close to the sea. General Sir Harold Alexander would call this 'the strongest position in Libya'.

In Egypt, the strongest position took its name from a railway station that stood on a small ridge – Tell el Alamein, the hill of twin cairns. Inland other more prominent ridges could be found, until, 38 miles to the south, Qarat el Himeimat (Mount Himeimat) rose to nearly 700 feet. But beyond Himeimat, the ground fell away sharply into the Qattara Depression, a vast chocolate-coloured quicksand lying 200 feet below sea level, through which no vehicles could pass; beyond which again was the almost equally impassible Great Sand Sea. The Alamein position was also dangerously close to Alexandria, but the logistic considerations previously described meant that this was really one of its advantages.[2]

General Sir Archibald Wavell, the British Commander-in-Chief, Middle East, was well aware of the value of Alamein as a defensive position, but his main concern in the closing months of 1940 was with planning to attack the Italians at Sidi Barrani. Though heavily outnumbered, he was emboldened by the knowledge that his enemies were not adequately equipped to fight a modern war – their tanks, artillery and fighter aircraft all being grossly inferior. In addition, their forts, though stocked with every available luxury, were neither properly protected nor mutually supporting, while south of one of them – Nibeiwa – there was a gap in the defences, 15 miles wide, which was not even patrolled.

On the night of 8th/9th December, Wavell's Western Desert Force, under the tactical command of Lieutenant General Sir Richard O'Connor, passed through this gap to assault first Nibeiwa, then the other forts in sequence, from the rear. By the 11th, all the Italian positions from Sidi Barrani south-ward were in British hands, and 73 tanks, 237 guns, over 1,000 vehicles, over 38,000 men had been captured. British casualties totalled 624. According to General Sir William Jackson in *The North African Campaign 1940–43*, the operation – it was code-named COMPASS – was 'fought with professional standards which were never again achieved by the British in the Western Desert until Montgomery won El Alamein'.

Encouraged by this success and by the fact that the Royal Air Force had achieved complete superiority over the battlefield, Wavell authorized O'Connor to strike westward into Cyrenaica. His offensive culminated in a daring dash across the base of the Cyrenaican 'Bulge' south of the Djebel Akhdar by 7th Armoured Division, which on 5 February 1941 cut the coastal road at Beda Fomm, trapping the retiring Italian forces. By the 7th, their last attempt to escape had been broken – 120 tanks, about 200 guns and 20,000 prisoners were taken, while 100 more tanks were found wrecked on the battlefield. In almost exactly two months the Western Desert Force had captured a total of 130,000 men, 1,300 guns and 400 tanks. Its own losses had been 500 killed, 1,373 wounded and 55 missing. Marshal Graziani resigned. It seemed that the war in North Africa was as good as over.

It was not to be. On the contrary, the Allied soldiers had only just begun that series of advances followed by retreats, of successes followed by failures that would characterize the Desert War prior to Alam Halfa. This depressing pattern, which would be known by various sardonic names – 'The Gazala Gallop', 'The Benghazi Handicap', 'The Djebel Stakes' – and which would eventually cause a creeping cynicism to spread through the Middle East, was already being foreshadowed even while 7th Armoured was sealing the fate of the Italians.

For on 6 February, Adolf Hitler was giving his orders to General Erwin Rommel, whom he had personally selected to command the troops he intended to send to the aid of his faltering ally – they were formally named the *Deutches Afrika Korps* on the 19th. This contained 150 tanks, half of them Mark IIs mounting only machine guns, but the rest were Mark IIIs or IVs armed with a short-barrelled 50mm or 75mm gun respectively. The Italian Ariete Armoured Division had also been placed under Rommel's orders. He could call on four Italian infantry divisions, stiffened by two German machine-gun battalions. Best of all, he commanded two *Panzerjäger* (anti-tank) battalions equipped with not only old 37mm weapons but also a fair number of highly efficient long-barrelled 50mm ones. He even had a handful of the magnificent 88mm anti-aircraft guns, which in their desert role of tank-destroyer would earn a reputation as formidable as it was well deserved.

By contrast, the Western Desert Force, now in the hands of Lieutenant General Philip Neame VC, was woefully weak, for Prime Minister Winston Churchill, with Wavell's approval, had decided to dispatch large military and air forces to Greece, a country already at war with Italy and now threatened by a German invasion as well. The only units still remaining in Cyrenaica were Major General Leslie Morshead's 9th Australian Division, then only partially trained, and Major General Gambier-Parry's 2nd Armoured Division, which was new to the Desert. The majority of its seventy tanks were light ones, less than half being cruisers with the 2-pounder guns that could match those of the Germans, and only twenty-two of these cruisers were fit for combat.

On 31 March, Rommel in his turn embarked on an audacious offensive, and by 8 April, his success appeared to be total: the Cyrenaican 'Bulge' was in his hands; every one of 2nd Armoured Division's tanks had been destroyed; Neame, Gambier-Parry and O'Connor, who had recently joined Neame as his adviser, were all prisoners of war.[3]

Fortunately Morshead's Australians had retreated safely to Tobruk, thus depriving Rommel of a valuable port and posing a constant threat to his supply lines. German light forces, slipping round Tobruk, pressed on to the Egyptian frontier, but beyond Sollum they were brought to an abrupt halt by the British 22nd Guards Brigade, led by a man who would become legendary in the Desert, Brigadier William 'Strafer' Gott.

Wavell, having been reinforced, then launched two offensives of his own on 15 May and 15 June, but both ended in failure, the latter – operation BATTLEAXE – with heavy losses of tanks, mainly inflicted by the German 88s. Casualties in men were light but among them indirectly was the British Commander-in-Chief. On 21 June, the day before the German invasion of Russia, Churchill, feeling that Wavell had been exhausted by his continuous responsibilities, replaced him with General Sir Claude Auchinleck, previously C-in-C, India. Provided with massive reinforcements originally designated for the Far East – to such an extent that Captain B.H. Liddell Hart in his *History of the Second World War* has claimed that it was really Rommel who 'produced the fall of Singapore' – Auchinleck set about preparing for yet another offensive.

At midnight on 26 September, the soldiers entrusted with this offensive received a new title which they were to make immortal: the Eighth Army. To command this, Auchinleck – against the advice of Churchill and the Chiefs of Staff – appointed Lieutenant General Sir Alan Cunningham. It was an odd decision for Cunningham had only recently reached Egypt from East Africa and was quite inexperienced in armoured warfare.

The Army's main infantry unit was XIII Corps under Lieutenant General Godwin-Austen. This contained the three brigades of 2nd New Zealand Division, led by Major General Bernard Freyberg, and the three brigades of Major General Frank Messervy's 4th Indian Division – in reality a British-Indian Division since it was the usual practice for the men of one battalion in each Indian Army brigade to be British while those of the other two were Indians or Gurkhas. The 1st Army Tank Brigade provided support.

The main body of the armour, however, was to be found in 7th Armoured Division which contained three armoured brigades plus the infantry and artillery of a support group. Commanded by Gott, now a major general, it formed part of Lieutenant General Willoughby Norrie's XXX Corps, as did the infantry of 1st South African Division – 22nd Guards Brigade and two South African brigades – under Major General Brink. Eighth Army also controlled the garrison of Tobruk which now consisted of 70th (British) Division, 1st Polish Brigade and 32nd Army Tank Brigade. 2nd South African Division was in reserve. So were some 500 tanks to reinforce the 710 gun-armed tanks already in the front line. The Army Tank Brigades had heavy tanks – Matildas or the later Valentines – while 7th Armoured had the faster, lighter cruisers, mainly Crusaders or the new American Stuarts, which were rechristened 'Honeys' by their delighted crews.

Against these forces was ranged an Axis army nominally commanded by the Italian General Ettore Bastico, but taking its operational orders from Rommel. Its armoured strength was contained in the *Afrika Korps* and the Italian XX Corps. The former under Lieutenant General Ludwig Crüwell contained the 15th and 21st Panzer Divisions; the latter under Lieutenant General Gastone Gambara consisted of the Ariete (Armoured) and Trieste (Motorized) Divisions. Crüwell had only 174 gun-armed tanks; Gambara only 146 obsolete ones. The infantry numbered five Italian divisions plus a newly-formed German one which included former members of the French Foreign Legion and which was shortly to be given the famous name of 90th Light Division. Finally Rommel had the priceless aid of thirty-five 88mm and ninety-six 50mm anti-tank guns.

Eighth Army's supporting air arm, the Western Desert Air Force – in practice the word 'western' was rarely used – also outnumbered its opponents. Under the command of the New Zealander Air Vice-Marshal Arthur Coningham, who in turn was responsible to the Air Officer Commanding-in-Chief, Air Marshal Sir Arthur Tedder, were one Free French and five British squadrons equipped with Blenheim bombers, two South African squadrons flying Marylands, No. 24 Squadron SAAF with the latest Bostons, and the equivalent of no less than nineteen fighter squadrons: thirteen British, three South African, two Australian and one Southern Rhodesian. These flew half-squadrons of Beaufighters and Fleet Air Arm Martlets, five full squadrons of Tomahawks and thirteen squadrons of Hurricanes, among them No. 80 Squadron RAF equipped with 'Hurribombers' which carried four 40lb bombs under each wing. In all Coningham controlled some 500 serviceable aircraft, while there were large reserves, including Wellington bombers, back in the area of the Nile Delta. By contrast, Major General Frölich, the *Fliegerführer Afrika*, could muster about 300 serviceable machines, only one-third of which were German.

In addition, Rommel's ground and air forces alike were desperately short of supplies, especially petrol. The main reason for this was that the convoys across the Mediterranean were coming under constant attack from Malta. In September, 28 per cent of all cargoes sent to Rommel failed to reach him. In October, the proportion lost was 21 per cent. In November, it rose to a staggering 63 per cent.

Yet when Eighth Army began its great offensive, which was rather dramatically code-named Operation CRUSADER, on 18 November 1941, all these numerical advantages were forfeited by a singularly bad plan. For this, as the British Official History[4] makes clear, the main blame must fall on Auchinleck. His staff prepared it; he personally approved it; and it was then presented by him as an established entity to his newly-arrived and inexperienced Army Commander.

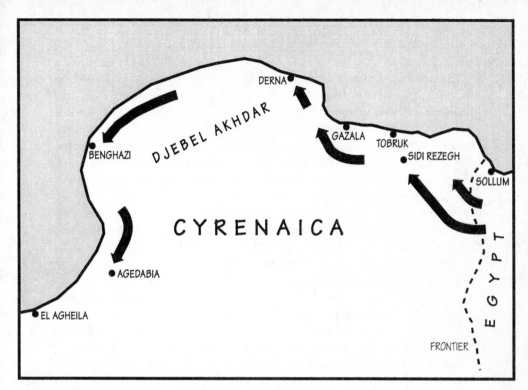

MAP 2A: The Djebel Stakes. Eighth Army's offensives.

MAP 2B: The Djebel Stakes. *Panzerarmee Afrika's* offensives.

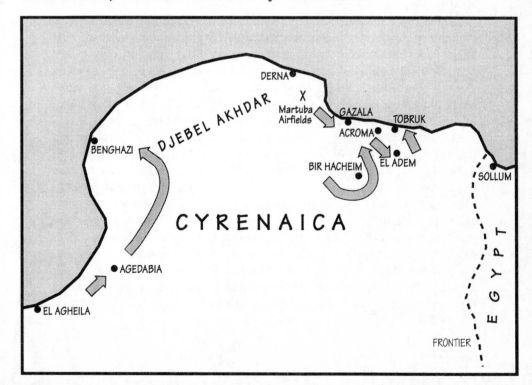

The basis of Auchinleck's plan was that while XIII Corps pinned down the Axis troops in the frontier positions, XXX Corps would destroy the German Panzer Divisions, after which the relief of Tobruk, the reconquest of Cyrenaica, the advance to Tripoli, would follow as a matter of course. Unfortunately Auchinleck never gave any indication as to how this desirable aim might be achieved. As Captain Liddell Hart points out, 'an armoured force is not in itself suited to be an immediate objective. For it is a fluid force, not easily fixed as infantry formations can be.'

It was perhaps inevitable therefore that during the first three days of Operation CRUSADER, 7th Armoured Division should have been split up in an attempt to track down its elusive target. Fortunately Rommel made the same mistake, dispersing the tanks and infantry of Crüwell's *Afrika Korps* equally widely.[5] Thereby, as Major General Freiherr von Mellenthin, who was then on his Intelligence staff, bluntly states in *Panzer Battles*, he 'missed a great opportunity' of winning the battle 'very easily'.

Even so the British suffered the heavier losses in the series of individual clashes with enemy tanks or anti-tank guns that now took place. On 19 November, a British armoured brigade, aided by the anti-tank guns of Brigadier 'Jock' Campbell's Support Group, seized the Sidi Rezegh aerodrome to the south-east of Tobruk, destroying nineteen enemy aircraft on the ground; but by the evening of the 22nd, despite desperate resistance during which Campbell's inspirational leadership won a VC, the Germans had regained this vital position and it was they who had the greater number of tanks in the battle-zone.

Elsewhere events had proved more satisfactory. The Desert Air Force, though suffering severe losses, was slowly gaining control of the skies. XIII Corps had wheeled round the flank of the frontier defences, with Freyberg's New Zealanders already moving westward towards Tobruk. Nonetheless Crüwell believed he could break British resistance with one last great effort on 23 November. This happened to be the Sunday before Advent, or in the Lutheran calendar, '*Totensonntag*' – the 'Sunday of the Dead'.

At 1500 on '*Totensonntag*', Crüwell's tanks, accompanied by artillery and infantry in lorries, accordingly made what General Jackson calls a 'charge en masse' against 5th South African Brigade which had now joined the remnants of 7th Armoured. The South Africans were not easily broken. By nightfall when their defence finally disintegrated, Crüwell had lost seventy-two of his 162 remaining tanks. In one panzer regiment alone, both the battalion commanders and five of the six company commanders were dead or wounded. The *Afrika Korps* could not survive that scale of casualties for very long. Crüwell, says Ronald Lewin in *The Life and Death of the Afrika Korps*, had 'cut the heart out' of his command. As if that was not enough, on 24 November, Rommel removed his surviving panzers from the battle area altogether, sending them eastward in a daring but reckless attack on the forces engaged with his frontier garrisons.

Yet these actions did have one dangerous consequence. The inexperienced Cunningham, who had already received greatly exaggerated accounts of the losses incurred by his own armour, began to think that the situation was lost. Happily, Auchinleck, not being so closely involved, was able to take a more realistic view, aided by the fact that Norrie, Godwin-Austen and even the senior General Staff Officer at Eighth Army HQ, Brigadier Galloway, all made clear their belief that the offensive should continue. On the 26th, Cunningham was relieved of his command. It is only just to relate that on his return to Britain he filled several important posts with distinction.

Cunningham was replaced by Auchinleck's Deputy Chief of the General Staff, Major General Neil Ritchie. This too was a strange choice for Ritchie lacked experience of high command in battle as well as of desert operations generally; he was also junior to both his corps commanders. Not that this mattered for the moment, because, ironically enough, as Field Marshal Lord Carver, who at that time was one of Norrie's staff officers, points out in his *Dilemmas of the Desert War*, while all this drama was taking place, 'the situation had been largely restored, not by any direct contribution of Auchinleck's, but by the toughness of the New Zealanders and the determination of Freyberg, egged on by Godwin-Austen, to push westward towards Tobruk'. Ignorant alike of the activities of Auchinleck and Rommel, Freyberg on the night of 26 November linked up with the Tobruk garrison. This compelled Rommel to hurry back from the frontier. By 1 December, he had driven Freyberg away from Sidi Rezegh, again isolating Tobruk, but suffering further crippling losses in the process. By the 6th, he had only forty tanks left.

Both sides were by now exhausted, but whereas the British could throw fresh soldiers, notably 2nd South African Division, into the fight, Rommel learned on 7 December that he could expect no troop reinforcements for at least a month. With considerable moral courage therefore, he abandoned his frontier garrisons – whom the South Africans had forced to surrender by 17 January 1942 – to fall back, first to Gazala, then all the way to El Agheila. By 6 January he was safely behind 'the strongest position in Libya'.

Meanwhile other factors were conspiring to reverse the result of CRUSADER. Rommel's Führer had come to appreciate the importance of Malta. On 2 December, he had ordered *Fliegerkorps* II, previously operating in Russia, to Sicily. Here it joined with *Fliegerkorps* X in the Balkans to form *Luftflotte* (Air Fleet) 2 under the command of Field Marshal Albert Kesselring. If Italian aircraft are added, Kesselring could muster some 2,000 warplanes. His orders from Hitler were admirably precise. He was to 'ensure safe lines of communication to North Africa' by bringing about 'the suppression of Malta'.

Kesselring duly embarked on his task to the utmost of his very considerable ability. Supplies began to reach Rommel again, but although Auchinleck was warned of this by intercepted enemy signals – the celebrated 'Ultra' Intelligence – he ignored the danger, informing Churchill that he was 'convinced the enemy is hard pressed, more than we dared think perhaps'. Just nine days after this optimistic forecast, on 21 January 1942, Rommel's command, now rechristened *Panzerarmee Afrika*, again took the offensive. Rommel could collect together only eighty-four German and eighty-nine Italian tanks and in practice his advance was carried out almost entirely by 15th and 21st Panzer and 90th Light Divisions, but he enjoyed all the advantages conferred by having achieved total surprise.

Moreover Eighth Army's logistic situation was most unhealthy – the 'piece of elastic' was stretched to breaking-point. The only troops west of Tobruk were the men of Godwin-Austen's XIII Corps, which now consisted of 1st Armoured Division under Messervy, 4th Indian Division under Major General Francis Tuker and 200th Guards Brigade (the old 22nd Brigade renumbered). Their commanders wished to concentrate them at Benghazi or Agedabia, 80 miles by road north-east of El Agheila, but Auchinleck, believing Rommel to be 'hard pressed' was determined to keep in contact with his enemy at El Agheila, and Ritchie, 'knowing his Commander-in-Chief's wishes', as the Official History puts it, 'was not the man to act otherwise than with energy and enthusiasm in giving effect to them'. The result was that XIII Corps had been scattered all over western Cyrenaica.

According to Field Marshal Carver, 'Auchinleck must bear the blame for placing Ritchie, Godwin-Austen and their subordinates in a fundamentally unsound position.' This was made worse after Rommel's attack had achieved an initial success. Godwin-Austen now wished to withdraw from Benghazi, Ritchie reluctantly agreed, but on 25 January, Auchenleck, who had just arrived at Eighth Army Headquarters, countermanded the orders. As Captain Liddell Hart points out, his intervention merely 'resulted in the British becoming spread out and static', as well as completely confused as to their leaders' intentions.

By 5 February, the conflict had died down. Rommel was back at Gazala, Godwin-Austen, disgusted by the way command had been taken out of his hands, had resigned, and the British were left to wonder how they had let the same disaster happen two years running. Worst of all, since Gazala was 70 miles south-east of Derna, the Martuba airfields were again in German hands. As a result, Kesselring's aircraft could dominate the convoy routes to Malta, which faced an ever-mounting danger of being starved into submission.

Churchill was horrified both by the threat to the island-fortress and by Auchinleck's apparent lack of concern over its fate. His views were shared by the Chief of the Imperial General Staff, General Sir Alan Brooke, who considered that Auchinleck had 'entirely failed to realize the importance of Malta'. It was therefore with the full consent of the Chiefs of Staff that on 10 May, Churchill signalled to Auchinleck: 'We are determined that Malta shall not be allowed to fall without a battle being fought by your whole army for its retention.'[6] Faced with this choice of obedience or resignation, Auchinleck reluctantly agreed to attack in mid-June. Hardly had he done so, however, when the 'Ultra' Intelligence revealed that Rommel intended to attack first on 27 May.

Auchinleck awaited the assault with considerable confidence. Eighth Army's defensive positions, collectively called the Gazala Line, were strongly held and well protected by minefields. They were occupied by XIII Corps now led by Gott, who had been promoted once more to lieutenant general. In the north was 1st South African Division under Major General Dan Pienaar. Then came Major General Ramsden's 50th (British) Division, of which one brigade, the 150th, was positioned some five miles south of the other two. Finally ten miles further south still, Brigadier General Koenig's Free French Brigade manned the fortified 'box' at Bir Hacheim (pronounced and sometimes spelt Bir Hakim). 1st and 32nd Army Tank Brigades containing 110 Matildas and 167 Valentines supported the infantry. 2nd South African Division held Tobruk. 5th Indian Division was in reserve.

Norrie's XXX Corps was made up of 1st Armoured Division under Major General Herbert Lumsden and 7th Armoured Division under Messervy, which between them contained 257 Crusaders, 149 Stuarts and 167 new American Grants which out-gunned their German rivals; 145 more tanks, including 75 Grants, were on their way to the front. In addition the British had received 112 of the new improved 6-pounder anti-tank guns, though Rommel's forty-eight 88mms were still the finest on the battlefield.

Panzerarmee Afrika consisted of the *Afrika Korps*, led by Lieutenant General Walther Nehring, with 15th and 21st Panzer, the Italian XX Corps containing Ariete and Trieste Divisions, 90th Light under Major General Kleemann, and four Italian infantry divisions which were directed on this occasion by Crüwell, now a full general. Its armoured strength was 332 German tanks, of which fifty were Mark IIs carrying only machine-guns, plus 228 of the useless Italian ones; seventy-seven more German tanks were in reserve, while the not very efficient Italian Littorio (Armoured) Division arrived at the front in the final stages of the fighting.

On paper the opposing air-arms were roughly equal in strength. Coningham's Desert Air Force contained some 380 fighters or fighter-bombers, 160 bombers and 60 reconnaissance aircraft. At the expense of abandoning his sustained raids on Malta, Kesselring had sent sizeable reinforcements of fighters and Stuka dive-bombers to North Africa, bringing the Axis strength there to some 350 fighters, 140 bombers and 40 reconnaissance machines, though in practice the Italians, whose aircraft made up almost half this total, played a very small role in the coming struggle. Coningham had also received improved types of aircraft. The Kittyhawks, of which there were six squadrons, were steadily replacing the older Tomahawks, of which only two squadrons now remained. Both the Kittyhawks and the Hurricanes of which Coningham could use six squadrons in varying roles, were being adapted so as to carry a 250lb bomb under each wing, though only about a third of them had been so converted by the time the battle began. Nos. 55 and 223 Squadrons now flew new Martin Baltimore bombers. The first Spitfire fighter squadron, No. 145, saw action as from 1 June, while seven days later, No. 6 Squadron, flying Hurricane IIDs armed with two 40mm armour-piercing cannons, also joined in the fighting.

Both before and during the battle, according to de Guingand, who was then Auchinleck's Director of Military Intelligence, the Commander-in-Chief 'had a lot to say regarding the major decisions within Eighth Army. If he was not up there himself, frequent signals would be exchanged. In addition he would send up one of his principal staff officers every day or two to convey his views to the Army Commander.'

On 20 May for instance, Auchinleck wrote a long letter to Ritchie in which he made three main suggestions: the armoured forces should be concentrated; they should be stationed well to the north; they should be prepared to meet a thrust against the centre of the British position. The first of these was excellent advice in theory, though if Axis reconnaissance aircraft located such a concentration then Rommel could choose a line of advance which would avoid this. The second was highly dangerous unless the third was a true estimate of Rommel's intentions, for if the panzers in fact moved round the south of the Gazala Line, they would have a clear run to Eighth Army's unprotected headquarters units and supply dumps.

Ritchie therefore believed it would be safer if the armour was not concentrated but so positioned as to be concentrated easily once the direction of Rommel's main thrust had become clear. In addition it should not be kept too far north since it must guard against moves both on the centre and round the flank of the Gazala Line. Of these Ritchie regarded the latter as the more likely – he had so advised his corps commanders three days earlier. He thus showed more foresight than Auchinleck, for von Mellenthin tells us that an advance on the British centre 'would have had no chance whatever' and was never even considered by Rommel.

Nonetheless Ritchie, with admirable loyalty but far less wisdom, passed on Auchinleck's prediction – with the result that when on the night of 26th/27th May, Rommel's attack came in from the desert flank, it was thought this was a reconnaissance in strength. Far worse though, Ritchie's change of tune made his subordinates feel, says Field Marshal Carver, that he was 'merely the mouthpiece of Auchinleck, far away in Cairo'. In consequence the battle would be marked by what General Fraser calls 'indiscipline at the top' as 'orders were received, doubted, questioned, discussed'.

Despite this, the battle began favourably for the Allies. Rommel had intended to make a feint with his Italian infantry on the north part of the Gazala Line, while the *Afrika Korps* swung south of Bir Hacheim which would be attacked by the Italian XX Corps. In fact everything went wrong. The Trieste Division lost its way during its approach march, to be brought to a halt by minefields north of Bir Hacheim. The attacks by Ariete on the Free French failed. XXX Corps, though realizing too late that the German thrust was more than a reconnaissance, still inflicted heavy losses on the panzers, to which the new Grant tanks proved deadly opponents.

By 29 May indeed, Rommel's assault had failed. He was desperately short of supplies, especially petrol. His long line of communications was under heavy pressure from the air. His chief subordinate Crüwell had been captured when his Fieseler Storch liaison aircraft had been shot down. Rommel did, however, have one ray of hope. The Trieste Division had cleared a lifeline to him through the British minefields.

To this area – aptly if unimaginatively named the 'Cauldron' – Rommel led his forces. By 1 June, he had eliminated the isolated 150th Brigade which threatened his new supply route, while Ritchie's attention, as Field Marshal Carver relates, 'was concentrated on trying to implement the general plan proposed by Auchinleck' – a move south of the battlefield which would threaten Rommel's supply bases. Not until 5 June was a major attempt made to crush Rommel in the 'Cauldron' and this failed with heavy casualties which were increased by an enemy counter-attack next day. So great were Eighth Army's losses, especially in tanks, that Rommel felt able to resume his advance. He first turned his entire strength against Bir Hacheim. The Free French garrison, superbly supported by the Desert Air Force, held out until the night of 10 June, when the survivors broke out of their now untenable position, having done much to restore the reputation of their country's armed forces.

Rommel next thrust northward. Ironically the British armour was now concentrated but on 12 June, something like 100 tanks were destroyed, chiefly by the German anti-tank guns. Two days later, after further losses, Ritchie, despite previous orders to the contrary from Auchinleck, wisely authorized 1st South African and 50th Divisions to fall back before they were cut off. They did so only just in time.

Before the battle started, it had been agreed that if the Gazala Line was breached, the next defensive position would be on the Egyptian frontier; there would be no second siege of Tobruk. Yet now Auchinleck came under strong pressure from Churchill not to abandon a base which had become a symbol of British determination. On 14 June therefore, the Commander-in-Chief ordered Ritchie to form a new line running through Acroma, just west of Tobruk, to El Adem, just south of it.

Ritchie had in fact already intended to make a stand in much the same area, but he warned Auchinleck that the German panzer strength was such that this might not be possible. He asked if in that case he should 'accept a risk of temporary investment in Tobruk' or abandon it, to withdraw to the frontier. Auchinleck, after further appeals from Churchill, signalled on 16 June that Tobruk could be allowed to become 'isolated for short periods'.[7] By the early hours of the 18th, Rommel, as feared, had scattered the defences at El Adem, the coastal road east of Tobruk had been cut and the fortress was isolated indeed.

Moreover Rommel's advance had driven the Desert Air Force from its forward airfields. There were thus no fighters to oppose the Junkers Ju 87 Stuka dive-bombers which Kesselring now massed for a crushing onslaught against Tobruk's defences. Under cover of their bombardment, the Axis soldiers burst into the town. At dawn on the 21st, the South African Major General Klopper ordered his men to surrender, though a few units continued the fight for another twenty-four hours. Some 32,000 men, British, South African, Indian, passed into captivity. Rommel had gained equipment, guns, ammunition, 2,000 serviceable vehicles, 5,000 tons of food, 1,400 tons of petrol – and his Field Marshal's baton.

He can be forgiven for allowing success to turn his head. At this moment of greatest triumph, Rommel made a terrible mistake. It had always been intended that once Tobruk had fallen he should pause on the frontier while his supply lines were guaranteed by the conquest of Malta. On the 21st, Field Marshal Kesselring in a personal meeting with Rommel pointed out that he needed to withdraw the bulk of his units to Sicily to resume operations against Malta, from which the Axis convoys were again being threatened. They would thus be unable to support any further advance. Accordingly, Kesselring, says von Mellenthin, who was present at this conference, urged that 'the only sound course was to stick to the original plan and postpone an invasion of Egypt until Malta had fallen'.

But Rommel would heed no advice. He was determined that his army should dash for the Suez Canal immediately, leaving the island-fortress still unsubdued. Appealing directly to Hitler and Mussolini, he won the support of both for his venture.

It was a catastrophic decision. Even after the fall of Tobruk, Eighth Army still had many more men, tanks, guns and supplies than did Rommel. Every mile he advanced into Egypt his supply line, that 'piece of elastic', would become more dangerously stretched. It did not seem to occur to him that the booty of Tobruk offered false promises; that without spare parts his captured vehicles would become unserviceable; that once his captured ammunition had been fired, his captured guns would be useless. Or perhaps it did, but he meant to take the risk anyway: he later called his move 'a plan with a chance of success – a try-on'.

Rommel's supply problems were aggravated by Ritchie having decided to retire from the frontier to Mersa Matruh, 90 miles east of Sidi Barrani. XXX Corps indeed fell back for another 120 miles to El Alamein, leaving the fighting at Mersa Matruh to XIII Corps and the newly arrived X Corps of Lieutenant General William Holmes. This had originally contained only the three brigades of 10th Indian Division but it now also took over the two remaining brigades of 50th (British) Division. All these forces were stationed behind minefields stretching from the coast to an escarpment some 10 miles to the south. A further 10 miles away was a second, larger escarpment on top of or to the south of which was XIII Corps: 29th Brigade from 5th Indian Division, the 4th and 5th Brigades of Freyberg's 2nd New Zealand Division and Lumsden's 1st Armoured Division with 159 tanks, sixty of them Grants.

Against these defences, Rommel's attack, which began late on 26 June, should really have stood no chance. His lines of communication were already perilous, under increasing attention from the Desert Air Force. His own supporting aircraft had fallen behind his advance, as had the Italian ground troops, who in any case could muster only seventy tanks of no great value and 6,000 infantrymen. His striking force, 15th and 21st Panzer and 90th Light, consisted of a mere sixty tanks (about a third of them Mark IIs) and some 2,500 infantrymen.

On 25 June, however, Auchinleck had relieved Ritchie – who it should be mentioned would later command XII Corps with distinction throughout the victorious campaign in North-West Europe – and had assumed personal leadership of Eighth Army. He promptly announced that he 'no longer intended to fight a decisive action at Matruh' but would engage the enemy over the whole area between 'Matruh and the El Alamein gap' with 'fluid and mobile forces'. As a result, declares Field Marshal Carver: 'Everybody assumed withdrawal was being planned.' Von Mellenthin echoes this criticism, adding sternly – and correctly – that 'a battle cannot be fought in this fashion'.

As ill-luck would have it, Rommel's main attack was made between the escarpments where the defences were weakest, though again protected by minefields. Shortly after dark on 27 June, 90th Light broke right through to the coastal road east of Matruh. This looked serious, but 90th Light contained only 1,600 men who in reality could have been destroyed before help reached them. The two panzer divisions were in an even worse state – pinned down, separated from each other, and very short of both ammunition and fuel.

'Concerted attacks by the greatly superior British forces,' von Mellenthin considers, 'would have terminated the existence of *Panzerarmee Afrika*.'

Unfortunately, as a result of Auchinleck's orders, the British were mentally unprepared for a counterstroke. Instead, as Field Marshal Carver sadly records, there was 'a precipitate and ill-organized withdrawal'. Rommel captured 6,000 prisoners, forty tanks and numerous supplies. This incredible – and frankly undeserved – victory convinced him that he should follow his star onwards to Alexandria and Cairo.

Kesselring and Marshal Ugo Cavallero, Chief of Staff of the Italian Armed Forces, were less sanguine. When they had joined Rommel for a conference on 26 June, both had insisted that in view of the serious supply difficulties which must be expected, he should not in any event advance beyond El Alamein.

Notes

[1] *The Rommel Papers* edited by Captain B.H. Liddell Hart. All quotations from Rommel come from this source.

[2] It may be appropriate to detail here the approximate distances by the coastal road between the places mentioned: Alexandria to El Alamein: 70 miles; El Alamein to Sidi Barrani: 210 miles; Sidi Barrani to Tobruk: 160 miles; Tobruk to Derna: 110 miles; Derna to Benghazi: 180 miles; Benghazi to El Agheila: 180 miles; El Agheila to Tripoli: 480 miles.

[3] The loss of O'Connor in particular was a severe blow but claims that he would have proved the answer to Rommel should be treated with some reserve. He was released from captivity when Italy surrendered in 1943, but though he rendered further distinguished services in Normandy, he found it a very different experience against German troops using German weapons.

[4] *The Mediterranean and Middle East* Volume III (September 1941 to September 1942) *British Fortunes reach their Lowest Ebb*, by Major-General I.S.O. Playfair with Captain F.C. Flynn RN, Brigadier C.J.C. Molony and Group Captain T.P. Gleave.

[5] Both German panzer divisions contained one tank regiment and one regiment of motorized infantry.

[6] All quotations from Churchill are from his massive history of *The Second World War* Volume IV: *The Hinge of Fate*. Those from Brooke (unless otherwise stated) will be found in Sir Arthur Bryant's *The Turn of the Tide 1939–1943* which is based on Brooke's wartime diaries.

[7] Full details of the signals between Churchill, Auchinleck and Ritchie will be found in Field Marshal Carver's *Dilemmas of the Desert War*.

Chapter 2

THE JULY BATTLES

Why was it that the British, despite their numerical advantages, had suffered so many misfortunes? Both at the time and later, one excuse was invariably offered: Allied tanks were inferior to German ones. General Auchinleck states this, not as an opinion but as a fact, in his Official Despatch.

Certainly the Allied tanks in the Desert had their faults. The heavy Matildas and Valentines, designed for co-operation with the infantry, lacked speed, particularly the former. Of the cruiser tanks, the Crusaders lacked mechanical reliability; the Stuarts lacked range. Yet in gun-power and armour, all were, if anything, superior to their German rivals.

At the time of CRUSADER, Rommel's Mark IIIs and Mark IVs carried a short-barrelled, low-velocity 50mm gun or a short-barrelled, low-velocity 75mm gun respectively. Both of these had less penetrative power than the 2-pounders used in all the British tanks or the equivalent 37mm of the Stuarts.

All German tanks originally had 30mm armour over the entire hull and the turret. This was considerably less than the Matildas with 78mm of armour on the hull and 75mm on the turret, or the Valentines with 60mm of armour on the hull and 65mm on the turret; both were virtually immune from enemy tank-guns save at very short range. The side plates of the Crusaders (28mm) and the Stuarts (25mm) were slightly less strong than those of the panzers but their front hull plates (33mm and 44mm) and their turret armour (49mm and 38mm) were thicker. For this reason the Germans had begun to modify their tanks by adding a further plate to the front of the hull. This doubled their width of armour which was thus superior to that of the Crusaders or Stuarts but not to that of the British heavy tanks. On the other hand the panzers' turrets remained as vulnerable as before. In any case, though some conversions took place during the winter of 1941–42, the majority of the German tanks had still not been improved by the end of CRUSADER.

During the Battle of Gazala, the panzer divisions presented a considerably more formidable picture. Not only did all their tanks now boast the additional frontal protection, but new Mark III or Mark IV Specials had also made their appearance. These had 50mm front hull armour, though the Mark III Specials normally had only 30mm turret armour and both had only 30mm side plates. They also both had long-barrelled high-velocity guns – 50mm in the Mark III Specials, 75mm in the Mark IV Specials.

Thus all German tanks were now superior to the Allied cruisers in hull armour though not in turret armour. They were still inferior, however, to the Allied heavy tanks. The standard Mark IIIs or IVs were still inferior to all Allied tanks in gun-power but the new Specials could out-gun all those types that had previously been in use. Fortunately there were only nineteen Mark III Specials on hand when the Battle of Gazala began; only twenty-seven by 10 June. As for the Mark IV Specials, there was at first no ammunition available for them and their number had still not reached double figures by as late as the end of July. They would only become a threat at a subsequent date.

Any progress made by the Germans moreover was completely overshadowed by the appearance in strength on the battlefield of the American Grant tanks. These had a thickness of armour at least equal to and in most respects superior to that of their German rivals: 50mm on the front of the hull, 38mm side plates, 57mm on the turret. They thus had nothing to fear from the standard German tanks even at close range. Ronald Lewin in his study of the *Afrika Korps* reports its men watching 'with horror the shot from the German 50mms bouncing off the Grants' armour'. Major General 'Pip' Roberts in his memoirs, *From the Desert to the Baltic*, reports that during the early exchanges at Gazala, in which he commanded 3rd Battalion, Royal Tank Regiment,[1] his own Grant was hit eight times without a shell penetrating it, while another Grant resisted twenty-five hits successfully.

Roberts also points out that the Grants' armament at this time was 'superior in anti-tank capability to any guns mounted in the German tanks'. Grants carried not only a 37mm in the turret but also a 75mm in a sponson on the side of the hull with a greater penetrative power even than the guns of the new long-barrelled Mark III Specials. Not that the Grant was perfect either: its 75mm had a limited arc of fire; it possessed an unnecessarily high silhouette; and it was somewhat slower than the German tanks. These defects though did not prevent it being more than a match for any opponent which it had to face before the Mark IV Specials began to arrive in large numbers.

That the British mishaps did not arise from inadequate tanks can be seen most clearly from a study of the Italian ones. These were slower than any of the Allied types except Matildas, mechanically unreliable, poorly armoured – 30mm on the hull, 40mm on the turret – and equipped with a low-velocity 47mm gun which was inferior to any on the Allied side. They aroused, says the German historian Paul Carell in *The Foxes of the Desert*, 'the contempt of their enemies and the compassion of their allies'. Yet the Ariete Armoured Division on more than one occasion during CRUSADER and Gazala successfully held off superior numbers of British tanks.[2]

This point illustrates one of the real causes of Eighth Army's failures. It has frequently been said that the British armoured commanders were staid and conservative in comparison with the dashing Rommel. In reality they were often too brave, too daring. They scorned standing on the defensive. They persisted in regarding the tank not as a mobile protected gun, but as a steel-plated horse. They delighted in making charges at the enemy armour, although in the tanks of that period it was extremely difficult to fire the gun accurately whilst on the move. Their charges broke down time after time on the iron defence of the 88mms.

For in anti-tank guns, the Germans did have the advantage – although to nothing like the overwhelming extent usually claimed. During CRUSADER, the main German anti-tank weapons were the long-barrelled 50mms which were more effective than the British 2-pounders or indeed than the short-barrelled 50mms carried on their own tanks. Prior to Gazala, however, Eighth Army received 6-pounders which possessed a considerable superiority in pen-etrative power over the German 50mms and were approximately equal to the captured Russian 76mm anti-tank guns that had now reached Rommel. The Germans' 88mms remained the most deadly guns on the battlefield, though their high mounting made them also more vulnerable than any others on either side. Fortunately for Eighth Army their numbers were always strictly limited.

Again, though, the real German superiority lay not in equipment but in tactics. The British success against the Italians, as General Jackson shows, had been achieved by 'close and intimate co-operation between tanks, artillery and infantry' – and, he might have added, aircraft. Under Auchinleck, however, co-operation had largely disappeared – this was another reason for that 'indiscipline at the top' which has already been noted. The Germans by contrast still used the different branches of their army in deadly combination. The anti-tank guns in particular formed a screen for their own armour in defence, while in attack they pushed boldly ahead to engage the British tanks, allowing the panzers to fall on weaker targets – supply echelons or unprotected infantry.

This tactic was aided by Auchinleck's policy of decreasing the integrity of his infantry units. As Jackson explains, he first made 'the brigade group the basic fighting formation instead of the division', and he tended to commit his brigade groups to action separately and without co-ordination. Then, shortly before Mersa Matruh, Auchinleck ordered a further fragmentation by creating 'battle groups' within each brigade. These contained artillery plus only as many infantrymen as were needed to protect this and had enough transport to keep them mobile. All other troops were sent to the rear, in some cases as far back at the Nile Delta. It is worthy of note that Freyberg refused point-blank to break up his brigades, claiming his responsibility to his own government as justification.

Fortunately all Eighth Army's tactical faults were more than balanced by Rommel's own strategic blunder of advancing into Egypt before Malta had been crushed. Liddell Hart says that 1 July 1942, when Rommel thrust into the 'El Alamein gap' between the sea and the Qattara Depression, was 'the most dangerous moment of the struggle in Africa'. In reality, Rommel was depending on a miracle. While Eighth Army was now so close to its base that its every need could be met quickly, Rommel's supply line, that fragile 'piece of elastic', was, as Kesselring and Cavallero had warned, on the point of snapping. Petrol, ammunition, food, water – all were desperately short.

Such difficulties were made worse by the fact that, as von Mellenthin confirms, 'the Desert Air Force commanded the battlefield'. This was scarcely surprising for the Axis air force was, in the words of the British Official History, 'still struggling to make its way forward'. On 30 June for instance, the Allied pilots did not encounter a single enemy machine. And even at best, Rommel might at any given moment expect the aid of no more than forty bombers and fifty-five fighters.

These numbers could not be compared to the aircraft available to the Desert Air Force, which had recently been receiving reinforcements. A second Spitfire squadron, No. 601, had joined No. 145, flying its first sorties on 27 June. Tedder – who on 1 July was promoted to Air Chief Marshal – had also sent forward two squadrons of Hurricanes previously defending the Canal Zone, together with the equivalent of two more from Operational Training Units. Moreover Tedder had other aircraft readily available in Egypt which were not part of the Desert Air Force as such, and a far higher proportion of Allied machines than Axis machines were serviceable. Against the handful of enemy aircraft on hand, Tedder could pit 65 Wellingtons, 30 Bostons, 30 Baltimores, 170 Hurricanes, 60 Kittyhawks and 20 Spitfires.[3] And within a week, he would also receive thirty-two Halifaxes from Nos. 10 and 227 Squadrons, the first four-engined bombers to reach the Middle East.

The Allied air arm was not only bigger than its opponent, it was infinitely more effective. This was the more commendable in view of the superior performances of the Messerschmitt Bf 109[4] and Macchi MC 202 fighters, both of which were faster than any of their Allied rivals, including, contrary to legend, the Spitfires.

Luckily for the Allied cause, the German airmen had succumbed to an 'ace' complex. In their account of the air battles in the North African campaign, *Fighters over the Desert*, Christopher Shores and Hans Ring state flatly that

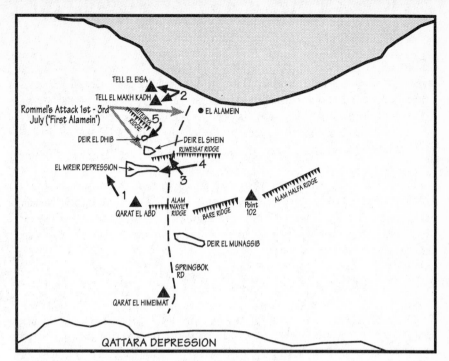

MAP 3: The July Battles. Auchinleck's five attacks are numbered in chronological order.

'some pilots were clearly more interested in increasing their personal scores than inflicting the most telling casualties'. While the Allied fighters flew constant missions against enemy ground forces, the 109s 'shirked this as often as possible'. They failed to protect their own bombers adequately and they rarely engaged Allied bombers as these 'had tail gunners'.[5] It was of no help to Rommel that his fighter pilots were 'conducting a private war of their own, divorced almost entirely from the actions of the main forces in the sands below'.

In the sands Rommel's army was equally weak. His 5,000 Italian infantrymen and thirty tanks had again fallen well behind the Germans, who in turn had been reduced to fifty-five tanks, of which only fifteen were the new Mark III Specials, and about 1,500 infantrymen. Yet Rommel's soldiers were not only few in number, ill-supplied and poorly supported. Worst of all, as the Australian war correspondent Alan Moorehead confirms in his book *The Desert War*, 'they had reached the limit of physical despair'. Von Mellenthin declares that 'the *Afrika Korps* and 90th Light' were now 'utterly exhausted'; 'exhausted and attenuated' is Field Marshal Carver's description. The German advance, Moorehead openly admits, was halted 'not because Rommel made a mistake, or because Auchinleck achieved an eleventh-hour miracle, but because the German army was exhausted. It could do no more. The German soldiers were wearied to the point where they had no more reserves either of body or of will-power.'

By contrast, the majority of the Allied formations were comparatively fresh. 1st South African Division for instance had had a week's break from combat, strengthening the defences at El Alamein. 4th and 5th New Zealand Brigades may not have benefited from their experiences at Mersa Matruh but they were much less tired than Rommel's men who had been in virtually continuous action for almost a month previously. Other units such as 6th New Zealand and 18th Indian Brigades were completely untouched by the recent conflicts.

Moreover, in practice, Rommel was restricted by geography to only three main avenues of advance. From the El Alamein railway station on its little ridge, level ground ran away to the south – though the long, low Miteirya Ridge lay to the south-west – until some eight miles away the rocky Ruweisat Ridge rose threateningly ahead. The first avenue of advance was north of this. The second lay between the ridge and another line of high points some seven miles further south. This began in the west with the peak of Qaret el Abd, continued with the Alam Nayil Ridge, became the Bare Ridge and finally rose triumphantly to the ridge of Alam el Halfa – or plain Alam Halfa as the soldiers called it. The final means of advance was between these features and the great Qattara Depression, though the approach to this was restricted by steep escarpments.

This southern route was not in fact particularly well guarded. It was defended by XIII Corps but the infantry formations – all three brigades of 2nd New Zealand Division together with 9th Indian Brigade from 5th Indian Division – did not enjoy the advantage of any real fortifications and were supported only by armoured cars. It may therefore have been just as well that lack of time and shortage of petrol ruled out any possibility of Rommel making the long wheel inland necessary if he was to attack in this area.

More important therefore were the defences in the north, where Rommel did attack. These were the responsibility of Norrie's XXX Corps and here the fortifications were much more worthy of the name. The most secure was the 'box' at El Alamein, where 3rd South African Brigade sheltered behind size-able minefields. The two other South African brigades held the gap between this and the Ruweisat Ridge. To the south of the gap, Norrie had hastily prepared a further 'box', also partially protected by minefields, at Deir el Shein, a shallow depression near the western end of the Ruweisat Ridge. This was manned by 18th Indian Brigade. 1st Armoured Division protected the South Africans' flanks, its 4th Armoured Brigade stationed in the gap, its 22nd Armoured Brigade astride Ruweisat Ridge. 50th Division was in reserve.

Against these forces Rommel's 'exhausted and attenuated' formations had no real hope of success – provided that Eighth Army held firm. Unfortunately there was the appalling risk that, as at Mersa Matruh, everyone might feel that only a delaying action was to be fought.

'It may be thought,' the Official History remarks with its usual restraint, 'that General Auchinleck should have declared that it was now "Backs to the

Wall" and that the Army, reinforced by every possible man and gun from Egypt, and fully supported by the Middle East air force, would die where it stood. Certainly such an order would have cleared away much bewilderment and doubt.'

Such an order, however, Auchinleck was not prepared to give. As the Official History states, he 'felt that although he had a good chance to stop Rommel and firmly intended to try, it would be wrong to ignore the possibility that once more his own rather loosely-knit army might be outmanoeuvred or outfought. Above all, he decided, it must be kept in being. Therefore it might have to retreat again.'

Auchinleck intended to retreat only as an unwelcome last resort, but he failed to make this clear to his subordinates, he issued warnings of the possibility of retirement, and, worst of all, as the Official History notes, 'some of the measures adopted at this time seemed to the men in the ranks inconsistent with a firm determination to fight'. In particular, though reinforcements were on their way to the front, it was certainly not the case that 'every possible man and gun' was used to hold the Alamein positions. On the contrary, X Corps, apart from 50th Division which had come under Norrie's command, had been sent all the way back to the Nile Delta, as had the surplus infantry from Auchinleck's new battle groups.

As a result, many did in fact believe that a withdrawal was imminent. Major General Sir Howard Kippenberger, later editor-in-chief of the New Zealand Official War History but then, as he relates in his memoirs, an *Infantry Brigadier* – he commanded 5th New Zealand Brigade – describes how Gott showed him a plan prepared by Auchinleck's staff to 'save Eighth Army' by a 'general retirement and evacuation of Egypt'. Kippenberger protested that this would be 'criminal', but that evening, 'a provisional order for our retirement arrived from XIII Corps. It certainly envisaged the abandonment of Egypt.'

By an extraordinary irony, however, Eighth Army was saved by one of its greatest faults – 'indiscipline at the top'. Lieutenant General Willoughby Norrie is normally described, rather slightingly, as brave, charming but indecisive. Yet it was Norrie who now, in the words of Field Marshal Carver, 'gripped the situation'. Carver was on Norrie's staff, so perhaps it would be more objective to quote the judgement of General Jackson: 'Fortunately Norrie, on whom Rommel's main blow was to fall, had made up his mind and had told his subordinates that this *was* the last ditch. XXX Corps would fight and die where it stood.' Moreover his attitude was backed by Major General Pienaar, commanding 1st South African Division, for though that officer – more irony – was all in favour of a retreat, he was equally determined that the South Africans should fight to the utmost at El Alamein so as to wipe out the stain of Klopper's surrender at Tobruk.

Still further irony followed. The indiscipline of Auchinleck's subordinates, notably Norrie and Pienaar, was then taken a stage forward. The basis of Auchinleck's plans, as the Official History reports, was to keep his forces 'fluid and mobile' and 'give no hostage to fortune in the shape of immobile troops holding localities which can easily be isolated'. These ideas were simply disregarded by Norrie and Pienaar. They were determined instead that Eighth Army should remain static, 'anchoring its operations' says Carver, 'on the fixed defences of El Alamein and taking little account' of Auchinleck's 'concept of moving columns of artillery around'. This resulted in the British artillery for once being concentrated in practice rather than co-operating in theory.

If Rommel was relying on a miracle on 1 July, he did nothing to deserve it, for he spared insufficient time for proper preparations and none at all for reconnaissance. As a result, Nehring's *Afrika Korps* collided unexpectedly with the Deir el Shein 'box', of the existence of which Rommel was unaware. The gallant 18th Indian Brigade, reinforced by nine Matildas, sixteen 6-pounder anti-tank guns and twenty-three field guns, held out until the evening, by which time the *Afrika Korps* had lost eighteen tanks – one-third of its strength.

On the coast, 90th Light Division, moving too far north, ran into, instead of avoiding, the Alamein defences, where it was thrown back by 3rd South African Brigade. In the afternoon, it tried to circle south of the 'box' but was halted in short order by the artillery of all three South African brigades and 1st Armoured Division. Next morning, 90th Light once more attempted to resume its advance but the South Africans continued to thwart all its efforts.

On the afternoon of 2 July, the *Afrika Korps* also advanced – on the Ruweisat Ridge – only to be checked by 1st Armoured Division. Nehring renewed his efforts on the 3rd, but since he could now muster only twenty-six panzers while his opponents possessed 119 gun-armed tanks, thirty-eight of them Grants, he naturally made little progress. At the same time the New Zealanders counter-attacked from the south, their assault falling on the Ariete which had just come up on the German flank. The Italians collapsed with little resistance, losing forty-four guns and 350 prisoners – 'a clear sign', as Liddell Hart remarks, 'of overstrain'.

By 3 July, Rommel's airmen had also come up at last and he made a final attempt to break through by turning his Stukas on the Alamein 'box'. Once again the South Africans played the major role in saving the day. While the Hurricanes of No. 274 Squadron RAF kept away the escorting enemy fighters, the Hurricanes of Major Le Mesurier's No. 1 Squadron SAAF tore into the dive-bombers. Hopelessly trapped, these jettisoned their bombs, but the South Africans, for the loss of one of their own machines which force-landed, shot down nine of them, all confirmed from the ground, then pursued the survivors for miles, claiming to have destroyed at least four more.

Rommel had played his last card – for the time being at any rate. That evening he finally called off the offensive. Three days later, Norrie, who had been mainly responsible for that desirable result, like Godwin-Austen before him, left Eighth Army at his own request, his place being taken by Ramsden.

Despite later claims in certain quarters, however, Rommel's prospects of victory in the Desert War had by no means disappeared. Indeed provided he could hold the ground he had won, he had two chances of success considerably better than his 'try-on'. In the first place, he was expecting substantial reinforcements by the end of August; once these had arrived, he could renew his advance in strength. Or if he again failed, as long as he could prevent Eighth Army from recapturing the Martuba airfields, then all his major problems would soon be solved by the fall of Malta, now being slowly starved into surrender.

It would be more accurate then to say that Rommel's prospects of victory should have disappeared, for there seemed little liklihood that he would in practice be able to hold his ground. Fresh formations, including the three brigades of Major General Morshead's magnificent 9th Australian Division, were arriving to swell Eighth Army, but as yet few replacements were reaching Rommel's battered units. In the meantime, says Paul Carell, 'with his weakened forces, he lay day after day in front of the ever-increasing British might.' 'The position of *Panzerarmee Afrika*,' agrees von Mellenthin, 'was perilous.'

Furthermore Rommel's danger was well known to his opponent as a result of the 'Ultra' interceptions. It was with justifiable confidence therefore that on the night of 4th/5th July, Auchinleck ordered his troops 'to destroy the enemy as far east as possible and not let him get away as a force in being . . . Eighth Army will attack and destroy the enemy in his present position.'[6] Throughout the rest of the month, relates Brigadier Lucas Phillips in *Alamein*, Auchinleck would constantly repeat his intention to '"destroy" or "encircle" the enemy or to make deep penetrations and "exploit"'. In fact 'more attention', as General Jackson complains, 'seemed to be paid to the problems of pursuit than to the break-in'.

It is therefore most misleading to refer to the whole series of encounters during July as if they were one single battle – the 'First Battle of El Alamein'. From 1st to 3rd July, Eighth Army had fought a defensive action, which may be labelled 'First Alamein' if this is wished. Thereafter it was on the offensive. Moreover this was not one continuous offensive. General Sir Charles Richardson, then the Eighth Army staff officer in charge of plans, records in his memoirs, *Flashback: A Soldier's Story*, that there was instead a series of 'piecemeal unco-ordinated attacks' – five in all with pauses in between. These pauses enabled Rommel to recover his balance but never seemed to give Eighth Army sufficient time, in the words of the Official History, 'to prepare thoroughly'.

The sad fact was that Auchinleck had not learned from previous mistakes. His infantry still fought not in divisions but in brigade groups or battle groups, and for all his advice before Gazala to concentrate the armour, he did nothing of the kind now that he was in personal command of Eighth Army. Nor did he take any steps to end the increasing lack of co-operation between the various branches of his Army. Indeed he made this worse by setting up his Headquarters on the Ruweisat Ridge in an inaccessible piece of desert, unsuitably far forward, with poor communications. This was not a base from which speedy, flexible control or co-ordination could be achieved. It was also over 40 miles from the HQ of Coningham's Desert Air Force which remained on the coast at Burg el Arab. As a result, reports de Guingand – who became Eighth Army's Brigadier General Staff in mid-July – there were 'great difficulties in the laying on of the best air support'.

Nor did Auchinleck help his cause by what General Richardson calls his 'inability to make effective use of his staff'. Instead, states de Guingand, Auchinleck relied on 'a sort of personal adviser' who 'carried no responsibility in Eighth Army'. This was Major General Eric Dorman-Smith, always known as 'Chink' from his prominent teeth, an Irishman of immense charm, ready tongue and consuming ambition who had been appointed Deputy Chief of the General Staff in Cairo on 18 May 1942. As Field Marshal Carver relates in his autobiography *Out of Step*, Dorman-Smith 'mesmerized' his superior and came to acquire 'a sinister influence' over him.

'Sinister' because unhappily Dorman-Smith's 'appreciations and plans' were, says de Guingand tactfully, 'somewhat impracticable'. This was hardly surprising for Carver declares that Dorman-Smith's main aim was 'to make a splash'; when 'proposing a course of action', his 'principal motive seemed to be to suggest some startlingly novel solution, regardless of whether or not it had a hope of working'.

Certainly none of Dorman-Smith's suggestions appear to have worked during Auchinleck's five assaults on *Panzerarmee Afrika* in July 1942. The first of these began on the 5th, when XXX Corps was directed to contain the enemy's front while XIII Corps attacked his rear. Unfortunately Gott's infantry were supported by only eight Stuarts together with some armoured cars, and in any event, as even the usually undemonstrative Official History confirms, XIII Corps was 'very weak and becoming weaker by separating (or, as some would say, disintegrating) into its "mobile artillery battle groups"'. By 7 July, Auchinleck's first offensive had failed miserably and his forces in the south were in danger of being cut off. He therefore abandoned his fortified 'boxes' in this area, ordering all troops to withdraw to the line of a track called the 'Springbok Road' running almost due north to south from El Alamein to Himeimat.

As though Auchinleck did not enjoy enough advantages, he now had a wonderful stroke of good luck when Rommel sent his Italian infantrymen who were at last beginning to come up – though they were still only about 4,000 in number – to hold the northern and central sections of his front, while the Littorio Armoured Division, now brought up to a strength of fifty-four tanks, joined the three German divisions, increased by reinforcements to no less than 2,000 infantrymen and from forty-five to fifty tanks, in following up XIII Corps, in case Eighth Army, as at Mersa Matruh, was about to make an inexplicable and unnecessary retreat. This move played straight into Auchinleck's hands, for Rommel's striking force was now concentrated in the south at the very moment when, by sheer coincidence, Auchinleck was about to launch his second offensive, planned for 10 July, in the coastal area.

This was entrusted to Ramsden's XXX Corps, which in turn gave the main role to Morshead's 9th Australian Division. Its orders were to seize the low hill of Tell el Eisa near the coast, from which it was hoped that the Australians would be able to break through the Axis defences altogether and enforce the retreat or even the destruction of *Panzerarmee Afrika*. The inland flank would be covered by the South Africans who were directed against another smaller feature, Tell el Makh Kadh to the south-east of Tell el Eisa and almost due west of El Alamein. The Australians were fresh, greatly outnumbered their opponents and were aided by a concentrated artillery barrage, for Morshead, like Freyberg before him, had refused to split up his division into battle groups. In addition, as more good luck would have it, the attack fell on the Sabratha Infantry Division which was the weakest of the Italian formations, being inexperienced, well below strength and lacking supporting artillery.

Perhaps it was not surprising then that both the Australians and the South Africans gained their objectives. The luckless Sabratha Division was routed with the loss of 1,500 prisoners, and the German Wireless Intercept Section, whose Intelligence work was vital, was overrun, its leader Captain Alfred Seebohm being mortally wounded. Paul Carell calls this 'an irreparable loss for the whole army' and laments that 'this handicap could not be overcome during the decisive battles for the El Alamein positions' – an interesting comment as showing that the Germans do not consider that these had yet been fought.

A complete breakthrough was only prevented by von Mellenthin, in temporary charge of Rommel's Headquarters. He hastily formed 'a rough battle line' from his own staff personnel together with the advanced elements of Major General Lungerhausen's 164th (Saxon) Light Division who had only that day arrived at the front. These forces should have proved quite inadequate to check Eighth Army's advance had the attacking infantry been properly supported. As it was, co-operation with the Desert Air Force had fallen away and Auchinleck, who had 200 tanks at his disposal, had allocated only thirty-two Valentines to help the Australians and just eight of the now aging Matildas to aid the South Africans.

In consequence, von Mellenthin was able to hold his ground until Rommel could come racing back from the south and launch a series of counter-attacks which could not dislodge either the Australians or the South Africans from their captured hills but which ended any chance that their progress could continue. By the end of 11 July, Auchlineck's second offensive had failed. Admittedly it had only just failed. Yet if there were those in Eighth Army who hoped that one more effort would prove decisive, they would be sadly disillusioned by the battle which the Official History calls 'First Ruweisat'.

This was Auchinleck's third offensive, which was launched late on 14 July, by, principally, Gott's XIII Corps. While Eighth Army had retained most of the Ruweisat Ridge, the Axis troops held the western part. It was now to be attacked from the south-east, not unhappily by a division, but by three separate brigades: 4th New Zealand on the left, 5th New Zealand in the centre and 5th Indian Brigade (from 5th Indian Division) on the right. This time there was to be no preliminary bombardment in the interests of surprise. As a diversionary move, XXX Corps would push south from Tell el Eisa to capture the Miteirya Ridge. To support the main attack – and to exploit north-westwards thereafter – was Major General Lumsden's 1st Armoured Division, his 2nd Armoured Brigade containing 46 Grants, 59 Crusaders and 11 Stuarts, his 22nd Armoured Brigade containing 31 Grants, 23 Crusaders and 21 Stuarts – a total of 191 gun-armed tanks.

It was not one of those rare battles where everything went 'according to plan'. The diversionary attacks by XXX Corps did not begin until two days later and then failed with heavy losses, 24th Australian Brigade suffering some 300 casualties. 5th Indian Brigade was thrown back in disorder on the night of the 14th/15th, though it renewed its advance successfully next afternoon. Both New Zealand brigades secured their objectives, capturing some 1,600 Italians, but their own losses were very high and their ordeal had only just begun.

For the two armoured brigades – which it is worth noting were widely separated – simply did not proceed to the New Zealanders' support at first light on the 15th as had been intended. As a result, the panzers were able to deliver unimpeded counter-attacks – in the morning against 5th New Zealand Brigade forcing the surrender of 350 men; in the afternoon against 4th New Zealand Brigade taking another 380 prisoners including Captain Charles Upham, the Second World War's only 'double VC'. In all the battle had cost the New Zealanders 1,405 officers and men dead, wounded or captured.

Auchinleck's third offensive had failed – not just miserably but disgracefully. How deep was the disgrace is best expressed by Ronald Lewin, writing admittedly from the German viewpoint, who declares bluntly:

There is nothing in the whole record of the *Afrika Korps* to compare with the abandonment of the New Zealanders naked before an armoured attack in the opening stages of this first Ruweisat battle . . . The human quality was exceptional on both sides. But whereas in the case of the *Afrika Korps* one is never – even in a case like '*Totensonntag*' – affected by a sense of waste, of ardent young lives simply thrown away, until the arrival of Montgomery the record of the British too often haunts one with precisely that intimation of tragedy.

After which it is scarcely bearable to have to report that 'Second Ruweisat', which began on the night of 21st/22nd July, was more disgraceful still. As the name suggests, this was another attack by XIII Corps on the Axis positions around the western end of the Ruweisat Ridge – again unfortunately by separate brigades. 6th New Zealand Brigade was to advance from the south on the El Mreir Depression, south-west of the ridge, while 161st Indian Motor Brigade from 5th Indian Division attacked from the east against the ridge and the Deir el Shein Depression to the north of it. 9th Indian Brigade was in reserve. There was again to be a subsidiary strike by XXX Corps against the Miteirya Ridge; this was to be supported by 50th Battalion, Royal Tank Regiment from the newly-arrived 23rd Armoured Brigade which contained six Matildas and some forty-five Valentines.

In addition to their other tasks, 6th New Zealand and 161st Indian Brigades were instructed to clear a gap in the minefields which the enemy had hastily been preparing. The two other battalions of 23rd Armoured Brigade, 40th and 46th Royal Tanks, which between them had ninety-eight Valentines, were then to pass through this gap, thereby severing the Axis forces in two. The New Zealanders were also to be assisted by 2nd and 22nd Armoured Brigades which between them controlled 61 Grants, 81 Crusaders and 31 Stuarts, to say nothing of almost another 100 tanks in reserve. It may be noted that Auchinleck's main target was Nehring's *Afrika Korps*, for he believed, says Field Marshal Carver in *Dilemmas of the Desert War*, that 'in its current weak state, the *Korps* could not hold such a concentration and that, once it had been destroyed, the rest of Rommel's forces could easily be dealt with'. Auchinleck, agrees Ronald Lewin, 'went straight for the *Afrika Korps*, firmly intending to break and pursue a defeated enemy'.

There seemed every reason for such a belief. *Panzerarmee Afrika*, as well as being desperately short of anti-tank guns, possessed just forty-two German tanks (plus fifty Italian ones), of which only thirty-four were gun-armed and only eight were 'Specials'. As usual, however, any optimism in Eighth Army quickly proved unfounded. The diversionary attacks in the north failed. The attacks by 161st Indian Brigade failed. The later attacks by 9th Indian Brigade failed. The 6th New Zealand Brigade, after a night's ferocious fighting which cost it 200 casualties, seized the eastern part of El Mreir, but 2nd and 22nd Armoured Brigades once more failed to move to its aid at first light on 22 July, and its position was promptly stormed by both 15th and 21st Panzer Divisions. Inevitably the wretched New Zealanders were shattered. Some 700 men were killed, injured or taken prisoner and twenty-three guns, thirteen of them the new 6-pounders, were lost.

Disaster to the infantry was quickly followed by disaster to the armour. Although no gaps had been cleared for 40th and 46th Royal Tanks, these still made a valiant attempt to advance. They suffered heavy losses in the minefields but they finally got through these, only to be confronted by Axis anti-tank guns, few in number but superbly handled. In all forty Valentines were destroyed, forty-seven were crippled and 203 officers and men were killed or wounded. 2nd Armoured Brigade, belatedly approaching El Mreir, lost another twenty-one tanks to no avail. In the north, 50th Royal Tanks lost twenty-three more. Although some of the disabled tanks were later salvaged, the offensive had cost Eighth Army a total of 118. It had cost the Germans just three.

Auchinleck would attempt one more offensive. Since Gott's XIII Corps had endured the heaviest losses in the two Ruweisat battles, this was entrusted to Ramsden's XXX Corps, aided by the bulk of the armour. It began on the night of 26th/27th July, and unbelievably it repeated all the errors committed in the previous encounters.

For a start, the attack was to be made by brigade groups. 24th Australian Brigade was given the task of seizing the eastern end of the Miteirya Ridge, to protect the flank of South African units which were to break into the enemy minefields south-east of the Ridge. Here they would make gaps for the infantry of 69th (British) Brigade which was then to capture the small Deir el Dhib Depression, north of Deir el Shein, clearing a path through any further minefields discovered. This in turn would enable 2nd Armoured Brigade, followed by the light tanks and armoured cars of 4th Light Armoured Brigade, to burst through the enemy positions towards the north-west.

At first all went well. The Australians, the South Africans and 69th Brigade had all carried out their tasks early on the 27th. But of course co-operation with the armour broke down. 2nd Armoured Brigade, wrongly advised as to the extent of the South Africans' mine-clearing activities, held back until the gaps could be widened. 50th Royal Tanks, trying to support the Australians, was repulsed by anti-tank fire with the loss of thirteen Valentines. For the third time running, the infantry were left 'naked before an armoured attack'.

Because by mid-morning on the 27th, the panzers, backed up by 90th Light, were already counter-attacking. The isolated 69th Brigade was driven back through the minefields, having suffered 600 casualties which necessitated its removal from the front line. 24th Australian Brigade was pushed off Miteirya Ridge with a casualty list of 400. This brought the total of Australians dead, wounded and missing in a period of just over three weeks to 146 officers and 3,070 other ranks, and the Eighth Army's total casualties for July to over 13,000.

Auchlineck would order no sixth offensive. Despite having possessed advantages such as few generals have ever enjoyed, he had failed to destroy *Panzerarmee Afrika*. It had not escaped unscathed, losing over 7,000 officers and men as prisoners of war, but more than 6,000 of these were Italians, and if the Italians had suffered severely they had certainly not been eliminated, while the Germans were far less exhausted at the end of July than they had been at its beginning. Indeed the Axis soldiers had considerable cause for satisfaction. Not only had they survived their period of peril, not only had they held their ground against heavy odds, but they had good reason to believe that if Eighth Army could not defeat them in July 1942, then it was scarcely likely to stand up to them once they had received their own promised reinforcements of men and improved equipment.

No wonder then that von Mellenthin concludes his account of this series of actions on a note of triumph: 'The *Panzerarmee* had failed to reach the Nile, but on the 15th, 22nd and 27th July we had won important defensive victories and the balance of losses was highly favourable to us.'

'In the German Army,' reports Alan Moorehead, 'I saw no signs of any breaking of morale. Why should there have been? They were winning.'

Notes

1   At full strength a battalion of the Royal Tank Regiment was the equivalent of a normal armoured (cavalry or yeomanry) regiment.

2   Full details of the various Allied and Axis tanks can be found in the Official History, which has provided the main source for the facts set out above.

3   A more detailed breakdown of the strength of the two sides can be found in *The Desert Air Force* by Roderic Owen, one of its former personnel.

4   'Bf' was short for *Bayerische Flugzeugwerke* – Bavarian Aircraft Company. The abbreviation 'Me', though widely used, was not officially correct until 1944.

5   These admirably frank comments were made by *Oberleutnant* (Flying Officer) Werner Schroer, the top-scoring pilot to survive the Desert fighting, in interviews with Shores and Ring.

6   Quoted in Liddell Hart's *History of the Second World War*.

Chapter 3

THE CHANGE OF COMMAND

In Eighth Army by contrast, the end of July 1942 brought with it, says Liddell Hart, a mood of 'prevailing disappointment'. The men of Eighth Army were experienced, battle-hardened, increasingly cynical – and well aware, in the words of Ronald Lewin who joined them at this time as a young artillery officer, that 'the *Afrika Korps* should never have been allowed to break into Egypt: having made its entry it should have been expelled'. The humiliating failures to do so became known, reports Lucas Phillips, as 'the nonsenses of July'.

Inevitably in view of the lack of co-operation between the different branches of the army, 'the most general and the most dangerous tendency,' declares Field Marshal Carver in his book *El Alamein*, 'was that of different arms or formations to lay the blame on others'. The infantry, states Kippenberger, had 'a most intense distrust, almost hatred, of our armour'. The tank commanders, records Lucas Phillips, accused the infantry of 'always screaming for tank support on every possible occasion'.

There was also, Field Marshal Carver relates, a growing 'mistrust' of the Higher Command. His fellow Field Marshal, Lord Harding, who was then a staff officer at GHQ, Cairo, echoes this opinion, declaring that Auchinleck 'had got the Eighth Army into a pretty good muddle and he had lost its confidence'.[1] Even the majority of Eighth Army's own staff officers, as General Richardson reveals, 'felt that the removal of Auchinleck was essential'. Nor did the recollection of how Rommel's advance had been checked in the first three days of July serve to lift the gloom. It was not only Alan Moorehead who realized that success then had resulted mainly from the enemy's exhaustion. This did not auger well for Eighth Army's ability to meet the new attack which Rommel was known to be planning for late August.

To make matters worse, mistrust between the Army and the High

Command appears to have been mutual. Field Marshal Harding believes that there was at least 'a doubt' in Auchinleck's mind 'as to the ability of the army to hold its position' when Rommel's offensive was renewed. As a result, he states, 'the Auk decided to have plans prepared for a withdrawal' from the Alamein position 'and those plans were duly prepared . . . The plan was that part of the Army should withdraw into the Delta and should make its escape into Sinai and the other lot would go down south into the Sudan.'

Similarly General Richardson declares that he personally was ordered to 'draw up a plan for the possible withdrawal of Eighth Army to Khartoum'. Major General Sir Miles Graham who was then Eighth Army's Deputy Chief Administrative Officer in charge of personnel and logistics recorded in a BBC radio broadcast of 24 September 1958 that he too was responsible for arrangements to 'evacuate the Eighth Army' should this prove necessary; they included having 'different coloured flags put into the sand to take the various units out'. The High Command was 'looking over the shoulder' agrees de Guingand, 'work was being done' on 'defensive positions far to the rear' and 'a new site for the Headquarters had been selected on the Nile, sixty miles south of Cairo'.

The main reserve positions were at Amiriya south-west of Alexandria, at Khatatba north-west of Cairo, and at Wadi Natrun, situated between Alexandria and Cairo and blocking a rough desert road called the 'Barrel Track' which ran towards the Egyptian capital from the southern part of the Alamein position. The importance which Auchinleck and those who shared his views placed on these is shown by the size of the forces held back to man them. They included all three brigades of the 44th (British) Division, commanded by Major General Ivor Hughes, which had recently arrived in the Middle East.

On 27 July, Dorman-Smith produced an 'Appreciation of the Situation in the Western Desert', which was approved without qualification by his chief.[2] In it Auchinleck's personal adviser records with obvious relief that 'the critical period for the preparation and manning of the Delta and Cairo defences is now over', that 'the defences of Alexandria–Cairo–the Delta proper . . . and the Wadi Natrun area will be well forward by August 14', that 'all arrangements for demolitions in the Delta are being made' and that 'the soft sand areas of the country east of El Alamein, notably the "Barrel Track" axis, the Wadi Natrun, the sand area to its north, are all added difficulties for the enemy's movement' – none of which factors would become relevant unless Eighth Army was driven out of the Alamein position.

'Within this Appreciation' indeed, as General Jackson remarks, there is 'a ring of defeatism or of realism depending on the point of view of the reader'. Moreover its pessimism – if 'defeatism' be considered too strong – is constantly repeated in those groups of records (summaries, orders, reports, messages) which together make up the War Diaries of GHQ, Middle East, Eighth Army and XIII and XXX Corps.[3] All, but particularly the first-named, harp continuously on the 'defensive systems' guarding Cairo and Alexandria, the troops needed to hold them, the demolitions necessary to deny vital supplies or equipment to the enemy and the removal of civilians living between Alamein and the Nile 'should the Battle of the Delta have to be fought'.

Inevitably such plans and intentions seeped through to the men of Eighth Army – and deepened their lack of confidence. In Field Marshal Alexander's Official Despatch there appears the blunt statement that 'it was fairly well known' that Eighth Army 'would retreat again, in accordance with the theory that it must be kept in being'. Alexander does add that this would happen only 'in the last resort', but the mood of Eighth Army suggested that the qualification was not likely to be of much practical value. 'I don't say that it is not prudent to be prepared for the worst,' declares de Guingand, 'but on the other hand, if there is too much of this sort of thing it is most unlikely that the troops will fight their best in their existing positions. The wrong outlook is likely to be encouraged – one of hesitation.'

Nor was confidence likely to be re-established by the plans of the High Command for meeting Rommel's new offensive. Dorman-Smith's Appreciation again makes depressing reading, showing no concern over the danger to Malta, the splitting-up of the infantry divisions, the effectiveness of the enemy's anti-tank guns, the lack of co-operation within the army and between army and air force, and worst of all an encouragement of the tendency towards 'looking over the shoulder' by a discussion of further possible retirements, this time within the battle-zone for tactical reasons.

In his Official Despatch, Field Marshal Alexander states that the plan prepared by Auchinleck and his advisers was accepted in principle by their successors. Later he would claim that this comment had been inserted in his Despatch without his knowledge. Later still he would decide he had consented to it after all. It seems that Alexander's problem was that he had somehow to conceal the true source of inspiration for the tactics used against Rommel, the 'Ultra' Intelligence which was then still on the secret list. But the really interesting point is that according to Alexander, Auchinleck's intentions were: 'to hold as strongly as possible the area between the sea and Ruweisat Ridge and to threaten from the flank any enemy advance south of the ridge from a strongly prepared position on the Alam el Halfa Ridge'.

Certainly this was a good summary of the steps that Eighth Army in practice took to oppose Rommel's advance. It bears no relation, however, to the intentions of Auchinleck. On the contrary, in his own Official Despatch, Auchinleck expressly confirms that for him the whole 'essence of the defensive plan' was not holding firm but 'fluidity and mobility', while Dorman-Smith in his Appreciation declares that: 'We have to be prepared to fight a modern defensive battle in the area El Alamein–Hammam' – and El Hammam lay some 40 miles by road eastward of Alamein.

In his Appreciation, Dorman-Smith also refers to the existence of 'reserve positions' some way behind the front line. Known as 'Observation Posts', these were in fact 'boxes', ten in number, established on prominent features. In the north they lay around Qasaba – or to give it its formal name El Qasaba el Sharqiya – which was on the railway line some ten miles east of El Alamein, in the centre around Alam Baoshaza east of the Ruweisat Ridge, and in the south on the ridge of Alam Halfa. Dorman-Smith suggests that 'the main front' could be withdrawn to these, reducing the existing fortifications to a mere 'outpost line'.

This suggestion, General Richardson informs us, Dorman-Smith '"sold" to the C-in-C', and, as Field Marshal Carver confirms in his *Dilemmas of the Desert War*, 'the Operation Orders issued at the time' by XIII and XXX Corps 'make clear' that this was the course in fact planned by the High Command.[4] They direct 9th Australian Division to the northern group of 'boxes', 5th Indian – commanded by Major General Harold Briggs – to the central group, 2nd New Zealand to Alam Halfa and 1st South African to the 'Army reserve area' near the El Ruweisat railway station. On reaching their allotted positions, the divisions are ordered to split up into 'battle groups', some to man the Observation Posts, others, containing the bulk of the artillery, to manoeuvre between them against Rommel's attacking forces. 'I never quite understood how it was to be done,' remarks de Guingand sardonically, adding: 'It was all too uncertain and fluid a plan for a sound defence. There was a great danger of the guns being driven hither and thither and confusion setting in.'

The whole point of these plans therefore was that Eighth Army would leave its present defences and it was no doubt for this reason that, as General Jackson points out, the forward dispositions of XXX Corps were left 'too shallow and over-influenced by the possible need for quick withdrawal'. Nothing could be farther removed from Alexander's description of troops holding 'as strongly as possible' fixed defences 'between the sea and Ruweisat Ridge'.

It will also be noted that no special importance had been attached to the Alam Halfa Ridge. This is never once mentioned in Dorman-Smith's Appreciation and the Operations Orders envisage it as only one among the several reserve positions. 21st Indian Infantry Brigade was sent to Alam Halfa on 3 August but this was very much understrength and had made scarcely any progress in the construction of defences by the middle of the month.

Still less had any work been done on other strategic localities in the neighbourhood of Alam Halfa. The Bare Ridge between it and the forward positions of the New Zealand Division was completely undefended. It had been planned that the New Zealanders should construct an 'intermediate position' on Point 102, the high ground just to the west of Alam Halfa but no such action had been taken by mid-August. This was perhaps not surprising for 2nd New Zealand Division was also very much below strength. Its 4th Brigade had had to be withdrawn from the battle area altogether after its casualties in July, while both the remaining brigades had suffered heavily. The New Zealanders in fact simply did not have enough men to secure both their front line and their left flank which rested on the ridge at Alam Nayil, let alone the Bare Ridge and Alam Halfa Ridge as well. In the circumstances, Alexander's statement that an enemy advance would be threatened 'from a strongly prepared position on the Alam el Halfa Ridge' appears highly optimistic to say the least.

Eighth Army's armoured formations were also to be 'fluid and mobile'. The bulk of 23rd Armoured Brigade was kept well back east of the 'boxes' around Qasaba. 1st Armoured Division was pulled out of the combat zone entirely to refit after its losses in the July offensives, though its 22nd Armoured Brigade was transferred to provide the main strength of 7th Armoured Division. This was instructed to cover the withdrawal of 5th Indian and 2nd New Zealand Divisions, counter-attacking when necessary – presumably, as so often before, straight at the muzzles of Rommel's 88s.

Just how 'fluid and mobile' the tanks were to be is well indicated by Major General Roberts, who had taken command of 22nd Armoured Brigade at the end of July. 'On code word "so-and-so",' he tells us, 'we would move to a specific area with a certain task; on another code word we would move somewhere else, etc. etc.' Since the chances were high that the wrong plan might be followed in the confusion of combat or as a result of communications problems, and since he was also grimly aware that the British armoured units were not 'sufficiently well trained for a battle of manoeuvre', Roberts felt strongly that the situation 'did not inspire the greatest confidence'.

Such a lack of confidence was in fact general – and with good reason. Had Rommel known of Auchinleck's plans he would have been delighted for this type of 'fluid and mobile' battle was just the sort at which his troops excelled; it was his own desire that events should 'move fast', that 'on no account' must the engagement 'become static'. In Eighth Army therefore, 'a good many people, including notably Freyberg', declares Field Marshal Carver, thought the tactics proposed by Auchinleck must fail. 'It would be difficult,' complains General Richardson, 'to conceive a tactical plan more unsuited to the units of the Eighth Army at that time'. The 'suicidal notions' embodied in Dorman-Smith's Appreciation and set out in subsequent commands to formations, 'might almost' grumbles Lucas Phillips, 'have been written for Rommel's express benefit'.

Mercifully Rommel would never gain any benefit from them. In London also, discontent at Eighth Army's failure to destroy or even drive back *Panzerarmee Afrika* was growing. To both Churchill and Brooke it was becoming intolerable that Eighth Army should have received continual reinforcements of men and equipment, carried by vessels travelling the weary miles round the Cape of Good Hope at a time when a shortage of shipping was crippling all Allied plans, and at the cost of ruinous consequences in the Far East – yet still without any corresponding advantage having accrued.

The fate of Malta was also causing mounting concern – in London if not in Cairo. It seemed clear that no further convoys could hope to reach the embattled island from the east. Convoys from Gibraltar, for which aircraft-carriers could provide fighter cover for at least part of the way, stood a better chance of success. From one such, code-named 'Pedestal', four freighters loaded with a mixture of flour, ammunition and aviation fuel in cans and the vital American-built tanker *Ohio* did reach Malta in mid-August, but the loss of nine more merchantmen as well as of several warships including the aircraft-carrier *Eagle* warned that this costly success was unlikely to be repeated. Yet Malta had to receive fresh supplies by the end of November. The only way of ensuring that they arrived was to guarantee fighter protection for the convoy bringing them. The only way it could be guaranteed was for Eighth Army to retake the Martuba airfields.

In addition, great events were due to take place at the other end of the Mediterranean, where the Western Allies had agreed to carry out a joint invasion of Vichy French North Africa. This operation, given the inspiring code name of TORCH by the Prime Minister, was planned for the end of October. It was felt with some reason that the reception of the landing forces would depend very much on whether Eighth Army had previously gained a decisive victory.

Finally, on the fall of Tobruk, President Roosevelt and his Chief of Army Staff, General George Marshall, had promptly ordered the shipment of 300 of the latest Sherman tanks, which carried a 75mm gun in the turret instead of in the less satisfactory side-sponson of the Grant, to the Middle East. Neither Churchill nor Brooke, both of whom were in Washington at the time, ever forgot the generosity of this gesture. Both felt a consequent moral obligation to ensure that when the Shermans reached Eighth Army in September, they would be put to the most effective possible use.

Accordingly both the Prime Minister and the Chief of the Imperial General Staff decided they must fly out to the Middle East to see what was going wrong. Brooke reached Cairo in time for breakfast on 3 August; Churchill, with an impressive entourage, arrived soon afterwards.

The series of interviews, discussions and decisions which followed have been covered in numerous accounts, most notably perhaps in Field Marshal

Carver's *El Alamein* and General Sir David Fraser's biography *Alanbrooke*. The key moment it seems, was a tour of Eighth Army which Churchill and Brooke made on 5 August. The opinions which they heard, says General Jackson, 'were many and varied and did not flatter the senior commanders'. The leaders of the divisions from the Dominions, as the self-governing parts of the British Commonwealth were then called, were particularly direct in their comments. Nor were such opinions held only by army officers – 'it was not difficult,' notes Churchill in his *Second World War*, 'to perceive how critical the Air was of the Army'.

By the end of that day, declares General Fraser, Brooke was willing 'to agree with any solution which took Auchinleck from Cairo'. The decision was ultimately his for, as Churchill recognized, it was Brooke who, as the professional head of the Army, had 'to appraise the quality of our generals'. In practice though, the Prime Minister was in full agreement and although much stress has been placed on his eagerness that Auchinleck should renew the offensive earlier than that officer intended, the main reason for his disapproval lay elsewhere. Churchill knew, from the 'Ultra' interceptions, that Rommel planned to attack at the end of August. He was naturally anxious to learn how Auchinleck proposed to meet this threat.

Unfortunately Auchinleck appeared to have little confidence in the ability of his men to do so and certainly inspired no confidence at all in Churchill when the Prime Minister raised this subject. Brigadier Sir Edgar Williams, then a young officer on the Eighth Army staff dealing with the 'Ultra' Intelligence, was one of those waiting outside Auchinleck's operations caravan at the time this exchange took place. He would later tell Montgomery's biographer Nigel Hamilton that 'I virtually heard Winston Churchill sack the Auk.' Churchill, Williams states, 'gave this astonishing description of what Rommel was doing and said to the Auk: "Well, what are you going to do about that? What's your plan?" . . . The Auk, he wasn't very articulate.' As Williams walked away afterwards, he remarked: 'Well, we'll get a new Army Commander now. Who the hell will it be?'

During 6 August, Churchill and Brooke made up their minds. Auchinleck would leave his dual posts of Commander-in-Chief, Middle East and Commander, Eighth Army. He would later be reappointed C-in-C, India, in which role, it is only right to state, he would prove a conspicuous success. Dorman-Smith would also depart – to the great relief of most of Eighth Army. In March 1944, he would be given an infantry brigade in Italy, only to be removed less than six months later as unfit for brigade command, all three of his battalion commanders having refused to serve under him any longer. He retired to Ireland, changing his name to Dorman-O'Gowan in the process, to regale anyone willing to listen with the story of how the 'Military Establishment' had decreed his ruin.

Auchinleck was replaced as C-in-C, Middle East by General Sir Harold Alexander, who had achieved so much at Dunkirk and at least more than anyone else in Burma. He would reach Cairo early on 9 August. In Brooke's view, the imperturbable Alexander was the ideal choice – a man who would cope with the political problems of the Middle East with tact and charm, support his subordinates loyally but only intervene if matters were going badly, and be able to win the affection and trust of all.

As Commander, Eighth Army, Brooke had initially favoured Lieutenant General Bernard Law Montgomery, who had proved superb under his command during the retreat to Dunkirk. Finally though, he accepted Churchill's wish that an officer already on the scene should be appointed. He therefore agreed that Eighth Army should be entrusted to Gott, who was ordered back to Cairo for consultation. He flew in a Bristol Bombay transport which tragically was compelled by an overheated engine to climb to 500 feet instead of proceeding at ground level as was usual. It was attacked by two 109s and shot down. Gott was killed. His replacement had after all to be sent out from England, arriving on the morning of 12 August, by which time Churchill and Brooke had already left Egypt.

Major General Fuller describes Montgomery in *The Decisive Battles of the Western World* as

> a man of dynamic personality and of supreme self-confidence. Known to his officers and men as 'Monty', he was a past master in showmanship and publicity; audacious in his utterances and cautious in his actions. Though at times smiled at by his officers, his neo-Napoleonic personal messages . . . electrified his men. He was the right man in the right place at the right moment; for after its severe defeat the Eighth Army needed a new dynamo and Montgomery supplied it.

Moreover after the bitter lessons of Dunkirk, Montgomery was well aware of the implications of fighting Germans, and if he had had no experience of fighting them in the Desert, he had at least conducted mock battles and training exercises in the area of the present fighting between the wars, when he had been a battalion and acting brigade commander – which was considerably more than Rommel could have said on his arrival in North Africa. Montgomery was also delighted to have a command in the field again, eager to take up his post and full of ideas. Indeed on the afternoon of his arrival, he would request Major General Harding to draw up plans for a mobile reserve corps. This would become a reformed X Corps and though not really very different from XXX Corps as envisaged before CRUSADER, it was certainly a change from Harding's previous task for Auchinleck – that of planning for possible withdrawals to Sinai and the Sudan.

Unhappily no orders with regard to X Corps could be issued as yet. Eighth Army was not to get its 'new dynamo' immediately. Auchinleck had accepted his fate with outward dignity. A meeting with Churchill had been, says the Prime Minister, 'at once bleak and impeccable'. But to Brooke, with whom as he knew the final responsibility for his dismissal lay, Auchinleck 'showed his bitterness'. 'Brooke had a stormy interview on 9th August with Auchinleck,' reports General Fraser. '"I tried to soften the blow as much as I possibly could. In the end I had no alternative but to turn on him and put him in his place," Brooke recorded afterwards. "He left me no alternative . . . I had to bite him back as he was apt to snarl, that kept him quiet".'

It was perhaps wounded pride therefore that prompted Auchinleck, after Churchill's departure and contrary to Churchill's wishes, to propose that the transfer of both his Middle East and Eighth Army Commands should be postponed until 15 August. Alexander, with his usual good nature, unwisely agreed, with the result that when Montgomery arrived it was felt that his plans should be held in abeyance until after the changeover. Worse still, though Montgomery left for Eighth Army HQ on the morning of the 13th, it was under instructions from Auchinleck, in the cynical words of Field Marshal Carver, to 'look round but not to take command until the 15th'.

Yet as Carver relates, Intelligence reports clearly indicated that Rommel was preparing for a fresh attack and 'it was thought likely that he would aim to deliver it near the period of the full moon which fell on August 26th'. Thus Montgomery might have as little as fourteen days to prepare for a major battle and one which would come at a time when Eighth Army had not yet received its planned reinforcements but *Panzerarmee Afrika* had. In the circumstances, Auchinleck's wish that the new Army Commander should in effect waste one-seventh of his precious time before the anticipated attack is utterly astounding.

Despite later criticisms, therefore, it is difficult to blame Montgomery for the action which he now took. Montgomery had already received forceful summaries of the maladies affecting the Allied cause in the Middle East from Harding on the 12th and from de Guingand who had driven out with him to Eighth Army's Headquarters on the Ruweisat Ridge on the morning of the 13th. On his arrival, he had cross-examined Ramsden, to whom Auchinleck had entrusted temporary command of Eighth Army. 'By the time he had finished,' reports Field Marshal Carver, 'Montgomery had decided that he could not tolerate two days hanging about under these conditions. He therefore told Ramsden to return to his corps, having decided in spite of Auchinleck's orders to assume command immediately' – at 1400 to be precise.

Montgomery had not taken over an easy command. Lieutenant General Sir Brian Horrocks who reached Eighth Army on 15 August, having been personally selected by Montgomery to command XIII Corps, states in his book *A Full Life*, that 'the desert veterans, who had been fighting continually in the Middle East, resented the arrival of Montgomery and myself.' This no doubt was an exaggeration, but certainly the men of Eighth Army were, in General Jackson's words, 'too disillusioned by all they had been through to accept at face value the views of some unknown general out from England with "his knees still pink"'. They had heard too many 'election promises'. This time they wanted proof.

Yet the only convincing proof was victory. Once Montgomery had displayed his ability in action, once Eighth Army with its armour, infantry and artillery integrated for the common good and backed by its air arm, had achieved an undisputed victory, then anything was possible. Unfortunately Montgomery here faced a seemingly unbreakable dilemma. His problem is neatly summed up by Jackson: 'Eighth Army's morale could not be fully restored until Rommel had been demonstratively beaten; and yet he would not be beaten unless morale was restored.'

Happily by one more extraordinary irony, that aspect of the situation which had most caused but had also been caused by Eighth Army's poor morale was now to provide the solution to the dilemma. It thereby brought about Eighth Army's salvation, for it gave Montgomery the chance to take immediate decisive action which would impress his men with his ability, silence the grumblers and unite his entire command behind him in relieved approval.

At 1830 on 13 August 1942, Montgomery addressed the staff officers of Eighth Army. Naturally they appeared outwardly respectful but inwardly, as Williams would tell Nigel Hamilton: 'I think we had this rather arrogant view that we'd had rather a lot of generals through our hands, in our day.' Also Montgomery, small, wiry, sharp-faced and sharp-nosed, was scarcely an impressive figure. Williams personally was amused because the fighter patrol which Montgomery had ordered to cover the Headquarters had left before the general arrived. Richardson considered that Montgomery did not 'look the part'. De Guingand was depressed by a feeling that he would not 'remain long in office. It was only natural that he [Montgomery] would bring out his own Chief of Staff.' Everyone noted how white the newcomer's knees were.

But once they had heard what their new leader had to say, their attitude changed completely. 'We all felt,' reports de Guingand, 'that a cool and refreshing breeze had come to relieve the oppressive and stagnant atmosphere. The effect of the address was electric – it was terrific! And we all went to bed that night with a new hope in our hearts, and a great confidence in the future of our Army.'

De Guingand must have experienced great pleasure in hearing Montgomery not only confirm his appointment but increase his powers and responsibilities – he was to be not just the Brigadier General Staff but a Chief of Staff through whom the new Eighth Army Commander would issue all orders; whose own orders were to be treated as those of the Army Commander, to be acted on at once. This, however, was only a minor part of Montgomery's message, for he had, to an uncanny extent, already detected the major weaknesses of Eighth Army and had directed his thoughts towards dealing with them.[5]

The least commendable part of Montgomery's speech was his attempt to assure his listeners that 'fresh divisions' were 'now arriving in Egypt' and that '300 to 400 Sherman new tanks' were 'actually being unloaded at Suez *now*'. In reality no new divisions would arrive until after Rommel had launched his anticipated offensive. Two divisions – 44th and 51st – had arrived comparatively recently but the latter at least was not considered sufficiently battle-worthy to help meet that offensive. Nor would the Shermans reach Suez until early September, again only after Rommel's attack. Had this been all that Montgomery's address contained, it might have raised spirits temporarily but the loss of trust which would have ensued when the truth came out must have been appalling.

Luckily these remarks passed almost unnoticed amid the admiration induced by Montgomery's ideas. It was Montgomery's intention to end the suspicions between the various branches of the Army and also the 'indiscipline at the top' by uniting his entire force in a common cause under his own firm control. 'We must have confidence in each other,' he told his staff. Then they would 'work together as a team; and together we will gain the confidence of this great Army and go forward to final victory in Africa.' They were to ensure that this mutual respect 'permeates right down through the Eighth Army to the most junior private soldier. All the soldiers must know what is wanted and when they see it coming to pass there will be a surge of confidence throughout the Army.' Obviously that would take time, but meanwhile as a first step towards a united effort, the Eighth Army Headquarters was to be moved forthwith to the coast so that it could be set up 'side by side with the HQ of the Desert Air Force'.

These factors were, however, as nothing compared with another decision that Montgomery now announced, namely his countermanding of all existing plans for retreat, either to the Observation Posts or to the Nile Delta.[6] He had indeed issued such instructions immediately on taking his premature command of Eighth Army and de Guingand states that a signal to that effect 'had already gone out', but if so, few of the staff who had had to be 'summoned from far and wide', had learned of it. Consequently it came as a surprise to them when their new leader announced curtly: 'I do not like the general atmosphere I find here. It is an atmosphere of doubt, of looking back to select the next place to which to withdraw, of loss of confidence in our ability to defeat Rommel, of desperate defence measures by reserves in preparing positions in Cairo and the Delta'.

Calling for a 'new atmosphere', Montgomery proclaimed:

> The defence of Egypt lies here at Alamein and on the Ruweisat Ridge. What is the use of digging trenches in the Delta? It is quite useless; if we lose this position we lose Egypt; all the fighting troops now in the Delta must come here at once, and will. *Here* we will stand and fight; there will be no further withdrawal. I have ordered that all plans and instructions dealing with further withdrawal are to be burnt, and at once. We will stand and fight *here*. If we can't stay here alive, then let us stay here dead.

In those few sentences, Montgomery ended for ever the doubts that had so crippled Eighth Army, the uncertainties, the glances 'over the shoulder'. The news spread like wildfire. It was soon confirmed by formal instructions to the individual corps[7] and by the emphatic approval of General Alexander immediately he took over as C-in-C, Middle East on 15 August. The effect, relates Horrocks, 'was magical'. 'There was no more talk of the alternative positions in the rear,' reports Kippenberger. 'We were delighted and the morale of the whole Army went up incredibly.' 'A sigh of relief,' states Lucas Phillips, 'went up from the whole Army. Morshead, the Australians' commander, said "Thank God!"'

Already then Montgomery had gained the initial approval of his command and he now set out to follow up his success by embarking on what the Official History calls 'a strenuous programme of tours and visits' in order to 'impress his personality' on his men. As one means to this end, he acquired an Australian slouch hat, onto which he stuck the badges of the units he visited; it was later replaced by the famous black beret. His action delighted the troops at the time, aroused the wrath of the pompous later and was comparatively unimportant in the long term.

For what really mattered was not Montgomery's headgear but his words and actions. As well as reiterating his 'no withdrawal' orders, he put over clearly his plans for the repulse of Rommel's anticipated attack. These will be described later; for the present suffice to mention General Jackson's comment that they made 'sound sense' to Eighth Army. Moreover, by revealing his intentions to his soldiers, Montgomery demonstrated his trust in them and convinced them of his own confidence in the outcome. As a result, declares the Official History, while 'there had been no lack of activity and energy before, it was now that a renewed, strong sense of purpose made itself widely felt'.

That sense of purpose and the reasons behind it were noticed even by the enemy. Thus Paul Carell calls Montgomery simply 'the man who was to defeat Rommel' adding 'and how dangerous he was'. Major General von Mellenthin gives a more detailed but equally emphatic verdict:

> There can be no question that the fighting efficiency of the British improved vastly under the new leadership, and for the first time Eighth Army had a commander who really made his will felt throughout the whole force . . . Montgomery is undoubtedly a great tactician – circumspect and thorough in making his plans, utterly ruthless in carrying them out. He brought a new spirit to Eighth Army, and illustrated once again the vital importance of personal leadership in war.

So in a miraculously short time, Montgomery had achieved the first part of his aim: he had restored Eighth Army's flagging morale by giving it the leadership, confidence, discipline and unity it had previously lacked. Nonetheless his success still rested on extremely fragile foundations. His leadership and Eighth Army's confidence, discipline and unity had not yet been subjected to the acid test of combat. If either failed in that test, then Montgomery's success so far would have been wasted, for Eighth Army would certainly suffer a blow from which there could be no further recovery.

This was the fear that haunted many. Montgomery, says General Jackson, 'was given the benefit of the doubt by most people, because they were delighted to have a firm line; the more cynical awaited practical proof of his policies.' 'We had been impressed with his clear thinking and his amazing confidence,' confirms General Richardson, 'but in many minds, certainly in mine, there lingered doubts: "Is this just a technique, and will it fall apart when we face the crunch with Rommel, still the bogeyman?"'

Of this mood of anxiety, Montgomery personally was well aware. 'The general atmosphere,' he tells us in his *Memoirs*, 'was: it looks good, it sounds good, but will it work?'

Notes

1   Field Marshal Harding's comments were made in interviews with Nigel Hamilton, author of a monumental biography of Field Marshal Montgomery, *Monty Volume I: The Making of a General 1887–1942*. All quotations from Harding, unless otherwise stated, come from this source.

2   The full text of this Appreciation is set out in an Appendix to John Connell's biography *Auchinleck*.

3   These may be found at the Public Record Office, Kew. Any subsequent quotations from the War Diaries come from this source.

4   Carver can speak with particular authority on this point. He was the staff officer who wrote the XXX Corps Operation Orders. The relevant ones are No. 144 of

29 July for XIII Corps and Nos. 70 and 71 of 31 July and 10 August respectively for XXX Corps – see the Corps War Diaries at the Public Record Office.

5   The full text of Montgomery's address can be found in Nigel Hamilton's biography.

6   Montgomery never seems to have distinguished between the planned tactical retreats and the possible major retirements, regarding both as equally disastrous. This may be why in his *Memoirs* he gives the misleading impression that the latter would have taken place automatically when Rommel attacked.

7   See Operation Orders No. 145 of 14 August for XIII Corps and No. 72 of 16 August for XXX Corps at the Public Record Office.

Chapter 4

THE BATTLE OF ALAM HALFA

All doubts would soon be resolved. On 30 August, Rommel wrote to his wife: 'Today has dawned at last. It's been such a long wait worrying all the time whether I should get everything I needed together to enable me to take the brakes off again. Many of my worries have been by no means satisfactorily settled and we have some very grave shortages. But I've taken the risk, for it will be a long time before we get such favourable conditions of moonlight, relative strengths etc. again.'

Rommel might well refer to 'favourable conditions', for, as Liddell Hart remarks, 'the strength of the two sides was nearer to an even balance than it was either before or later'. The forces striking from Malta might attack Axis supply ships but Axis transport aircraft could still operate without interference and during July and August, these ferried out 24,600 soldiers to reinforce Rommel's army. By the end of August, the remaining formations of 164th Light had been brought up to the front line, Rommel's three original German divisions had been restored to full strength and *Panzerarmee Afrika* had been joined by Colonel Bernhard Ramcke's 288th Parachute Brigade, now used in an infantry role but still possessing all those ruthless fighting qualities traditionally associated with airborne units. In August also, there arrived the 'dismounted' Italian Folgore Parachute Division, described by Ronald Lewin as 'a first-class fighting formation'; containing, says Lucas Phillips, 'spirited troops of good training and physique' who collectively were 'as good as the average German division and better at night work'.

While the Axis infantry thus increased in both numbers and quality to two German and five Italian divisions, plus the one independent German brigade, Eighth Army at the time Montgomery took command had received no reinforcements for its existing four infantry divisions. Luckily though, the new leader's reluctance to waste fighting men on defences at Cairo or Alexandria would soon alter the situation.

With regard to armour, Eighth Army did receive a reinforcement by the end of August, but the 10th Armoured Division under the command of Major General Alec Gatehouse was no more than a replacement for 1st Armoured Division and it contained at this time only Brigadier Neville Custance's 8th Armoured Brigade. This consisted of the 3rd Battalion, Royal Tank Regiment, the Staffordshire Yeomanry and the Nottinghamshire Yeomanry (also called the Sherwood Rangers). Unfortunately while 3rd Royal Tanks was a veteran formation, both the Yeomanry regiments were totally inexperienced, having seen no action previously in the war, or indeed since they had ceased to ride horses.

The arrival of 10th Armoured Division brought the number of tanks in Eighth Army by the end of August up to 772 – on paper. In reality those serviceable were 693 – 197 Crusaders, 169 Stuarts, 163 Valentines and, most important, 164 Grants. This was a much higher figure than those available to Rommel but in fact the recovery of the Axis armour had been the more remarkable. The *Afrika Korps* which had mustered sixty tanks at Mersa Matruh, as few as twenty-six on 3 July, and only forty-two when it had won 'Second Ruweisat', now possessed 232 tanks, of which 203 were gun-armed. The Italian Ariete and Littorio Armoured Divisions could find another 243 medium and thirty-eight light tanks – albeit of dubious value.

In the case of the German armour, Rommel had again benefited in quality as well as quantity. His Mark III Specials which could outgun all British tanks except Grants, but of which he had never had more than twenty-seven in June or sixteen in July, numbered seventy-three on 30 August. He had also at last received suitable armour-piercing ammunition for his Mark IV Specials, of which he now had twenty-seven. They were thus more than a match for any of their opponents, for the Mark IV's long-barrelled 75mm – 'the devil of a gun' as Major General Roberts calls it – was 'far superior to the gun in the Grants'.

Rommel's finest anti-tank guns, his 88mms, had always been superior to those of his enemies. It was hardly possible for their quality to increase in August 1942, but their numbers did, for during that month, Rommel's original Flak Regiment 135 was joined by Flak Regiment 102.[1]

Equally welcome to Rommel must have been the build-up of the Axis air forces. Major General Max Seidemann, who had taken up the post of *Fliegerführer Afrika* in August, commanded 720 machines divided almost equally between the Luftwaffe and the *Regia Aeronautica*. The Italian aircraft were mainly fighters, ranging from biplane Fiat CR42s through Fiat G50s and Macchi MC200s to the excellent Macchi MC202s. Apart from reconnaissance machines, the German warplanes consisted of three *Gruppen*[2] of Junkers Ju 87 Stuka dive-bombers, the equivalent of three *Gruppen* of Junkers Ju 88 bombers, a *Gruppe* of Messerschmitt Bf 110 twin-engined fighter-bombers – which had arrived in late August – and four *Gruppen* of Messerschmitt Bf 109s. In addition, there were 230 German aircraft, mainly Ju 88s and Bf 110s, in Crete which could be used for long-range attacks on Allied bases or aerodromes.

By contrast, Coningham's Desert Air Force contained 565 machines. Apart from reconnaissance aircraft, among which was an entire Hurricane squadron, No. 208, the RAF contributed two squadrons of Baltimore light bombers, three squadrons of Spitfires, three of Kittyhawks and a further eight squadrons of Hurricanes, including No. 6 Squadron with its anti-tank Hurricane IIDs. There were also two squadrons of Royal Australian Air Force Kittyhawks, seven squadrons from the South African Air Force – two with Boston light bombers, two with Kittyhawks, one with Tomahawks, two with Hurricanes – and two squadrons from the United States Army Air Force, the 81st flying Mitchell bombers and the 64th with Warhawks, both of which had joined the Desert Air Force during August. Coningham, like Seidemann, also had the support of some 230 aircraft not under his direct control: six squadrons of Wellingtons, the equivalent of a squadron of Halifaxes, two squadrons of Beaufighters and two of Fleet Air Arm Albacores.

Admittedly, figures are as usual somewhat misleading. Of the Axis warplanes, only about 60 per cent were serviceable at any given moment, while the rate for Allied aircraft as a whole was about 70 per cent and for the rugged, reliable Hurricanes was as high as 75 per cent. Also apart from the Macchi MC202s, the Italian fighters were definitely inferior in performance, so were usually kept out of the thick of the fighting. It would perhaps be more fair, then, to consider the two air arms as being about equal in strength. Nonetheless for Rommel the contrast with the situation in July was immense, the more so since Seidemann's command was now well forward to provide close support.[3]

In the air too, the Axis gain had been in quality as well as numbers. As was mentioned, the Desert Air Force now contained a third Spitfire squadron, No. 92 having become fully operational on 13 August, but the finest fighters in North Africa were still the Messerschmitt Bf 109s, which had attained their greatest strength ever. By an odd coincidence there were exactly 109 of these in the fighter *Gruppen*, of which about sixty-five were serviceable – to them should be added about forty-five serviceable Macchi MC202s with an almost identical performance. Of course, whether the 109 pilots could be persuaded to protect their own bombers properly or to engage Allied bombers although these 'had tail gunners', remained to be seen.

Certainly Rommel still had his worries; it was these which had caused him to postpone his offensive from its originally planned date of 26 August. Chief of them was his supply line, that fragile 'piece of elastic' which his own decision to strike deep into Egypt before Malta had been conquered had made still more vulnerable. Petrol in particular was in short supply, though this was a problem which Rommel had had to face in virtually every previous encounter; his robust reaction had always been that if his men needed fuel, they had better 'go and get it from the British'.

In fact on this occasion, as Horrocks points out, the shortage of petrol was not 'quite so acute as Rommel claimed'. Four tankers had reached Tobruk in the last ten days of August, as had some ammunition ships. Three other tankers had been sunk en route, but on 30 August, Kesselring transferred 1,500 tons of fuel from Luftwaffe stocks, which when added to the supplies already with Rommel's units, gave *Panzerarmee Afrika* enough for a seven days' battle. In addition, Kesselring agreed to fly in a further 500 tons daily – a promise which, von Mellenthin confirms, he 'did in fact fulfill' though much of the fuel was 'consumed on the long journey to the front' – while Cavallero for his part stated that five tankers would reach Tobruk in the first week of September.

More important indeed, was Rommel's lack of motor vehicles which he needed not only for his front-line troops but to bring up his vital supplies. Almost 800 lorries reached him in August, but the difficulty remained acute, for by this time a shortage of spare parts for his captured British vehicles had rendered a high proportion of these unserviceable.

Even so, Liddell Hart's comment that Rommel not only 'still had a possibility of victory' but might well 'have achieved it if his opponents had faltered or fumbled as they had done on several previous occasions when their advantage had seemed more sure', appears to be a considerable understatement of the position. Rommel's advance this time was far more than just a 'try-on' – as he was very well aware. He called it a 'decisive battle' which would result in 'the final destruction of the enemy'; he urged his soldiers to give of their utmost 'during these decisive hours'; he told his wife that his blow 'might go some way towards deciding the whole course of the war'.

Despite these comments, the Official History considers that Rommel's 'old fire and enthusiasm were lacking', that 'the Rommel of Alam el Halfa was not the Rommel of Gazala and Tobruk'. This seems a reasonable suggestion at first glance for Rommel was suffering from stomach trouble and high blood pressure. On the other hand he had been similarly afflicted both before Gazala and when preparing for what he believed would be a decisive assault on Tobruk prior to CRUSADER. It may be that Nigel Hamilton is correct, in part at least, when he describes Rommel's problems as 'the nervous anxiety of the ambitious performer, mezmerized by the prize of Alexandria and Cairo'.

In any case, it appears that Rommel had got over the worst of his troubles by the end of August, perhaps because he realized how 'favourable' the 'relative strengths' of the two sides had become. In a moment of depression on 22 August, he had suggested that he might be recalled, but only two days later, he could reassure his Führer that he now felt well enough to command the coming offensive though he hoped he could have a long period of recuperation in Germany after completing his crowning conquest of Egypt. By the 30th indeed, he could tell his wife that he was 'feeling quite on top of my form'.[4]

Nor did Rommel's plan for his 'decisive battle', which the British would call the Battle of Alam Halfa, and which was to commence on the night of 30th/31st August, show the slightest lack of 'fire and enthusiasm'. It was not quite so dramatically daring as the one for Gazala, where he had intended to defeat Eighth Army and capture Tobruk all in four days, but it was most certainly, as Lucas Phillips says, 'typical Rommel'; 'genuine Rommel' in the words of Paul Carell.

Rommel entrusted the northern sector of his front to Lieutenant General Navarini's XXI Italian Corps which contained, reading from north to south, the German 164th Light Division, the Italian Trento Division, the bulk of the Ramcke Parachute Brigade and the Italian Bologna Division. Their task was to pin down the Allied forces opposite to them, for which purpose the 164th and Trento Divisions would make raids in the north, while Ramcke's parachutists would deliver a strong attack on the Ruweisat Ridge.

The main thrust, as at Gazala, would be made in the south, in the areas of good going between the Qattara Depression and the line of high ground running from Alam Nayil by way of the Bare Ridge to the ridge of Alam el Halfa. On the right flank of the advance were stationed the German 3rd and 33rd Reconnaissance Units, with armoured cars, infantry in lorries and supporting anti-tank guns. North of these came the *Afrika Korps* under Nehring, who by the way had been promoted to full general after the fall of Tobruk, with Major General Gustav von Vaerst's 15th Panzer Division on the right and 21st Panzer Division under the brilliant Major General Georg von Bismarck on the left. North again was the Italian XX Corps under Major General Giuseppe de Stephanis, containing Ariete (Armoured), Littorio (Armoured) and Trieste (Motorized) Divisions. Finally on the left flank came Major General Kleemann's 90th Light Division.

All these forces were to race eastward, the panzers for 30 miles, a distance that would outflank the whole of Eighth Army's defences, before wheeling into line facing north. Rommel intended to complete this preliminary move well before dawn on 31 August, but he was confident he could do so since his Intelligence staff had assured him that this sector was only 'weakly mined'.

While this main attack was taking place, Lieutenant General Orsi's Italian

X Corps would move up in support, his Brescia Division, reinforced by units from Ramcke's Parachute Brigade, attacking Alam Nayil, his Folgore Parachute Division proceeding to Himeimat. They would thus be well placed to guard against any Allied counter-attack that might develop in the south.

Then at 0600 on 31 August, the *Afrika Korps* would strike north-east directly towards the coast which it would reach near the El Ruweisat railway station some 35 miles to the east of El Alamein. Here it would attack the British supply area, while the Italian armour assaulted the Alam Halfa and Ruweisat ridges from behind. Eighth Army would doubtless move back its own tanks to the rescue, but past events had convinced Rommel that he could always master the British armour. Once this had been achieved, Eighth Army's infantry would be completely isolated, as Tobruk had been. Rommel would leave the bulk of his own infantry to deal with them, while 21st Panzer Division raced for Alexandria and 15th Panzer, 90th Light and the Italian XX Corps headed for Cairo, from which the Germans would push on to Suez while the Italians followed the Nile southward.

In fact it was not a case of 'the Rommel of Alam el Halfa' being different from 'the Rommel of Gazala and Tobruk' but of the conditions of Alam el Halfa being different from those of Gazala and Tobruk. For a start there was a new spirit in Eighth Army and a new officer in command. 'It was the first and typical Montgomery battle' declares Kippenberger. 'All our preparatory moves were made unhurriedly and in plenty of time, and we were completely ready when the blow fell.' He adds that he liked Montgomery's plan for the forthcoming battle 'more than that for any action I had taken part in'.

It would later be claimed in certain quarters that Montgomery had really only taken over the plan prepared by his predecessors, of which Dorman-Smith's Appreciation was the 'blueprint'. It is not a view supported by the officers who were in Eighth Army at the time – least of all by Major General Sir Francis de Guingand, who having been Chief of Staff to both Auchinleck and Montgomery, was in a unique position to judge. In *Operation Victory*, de Guingand implies that Montgomery was unlikely to have seen Dorman-Smith's Appreciation since he disliked reading documents – de Guingand kept those he did read 'to the very minimum' and normally summarized them first. Then in his later book *Generals at War*, de Guingand specifically confirms that: 'To the best of my knowledge, he (Montgomery) never examined any plans or appreciations that existed at the time.' On the contrary, de Guingand relates, Montgomery told him to 'burn the lot'.

Not that it was really very likely that Montgomery would turn to Auchinleck or Dorman-Smith for advice on tactics. In his *Memoirs*, he makes it clear that he had been contemptuous of Auchinleck when he had served under that officer in England and his feelings had in no way been altered by an unfortunate interview on his arrival in the Middle East, during which Auchinleck had singularly failed to inspire confidence – perhaps as on a former occasion, he had not been 'very articulate'. As for Dorman-Smith, Montgomery had considered him to be clever but shallow ever since he had been one of Montgomery's students at the Staff College, Camberley.

If Montgomery had needed any such advice, there was in any case a much more reliable guide close at hand. As Ronald Lewin states somewhat contemptuously: 'The old idea that Montgomery simply stole a visionary anticipation by Auchinleck and Dorman-Smith that Rommel would strike at Alam Halfa was never credible, and now seems a mere fantasy as we discover how "Ultra", thickened up by other Intelligence, kept him abreast of Rommel's intentions.'

'My Intelligence staff,' says Montgomery in his *Memoirs*, 'were certain the "break-in" to our positions would be on the southern flank; this would be followed by a left wheel, his armoured forces being directed on the Alam Halfa and Ruweisat ridges. I agreed and my plans were based on this forecast.'

Nonetheless if Montgomery then had no opportunity, no inclination and no need to study Dorman-Smith's Appreciation, it is still instructive to note how different his own ideas were. This was a matter of some significance for the future, because it is impossible to understand the trust which the men of Eighth Army came to have in Montgomery until it is appreciated – as they did – that victory at the Battle of Alam Halfa arose from just those alterations which Montgomery had made to the previous plans.

In the first place, Montgomery concentrated all his attention on the existing front-line positions. He showed no interest in 'the defences of Alexandria–Cairo–the Delta proper' which were considered so important by Dorman-Smith in his Appreciation. He cancelled all schemes for withdrawals to the 'reserve positions', the Observation Posts, suggested by Dorman-Smith in his Appreciation and set out in detail in subsequent Corps Operation Orders. He rejected the idea that a 'fluid and mobile' Eighth Army should 'be prepared to fight a modern defensive battle in the area El Alamein–Hammam' as directed by Dorman-Smith in his Appreciation. In short his aim was to do just what Rommel – and Auchinleck – least wanted: ensure that the fighting would 'become static'.

Montgomery's own Corps Operation Orders therefore, as mentioned earlier, ordered the divisions in XXX Corps – 9th Australian, 1st South African and 5th Indian reading from north to south – and 2nd New Zealand Division which provided the infantry strength of XIII Corps to defend their present positions to the end. Labour units, hitherto employed on tasks in the Delta, were summoned to strengthen and give as much depth as possible to the forward positions of all the infantry divisions, while food, water and ammunition were hurriedly brought up to enable them to conduct a lengthy resistance if needed.

Next Montgomery ended the existing obsession with battle groups. These had been mentioned with approval by Dorman-Smith in his Appreciation and their use is taken for granted in the later Corps Operation Orders. Montgomery, however, as de Guingand tells us, ordered that 'the expression ceased to exist. Divisions would fight as divisions and be allowed to develop their great strength.' In this objective, he once more enjoyed the support of Alexander who, according to the Official History, made it clear that 'the basic formation would be the division, which was not to be split up into detachments except temporarily for a definite task'.

This attitude further ensured that the artillery in each infantry division – which normally consisted of three regiments of field guns and one regiment of anti-tank guns – was also no longer scattered among battle groups or 'boxes', and in addition Montgomery ordered that every possible gun previously kept back to defend the positions to the rear should be moved up to the front line. He decreed that on future occasions Eighth Army's artillery would deliver concentrated fire – a task made easier at Alam Halfa by the decision that the fighting should remain static.

The area from the coast to the Ruweisat Ridge was now at last, and for the first time, really held 'as strongly as possible', but the situation of 2nd New Zealand Division still appeared perilous. Whereas the divisions in XXX Corps all mustered their full three brigades, Freyberg commanded only two. With these, moreover, he would now be expected to defend not only the existing front line but also his left flank on the Alam Nayil Ridge in case Rommel's breakthrough to the south should succeed. He naturally expressed concern that he did not have an 'adequate garrison' to carry out what he expressly described as this 'fresh policy'. Still less of course was Freyberg able to guard the ridges extending eastward from Alam Nayil. Fortunately Montgomery had made further decisions which would resolve the New Zealanders' difficulties.

As previously described, 44th (British) Division had been held back to guard the cities of Egypt since Auchinleck considered, probably correctly, that it was insufficiently trained for his 'fluid and mobile' battle. Montgomery, having no intention of fighting such a battle, believed, equally correctly, that it would fight well enough from fixed defences. On the evening of 13 August therefore, he demanded that it be sent to the front. Auchinleck, then still officially C-in-C, Middle East, weakly left the decision to Alexander. At 2200, 44th Division was ordered to proceed to the Eighth Army area.

Montgomery also claimed the 50th Division, under Major General Nichols, for his army reserve. This remained at Amiriya for the time being but would duly move up to the battle zone during the coming action – unfortunately it contained only one brigade, the 151st, after the maulings received by 150th Brigade in the Cauldron and 69th Brigade on the Miteirya Ridge.

Alexander did retain 51st (Highland) Division under Major General Douglas Wimberley to man defences in the neighbourhood of Cairo. It was not a decision that appealed to Montgomery – he would see that the division was sent forward as soon as the battle was over – but since 51st Division was not then considered fit for action even in a purely defensive role, Alexander really had little choice in the matter.

In any event it was the arrival of 44th Division that was crucial. On 16 August, its 131st and 133rd Brigades relieved 21st Indian Brigade on the Alam Halfa Ridge, while its 132nd Brigade joined the New Zealanders, thereby giving Freyberg sufficient troops with which to guard his front line and also his flank on Alam Nayil. It should be noted, however, that although detached from its parent division, 132nd Brigade did not operate on its own as Auchinleck's brigade groups or battle groups had previously done. It now formed part of 2nd New Zealand Division, benefiting from all that division's other elements – field artillery, anti-tank guns, engineers, medical staff, signals staff, and so on. Similarly at Alam Halfa, Major General Hughes had not only his two remaining infantry brigades but all his division's other resources. He at once set to work to lay minefields, organize gun positions and otherwise stiffen the defences – in short to establish at last, and for the first time, a really 'strongly prepared position on the Alam Halfa Ridge'.

Montgomery was equally determined that his armour should not become 'fluid and mobile' for he was well aware of the threat posed by Rommel's anti-tank guns – though this is nowhere mentioned in Dorman-Smith's Appreciation. He had made his views clear as early as 14 August. In a conversation with Major General Renton, commanding 7th Armoured Division, Montgomery was asked 'who would loose the armour against Rommel?' He replied, he states in his *Memoirs*: 'No-one would loose the armour; it would not be loosed and we would let Rommel bump into it for a change.' This was 'a new idea' to Renton. Most unwisely he 'argued about it a good deal' – as a result of which Montgomery transferred 22nd Armoured Brigade to the control of Gatehouse's 10th Armoured Division. Roberts was then directed to take his brigade to Point 102 where, reinforced by a number of anti-tank guns, it was to await the enemy attack in defensive positions of its own choosing. 'Gone were all the other plans,' declares Roberts, 'and we gladly destroyed the mass of traces with different code names which had been prepared with laborious staff work to indicate the alternative positions. There was one firm plan and one position to occupy and we all felt better.'

Of the other armoured units, Custance's 8th Armoured Brigade was stationed ten miles east of Roberts to the south-east of Alam Halfa. It too was strengthened by further anti-tank guns and both Custance and Roberts would also enjoy the support of 44th Division's artillery. 23rd Armoured Brigade, previously intended to be kept back east of Qasaba, was ordered by

Montgomery to transfer a squadron of tanks each to the Australians, the New Zealanders and 5th Indian Division, while its remaining Valentines were brought up close behind the Ruweisat Ridge to help to hold the existing front line. Then once it was clear that there was no danger of a breakthrough in the Ruweisat area, Brigadier Richards was to move south to occupy the Bare Ridge where he too would come under the command of Gatehouse.

That left only 7th Armoured Division which was holding the front between Alam Nayil and the Qattara Depression. It was always realized that this was the most vulnerable part of the defences and that ground might well be lost here. If that happened, Montgomery urged his armour to attack Rommel's vital supply units[5] – another idea not to be found in Dorman-Smith's Appreciation. According to Lieutenant General Horrocks, Montgomery constantly emphasized the need to 'shoot up his (Rommel's) soft-skinned vehicles'.

Yet in practice it seems clear that Montgomery hoped that his men would stand firm in this area also. Dorman-Smith's Appreciation had envisaged 7th Armoured imposing only delaying tactics on the enemy by means of a 'harassing defensive technique', while later Operations Orders, as we have seen, instructed it to cover the retirement of the infantry to the 'reserve positions'. Montgomery, having rejected all thoughts that the infantry might retire, was obviously free to use 7th Armoured in a different role.

In his *Memoirs*, Montgomery states that it was planned that 7th Armoured 'would give way' before an enemy attack; but he was always notoriously reluctant to admit that any part of any of his battles had not gone exactly 'according to plan' – to his own detriment, for his flexibility was in fact one of the hallmarks of his quality as a general. It is worth noting that in a previous work that had appeared under his name – *El Alamein to the River Sangro*[6] – he states only that 7th Armoured had been ordered to avoid 'becoming pinned to the ground'. He also comments on the importance of Alam Halfa 'if the enemy penetrated the Alamein defences in the southern sectors' – thereby at least implying a belief that the enemy might not do so.

That Montgomery came increasingly to hold such a belief is apparent from the instructions given at the time. Thus while for example XIII Corps Operation Order No. 146 of 17 August directs 7th Armoured merely to 'impose maximum delay' on the enemy, in the later No. 147 of 27 August, the Division is told to 'impose maximum delay and if possible stop' any Axis advance. Moreover during the battle the orders given by both Montgomery and Horrocks make quite clear their desire that 7th Armoured should do just that.

This might appear an unreasonable expectation, for the removal of Roberts had left 7th Armoured containing only Brigadier Carr's 4th Light Armoured Brigade with a limited number of Crusaders and Stuarts, and the mobile infantry of Brigadier Bosvile's 7th Motor Brigade, strengthened by anti-tank guns and the tanks of the 10th Hussars. In reality, though, Montgomery had still more new ideas to offer which would dramatically assist Carr and Bosvile to impede any attack on the southern part of the front.

In Dorman-Smith's Appreciation, no mention is made of minefields – it is difficult after all to think of any form of defence which is less 'fluid and mobile'. Some mined areas had been prepared but it appears that the general feeling, in Field Marshal Carver's words, was that 'to lay too many mines would only limit the ability of Eighth Army's own armoured forces to make a counter-thrust when their turn came'. Montgomery, not being interested in a 'fluid and mobile' defence, yet again had other ideas. As early as 14 August he had commanded that the minefields in the 7th Armoured Division area should be enlarged and strengthened, and every day thereafter, according to Carver, saw these minefields 'being extended southwards'. By the end of the month they formed two wide belts within which were contained a formidable number of both anti-tank and anti-personnel mines.

In order to familiarize officers and men with all the aspects of Montgomery's new plan, a number of exercises were conducted by both Corps. Some were 'telephone battles', in which no movement of troops took place but the Headquarters staff of corps, divisions and brigades issued orders as in a real action and assessed the results that would have followed in different situations. On 22 August, XIII Corps, under the supervision of appointed umpires, carried out a detailed rehearsal of its intended movements in which 22nd Armoured Brigade and units from both 2nd New Zealand Division and 44th (British) Division all took part; while on the 28th, another exercise rehearsed the co-operation necessary between 22nd, 8th and 23rd Armoured Brigades.

At last co-ordination between the different branches of the Army was being realized – as was co-operation between the services. For while Dorman-Smith in his Appreciation dismisses the Allied air supremacy with the casual comment that it was 'a very considerable if somewhat indefinable asset', Montgomery regarded it as one of the keys to success. By 16 August, his Headquarters was again side by side with that of the Desert Air Force, the two staffs co-operating fully in planning future moves. Their task was aided by the decision that the coming battle would no longer be 'fluid and mobile', for this inevitably reduced the possibilities of errors arising from mistaken identity.

The RAF Official History notes that:

> Beyond this, however, he [Montgomery] also brought to his post a remarkably keen, clear and vigorous appreciation of the part that could and should be played by air forces in a land battle. Commanders like Auchinleck and Ritchie had never been

anything but highly co-operative; but Montgomery insisted that goodwill was translated at all stages into practical action. If air co-operation was the gospel in the GOC's caravan, it would also be the gospel all the way from base to front line.[7]

Montgomery indeed, in his own words a few months later, 'always maintained that the Eighth Army and the RAF in the Western Desert together constitute one fighting machine and therein lies our great strength'. He exulted in 'his' 'magnificent air striking force', as he rather arrogantly considered it, in the same way that he took pride in the 'truly magnificent material' that composed 'his' Army. 'Monty' says Horrocks, 'was the most air-minded general I ever met.'

The new Eighth Army Commander, with the aid of enthusiastic subordinates and of his revitalized staff, and sustained always by the steadfast Alexander, had now done everything possible to prepare for Rommel's onslaught. All else depended on his soldiers and their comrades in arms in the skies above their heads.

And perhaps appropriately it was the airmen who saw action first. At 1925 on 30 August, the night-fighter Hurricane IICs of No. 73 Squadron RAF, a veteran unit which, since its arrival in North Africa at the end of 1940, had fought throughout the various Desert campaigns, operating for one brief but violent period from landing-grounds within the perimeter of a besieged Tobruk, took off to guard the Allied aerodromes. They had a number of encounters with Junkers Ju 88s from Crete, two of which were shot down by Squadron Leader Johnston and Warrant Officer Joyce. The raiders' bombs also did some damage but happily mostly among dummy machines which had been carefully provided to distract their attention.

Meanwhile the Albacores of Nos. 821 and 826 Squadrons, Fleet Air Arm were also airborne, heading towards a featureless area of desert north-west of Himeimat, where the 'recce' Hurricanes of No. 208 Squadron had reported enemy motor transport assembling. At about 2145, the slow, ungainly biplanes[8] illuminated these with parachute flares in preparation for an attack by Wellington bombers. This did little harm, but it provided the first example of those night attacks by the Allied air forces which were to continue throughout the battle and inflict mounting losses on Rommel's 'soft-skinned' vehicles.

Two hours later, *Panzerarmee Afrika* began its 'decisive battle'. As was mentioned earlier, Rommel had planned diversionary attacks on the XXX Corps front. The 164th Light Division launched a raid on the Australians but achieved little. The Trento Division, although one of the better Italian units, achieved even less, for the enterprising South Africans delivered a pre-emptive strike – an action they would scarcely have undertaken had they been

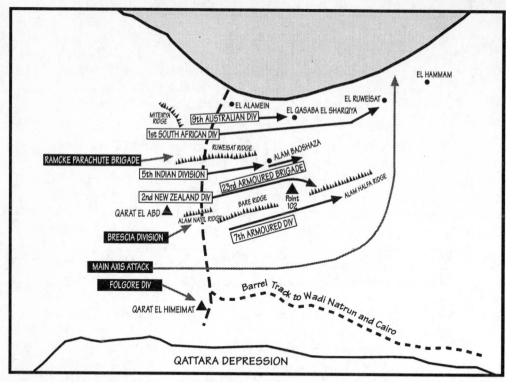

Map 4A: Alam Halfa. The battle planned by Rommel and Auchinleck.

Map 4B: Alam Halfa. The battle fought by Rommel and Montgomery.

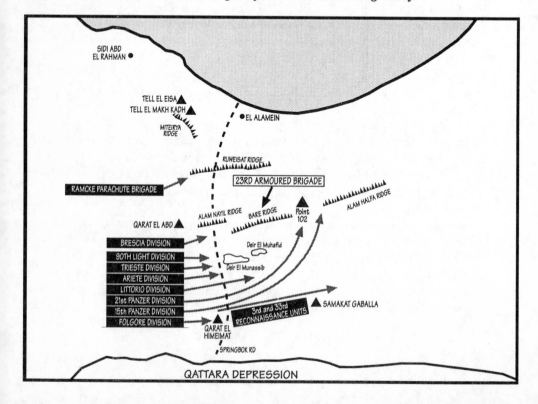

getting ready to retire to the Army Reserve area as Auchinleck had intended. They not only disrupted the Trento's attack but took fifty-six Italian prisoners. Further south, 2nd New Zealand Division also went onto the offensive against the Brescia Division, capturing thirty more Italians.

Far more dangerous was a most determined assault on the Ruweisat Ridge by Ramcke's pugnacious parachutists. This fell on 9th Indian Brigade, the brunt being borne by its British battalion, the 2nd Battalion, West Yorkshire Regiment, which suffered heavy casualties. Had 5th Indian Division followed Auchinleck's scheme of retiring to the reserve positions in the event of a heavy attack, leaving only outposts in the forward area, matters must have taken a very ugly turn. Instead the Germans gained some ground but they held this only until about 0700 on 31 August, when they were thrown back by a counter-attack delivered by 5th Indian Brigade's British battalion, the 1/4th Essex – a success which enabled Montgomery, at about 1100, to move 23rd Armoured Brigade to the Bare Ridge as he had previously planned.

It was in the south, however, where Rommel's main thrust was made, that the changes that Montgomery had wrought became most apparent. First of all, far from the area being 'weakly mined', the attackers, in Rommel's own words, 'came up against an extremely strong and hitherto unsuspected British mine belt', which was also 'thick with booby-traps'. As they tried to clear a way through this, they came under heavy fire from 4th Light Armoured and 7th Motor Brigades which, aided by the guns of 3rd and 4th Regiments, Royal Horse Artillery and those of the New Zealanders on their northern flank, held their ground with what Rommel calls 'extraordinary stubbornness'.

Then at 0240 on 31 August, 'there came' reports Paul Carell, 'a new blow. The RAF arrived.' So did the Fleet Air Arm, for the first arrivals were the flare-dropping Albacores, which provided illumination for what Rommel describes as 'relay bombing attacks', over which the Army and Air Force staffs, working in complete co-operation, exercised, in the words of General Richardson, 'minute by minute control'.

Despite its misfortunes, the *Afrika Korps* kept up its pressure, finally breaking through the first belt of British mines at about 0430, as did the valiant 90th Light Division soon afterwards. By 0700, the panzers had cleared a path through the second minefield also, and half-an-hour later, Himeimat fell to the enemy, while Carr and Bosvile slowly retired eastwards.

In theory therefore, Rommel had won the first round. In practice it had been won by Montgomery. In the first place the Axis forces had suffered heavy casualties which included a number of valuable senior officers. A bomb exploding just in front of Nehring's command vehicle had gravely injured the leader of the *Afrika Korps* and killed two of his staff officers. Von Bismarck had died at the head of his men, the victim possibly of mortar fire, probably of a mine. 90th Light's commander, Kleemann, had also fallen foul of a mine, like Nehring retiring from the battle badly wounded.

Rommel had also lost valuable time, which to him seemed the more important since he believed that 'a quick break-through in the south' would have
denied the British the opportunity of taking counter-measures. He would
have been amazed to learn that the Eighth Army Commander, warned in
advance by 'Ultra', had been so confident of the moves which his enemy
would make that he had been asleep when the action opened.[9] So disheart-
ened was Rommel that he seriously considered abandoning his offensive
entirely in the early hours of the 31st, and although he eventually yielded to
the pleas of his subordinates, he found that the problems caused by the minefields had still by no means been solved.

Indeed though the Littorio Armoured Division was able to follow the *Afrika
Korps* eastwards, the much more experienced Ariete, the Trieste and even
90th Light remained entangled in one or other of the minefields for much of
31 August. The minefields, backed by Freyberg's artillery, also provided an
insurmountable obstacle to the Italian Brescia Division when, stiffened by
detachments from Ramcke's Parachute Brigade, it attempted to attack the
New Zealand flank on Alam Nayil that morning. And the German supply
units found it extremely difficult to move through the gaps cleared in the
minefields so as to refuel and rearm their panzers – the more so since mines
and booby traps were not the only dangers they had to face.

For with the dawn the rival air forces went into action. The Junkers Ju 87s
and Ju 88s did their best to aid their ground forces but their raids caused little
damage, largely because their targets were sheltering in strong prepared positions. Moreover many of their raids did not even reach the targets. On the
morning of 31 August for instance, the Hurricanes of No. 213 Squadron,
which had begun the day by strafing enemy fighters on the ground, encountered a formation of forty Stukas. Pilot Officer Barnes, Flight Sergeant
Stephenson and Flight Sergeant Rebstock each destroyed a dive-bomber,
while the remaining ones jettisoned their bombs futilely. After gaining his own
victory, Barnes was also shot down but, although badly burned, escaped from
his blazing machine by parachute.

The Allied air attacks, on the morning of the 31st, were far more effective.
The Hurribombers, the Kittybombers, the RAF Baltimores, the South
African Bostons, all kept up a persistent assault, which was the more
successful because the Axis forces were exposed in the open. As a result, the
Afrika Korps could not commence its eastern drive until 1000, and two hours
later it was forced to halt west of Samakat Gaballa – high ground lying to the
east of Himeimat – so as to allow the supply echelons to reach it. These in
turn had been so delayed by minefields and air attacks that it was not until
1400 that the panzers were able to resume their advance. Unhappily a dust
storm had begun in the late morning which reached a peak of intensity in the

early afternoon. To Montgomery's bitter disappointment, this grounded the aircraft on both sides, enabling von Vaerst, who had taken over command of the *Afrika Korps*, to refuel unhindered.

Nonetheless the minefields and the air attacks had already caused sufficient delay to force Rommel into a disastrous change of plan. In the early hours of the 31st, he had met with Nehring's Chief of Staff, Colonel Fritz Bayerlein, to discuss further moves. 'One thing was clear,' Bayerlein would later tell Paul Carell, 'the main plan, the encirclement of the Eighth Army, was no longer possible for the enemy had had time enough to prepare counter-action. The surprise element had gone. Moreover in daylight it was no longer possible for us to by-pass the fortified heights of Alam Halfa.' 'With the British armour assembled for immediate action,' Rommel would later declare, 'it was impossible for us to continue with our wide sweep to the east, as our flanks would have been under a constant threat from the 7th Armoured Division in the south and the 10th Armoured Division in the north. This compelled us to decide on an earlier turn to the north than we had intended.'

Thus when the Axis forces resumed their advance, the German reconnaissance units continued eastward, capturing Samakat Gaballa, but von Vaerst turned north-eastward immediately to lead the *Afrika Korps* towards the western end of Alam Halfa, while the Littorio Armoured Division, followed later by Ariete, made for the Bare Ridge. The panzers thus moved straight into the heart of Eighth Army's prepared positions, just as Montgomery most desired.[10]

The men of 7th Armoured Division retired before this advance, Carr's 4th Light Armoured Brigade moving north-east of Samakat Gaballa and Bosvile's 7th Motor Brigade taking up a position to the north-east of Carr and about halfway between him and Custance. 10th Hussars, whom Horrocks had ordered to hold the Muhafid Depression, south of the Bare Ridge, rejoined Bosvile after a hurried move across the front of the advancing *Afrika Korps*, just in time to avoid being cut off.

Had 22nd Armoured Brigade also been falling back in this way, or trying to cover the withdrawal of the infantry divisions as envisaged by Auchinleck and his advisers, the situation might have been ominous in the extreme. As it was, the men of 22nd Armoured had spent the morning and early afternoon in their prepared positions at Point 102, waiting tensely but quietly for the action which they were certain was coming. They were disturbed by two bombing raids, plus another on the neighbouring Alam Halfa Ridge, but they suffered no casualties from these, though during the afternoon, a reconnaissance force which Roberts had sent out to keep track of the enemy armour came under fire, losing four Crusaders.

Roberts had stationed three of his four armoured regiments in the foothills south of Point 102 covering a front of about three miles. He describes these with some reason as 'a motley collection of combined units'. On the right or western front, were the combined 1st and 6th Royal Tanks, with twenty-three Grants and nineteen Stuarts. In the centre, came 4th County of London Yeomanry, with a squadron of 3rd County of London Yeomanry under command – in all twenty-one Grants and fifteen Crusaders. In the east, nearest to Alam Halfa, came another combination, 5th Royal Tanks and 2nd Royal Gloucestershire Hussars, which contained a total of twenty Grants and fifteen Crusaders.

Most of these tanks were now somewhat battle-worn as a result of long service, but while this would not have been very encouraging had the brigade been intended for 'fluid and mobile' operations, Roberts was confident that his command would do well enough in a defensive action. He also enjoyed good artillery support. 1st Battalion, The Rifle Brigade with its 6-pounder anti-tank guns was stationed to the left of 1st/6th Royal Tanks, and behind them lay an anti-tank battery; while the eastern flank had been similarly strengthened by the presence of the 25-pounders of 1st Regiment, Royal Horse Artillery.

Roberts personally took up his station just to the south-east of Point 102, four Crusaders being allocated to his Headquarters. His remaining armoured regiment, the Royal Scots Greys under Lieutenant Colonel Sir Ranulph Fiennes, mounted now not on horses but on, or rather in, twenty-four Grants and twenty-one Stuarts, remained on the north-eastern slopes of Point 102 about two miles behind the front line. Since its tanks were comparatively new ones which were thus the most mechanically trustworthy, Roberts intended to use it as his 'mobile reserve'.

Soon after 1730, the dust storm finally died away and in the improving visibility Roberts could clearly see through his binoculars the *Afrika Korps*, its two panzer divisions – rather ironically in view of what would follow – admirably concentrated, moving across his front, apparently preparing for an attack on Alam Halfa. Then discovering that Point 102 was also occupied, the Germans halted and turned north. Shortly after 0800, 21st Panzer headed straight for the centre of 22nd Armoured's position, while 15th Panzer circled to come in on the Brigade's left flank. It felt, Roberts tells us, like watching 'a snake curl up ready to strike'.

The Axis armour was now as deadly as any snake for at long last the Germans really did have a tank which could outgun any on the British side. At the head of 21st Panzer were a number of Rommel's new Mark IV Specials with their long-barrelled 75mms. With these they opened fire at a range of over 1,000 yards on Major Alexander Cameron's 'A' Squadron of the County of London Yeomanry which lay directly in front of them. Three of Cameron's Grants went up in flames 'before they had hardly fired a shot'. As the range decreased, the Grants could also fire effectively and the panzers halted temporarily, but by that time all twelve of 'A' Squadron's Grants had been destroyed. Roberts hastily called on his 'mobile reserve', the Royal Scots Greys, to come forward as quickly as possible.

Meanwhile 21st Panzer had begun to advance again, now heading for the position held by 1st Rifle Brigade. With splendid coolness, the British gunners held their fire until the panzers were within 300 yards. Then they opened up with their 6-pounders, inflicting heavy losses on the enemy – the gun commanded by Sergeant Griffiths alone was credited with knocking out five German tanks. At almost the same moment, a storm of artillery fire from all the British guns within range crashed down 'right on top' of the panzers. They halted, regrouped, edged forward once more, were again checked by artillery fire – and then the Greys poured over the crest of the hill from the north in a great cloud of dust. Moving into the gap left by the destruction of Cameron's squadron, they lost four Grants to enemy gunfire, but at about 1900, 21st Panzer Division finally fell back.

On 22nd Armoured's left flank, the Grants of 5th Royal Tanks were still in action against 15th Panzer Division. Roberts quickly transferred the remaining County of London Yeomanry tanks to a position north of the threatened left flank, whence they too engaged the panzers. 1st Royal Horse Artillery also directed a heavy fire on the enemy, as did 44th Division's artillery from Alam Halfa. At about 1930, 15th Panzer broke off its attack.

In all on 31 August, the Germans had lost twenty-two tanks destroyed plus several others disabled but later removed to safety – this being a field in which the enemy was always very skilful. Despite the vigour with which the action had been fought and despite its own losses in tanks, 22nd Armoured Brigade had had only three men killed and some fifty wounded.

It was a small price to pay for the success achieved. Though at 0500 next morning, Montgomery gave orders to guard against a possible breakthrough at Point 102, bringing 23rd and 8th Armoured Brigades closer, sending 2nd South African Brigade to reinforce the eastern part of the Ruweisat Ridge, and calling up his reserve 151st Brigade from Amiriya to south of Alam Halfa where it arrived on 2 September, in fact the moment of greatest danger had already passed. 'In that hour's battle,' says Field Marshal Carver, 'on a front of only a few miles, in which certainly not more and probably less than 100 tanks had actually fired their guns against each other, the tide of battle in the desert had turned.'

Notes

1. It will be recalled that the 88mms were anti-aircraft as well as anti-tank weapons.
2. A *Gruppe* was roughly equivalent to a British squadron but of noticeably larger size.

3   Horrocks relates that shortly before the new Axis offensive began, his HQ was attacked by Stukas at a time when it was being visited by Montgomery. 'I couldn't help feeling this time,' says Horrocks, as both officers went flat on the sand, 'that an unlucky strike which knocked out the commander of the Eighth Army before he had really got into his stride might alter the whole war in the Middle East.' Happily the bombs fell some distance away.

4   It can of course be argued that Rommel would in any event not want to alarm his wife. Yet during Auchinleck's offensive in July as well as Montgomery's later offensive in October, Rommel's letters were quite pathetically pessimistic. Indeed he seems to have used them as a form of 'safety valve' since on neither occasion did his remarks reflect his fixed determination to hold firm until his enemy eventually gave up – as in fact happened in the former case at least.

5   See for instance XIII Corps Operation Order No. 145 of 14 August at the Public Record Office where the British armour is specifically directed to destroy not only 'enemy main forces' but also 'their maintenance'.

6   In reality this, and its sequel *Normandy to the Baltic*, were written by Major General Belchem, who had been one of Montgomery's staff officers, under Montgomery's direction.

7   *Royal Air Force 1939–1945* Volume II: *The Fight Avails* by Denis Richards and Hilary St George Saunders.

8   The Albacore was really only an improved version of the famous Swordfish torpedo-bomber with an enclosed cockpit.

9   De Guingand reports that when he awakened Montgomery with the news, his leader merely muttered: 'Excellent, excellent!' then calmly went back to sleep.

10   To encourage Rommel to proceed in this direction, a false map indicating good going in the area south of Alam Halfa had been designed by de Guingand and Williams and hastily produced by the Directorate of Military Intelligence in Cairo. Appropriately crumpled and tea-stained to suggest long use, this map was placed in a scout-car which was deliberately blown up on a mine at the edge of the German front line a few days before the battle opened. It duly fell into German hands but, alas, it appears to have had little, if any, effect on Rommel's plans.

Chapter 5

'THE SWINE ISN'T ATTACKING!'

At the time, of course, it was far from obvious to the men of Eighth Army that the tide had turned in the Battle of Alam Halfa, let alone in the Desert War as a whole. Nor was Rommel ready to admit defeat just yet. He would later claim that only shortage of fuel prevented a renewed attack on Point 102 on the night of 31 August. It does seem that the wretched Axis supply echelons were still having difficulty in picking their way through the gaps in the mine-fields in the face of continuous air attacks. Nonetheless it is impossible to believe that the *Afrika Korps* would in any circumstances have considered assaulting after dark a position of unknown strength which had already put up a resolute resistance – particularly since the German positions were being shelled by 44th Division's artillery for much of the night. This meant that the panzers had to be dispersed far more widely than usual, with the result that most of the hours of darkness were spent in refuelling and rearming them.

With daylight, however, the offensive could be resumed. At 0640 on 1 September, 15th Panzer Division thrust towards the Alam Halfa Ridge, while 21st Panzer remained in position facing Roberts. Had von Vaerst succeeded in carrying out this manoeuvre he would have outflanked 22nd Armoured Brigade and could have fallen upon the British 'soft-skinned' vehicles which were bringing up fuel and ammunition to Roberts. With real luck he might have been able to capture some of these, thus getting his petrol 'from the British' as Rommel was fond of commanding.

Whatever the advantages of this action in theory though, Rommel has been criticized for executing it in the situation which existed in practice. The lack of movement by 21st Panzer has been ascribed to shortage of petrol. It does seem that the division had experienced problems with refuelling during the night, but it also seems that these were not as serious as is usually stated. 21st Panzer did in fact move later in the day – towards the right flank of 22nd

Armoured Brigade, coming under the fire of both 1st/6th Royal Tanks and the artillery of 23rd Armoured Brigade for its pains. Yet in any case it was a sensible idea to leave 21st Panzer where it was, either to act as the 'anvil' for 15th Panzer's 'hammer', or to be ready to push forward on Point 102 if Roberts was forced to leave this in order to engage the outflanking forces.

It is for his orders to 15th Panzer to advance single-handed on Alam Halfa, however, that Rommel has been most strongly condemned. Von Mellenthin states that this movement 'offered little hope of success', while Field Marshal Carver declares that it 'can only be explained' if Rommel believed that Point 102 'marked the extreme edge of Eighth Army's defences and that Alam Halfa itself was not properly held'.

Yet it seems quite possible that Rommel did entertain at least similar beliefs. After the Allies' successful offensive later in the year, high-ranking German officers would be captured, who under interrogation would declare explicitly that Rommel did not know that Montgomery had 'occupied' Alam Halfa. There was surely no reason why such statements – which scarcely reflected credit on the Axis High Command or its Intelligence staff – should have been made unless they were believed to be correct, although of course they may have been unintentionally exaggerated.

In his own account, written with the advantage of hindsight, Rommel states that air reconnaissance had revealed that Alam Halfa was 'now heavily fortified'. He considered that a fight for this 'would be very severe'. 'Field Marshal Kesselring' Rommel tells us, 'was accordingly asked to attack it heavily from the air.'

Interestingly enough, though, the Luftwaffe in reality made more attacks on Point 102 than on Alam Halfa. Moreover Rommel relates that 'we later discovered' Alam Halfa was held by '44th British Infantry Division, newly arrived from Great Britain'. If it was only later that the Germans learned of the presence of 44th Division on the ridge, they could well have been excused for believing that it 'was not properly held'. Without 44th Division, Eighth Army would indeed not have had enough troops to hold the front line and Alam Nayil and Alam Halfa securely – it was precisely for this reason that Montgomery had insisted 44th Division be brought to the combat area.

Rommel's attack therefore could well have been based on a belief that Alam Halfa, though certainly not wholly unguarded, was at least not defended adequately. Had the garrison on the ridge consisted only of the weak 21st Indian Brigade, while the New Zealanders fell back towards it, dispersing into 'boxes' and battle groups in the process, as Auchinleck and his advisers desired, Rommel's belief would have proved justified and an attack on Alam Halfa might well have triumphed.

As it was, von Vaerst was easily repulsed by 44th Division's artillery. He twice attempted to renew his advance but without success, and at about 0830,

Custance, whose 8th Armoured Brigade had been instructed, as already mentioned, to close in towards Roberts, appeared on the Germans' right flank with seventy-two Grants and twelve Crusaders. This action at least gave von Vaerst a chance of using his most effective weapons. In the words of the Official History, he 'established a strong anti-tank screen', which threw back both 3rd Royal Tanks and the Staffordshire Yeomanry. The Nottinghamshire Yeomanry, on the British right, tried to turn the enemy's flank, but at a range of 800 yards they too came under heavy fire, losing seven tanks. Happily before the battle could become 'fluid and mobile', Custance retired. His intervention had at least induced von Vaerst to abandon his advance – indeed that afternoon, the panzers fell back for a mile or so to the south. Rommel again refers to a shortage of petrol, but it seems that a more potent factor was another furious bombardment by every gun in 44th Division that could be brought to bear.

Rommel's last attack had failed. At about 1200, he announced that he was going onto the defensive in the positions which he now held. Yet to his credit, he had still not abandoned hope of winning his 'decisive battle', if only he could persuade his opponent to indulge in the 'fluid and mobile' warfare at which *Panzerarmee Afrika* excelled. According to Horrocks, 'the Germans tried over and over again' throughout the afternoon of 1 September 'to lure us out of our defensive positions' – but Montgomery was not to be tempted.

Montgomery's refusal to oblige may well have been prompted by an unsuccessful action away from the main battle-zone. At 0535 on 1 September, 2/15th Australian Battalion[1] commenced a raid to the west of Tell el Eisa, supported by aircraft and by a squadron of Valentines from 40th Royal Tanks. Code-named Operation BULIMBA, this was designed partly to distract enemy attention, but principally as an armed reconnaissance in an area where Montgomery intended to attack when the time came for his own offensive. Montgomery, as Williams remarks,[2] tended to think 'one battle ahead of the rest of us' – normally an admirable trait but one which did not have particularly happy results on this occasion.

At first the raiders achieved total surprise, taking some 140 members of the German 164th Light Division prisoners. Then the enemy recovered, launching a counter-attack which was made more effective by poor co-operation between the Australians and the British armour. Seven Valentines were knocked out and by 0900, the Australians had been driven back to their starting point with 135 casualties. Even though only fifteen of these were fatal, the attack had undeniably proved a failure.

This failure and the way in which Custance had been checked by von Vaerst's anti-tank guns warned Montgomery, in Field Marshal Carver's words, just 'how blunt was the weapon in his hand when it came to attack'. By the time the Eighth Army Commander reached XIII Corps Headquarters on the Alam Halfa Ridge in the early afternoon of 1 September – to be greeted by a heavy Stuka attack – he had determined, as he relates in *El Alamein to the River Sangro*, that any move 'to close the gap in our minefields through which the enemy had come' must be 'developed southwards from the New Zealand sector', must 'proceed methodically and by easy stages', and must above all 'resist any temptation to rush into the attack'.

Despite the cries of later critics who describe Montgomery's decision as over-cautious, unimaginative, even dull, and call for an all-out assault, no one who was present at the battle has denied that such an action would have been catastrophic. 'To any student of the techniques which Rommel and the *Afrika Korps* had evolved and refined;' declares Ronald Lewin, 'it will be plain that, had this happened', the *Afrika Korps*

> would have fallen back on the minefields and formed a protective hedgehog with its 88mms, 50mm Pak,[3] the good Russian anti-tank guns now in service, and the murderous Mark IV Specials of which a substantial number survived. Eighth Army was denied the possibility of out-flanking by the Qattara Depression. Some sort of head-on conflict in the old style must have materialised. Of the three [British] armoured brigades available, 8th was totally ignorant of desert warfare, 23rd consisted of the reinforced survivors from an almost total disaster, and only 22nd had maturity – but it was battle-weary and it is to be doubted whether it had grown out of all the bad old ways, though it had fought a most able defensive action on the 31st.

Far from Montgomery being at fault therefore, his refusal to launch a headlong attack was, Lewin considers, 'a final stroke of bad luck' for Rommel. 'Montgomery was wise to avoid the likelihood of another "Cauldron", and the *Afrika Korps* was unlucky, after what was an open defeat, to lose the opportunity for what must surely have been a certain revenge.'

Such was also Rommel's own view. 'Montgomery,' he states,

> had attempted no large-scale attack to retake the southern part of his line; and would probably have failed if he had. He had relied instead on the effect of his enormously powerful artillery and air force. Added to this, our lines of communication had been subjected to continual harassing attacks by the 7th Armoured Division. There is no doubt that the British commander's handling of this action had been absolutely right and well suited to the occasion, for it had enabled him to inflict very heavy damage on us in relation to his own losses, and to retain the striking power of his own force.

On 1 September, Field Marshal Kesselring visited the battle-area and Rommel poured out his troubles to him, declaring angrily that: 'The swine isn't attacking!' The 'swine' of course was Montgomery.

In practice, therefore, the main Allied weapon on 1 September, was Coningham's Desert Air Force. This had the duty not only of assaulting the Axis army but also of holding off the Axis airmen when these attacked Eighth Army's defences in the hope of fulfilling Rommel's aim of forcing the Allied soldiers to leave their fixed positions. Coningham's tasks were by no means easy for just as the Germans' 'murderous Mark IV Specials' and 88s were the finest tanks and anti-tank guns on the battlefield, so the Germans' Messerschmitt Bf 109s were, on paper, the finest fighter aircraft above it.

During 1 September, the 109 pilots, in particular their most brilliant 'ace', *Oberleutnant* Hans-Joachim Marseille, are said by Christopher Shores and Hans Ring in their *Fighters Over the Desert*, to have enjoyed a 'day of glory'. Only four 109s were destroyed, though three of the pilots died while the fourth became a prisoner of war. In return, they believed they had shot down twenty-six single-engined Allied fighters, of which Marseille alone claimed seventeen.

In reality the 109s failed almost totally. In the first place, they overestimated their achievements – particularly Marseille bearing in mind that some of the Allied machines lost were shot down by other pilots in his Gruppe or in combats where he was not even present. Twenty Allied fighters – nine Hurricanes, four Kittyhawks, four Tomahawks, two Spitfires, one Warhawk – really fell victim to the Luftwaffe on 1 September, and of these, four Hurricanes, two Kittyhawks, one Spitfire and the Warhawk were repairable, having crash-landed on Allied airfields after combat damage. Yet such exaggerations, inevitable in the sheer speed of air fighting, were minor blemishes. The true failure of the 109 pilots lay in the fact that their obsession with individual successes caused them to neglect both their own crucial duties. They failed to protect their bombers, preferring to intervene only when the Allied fighters had already engaged these and were thus at a height disadvantage – with the result that the Axis air raids proved completely ineffective. Worse still, they were so reluctant to encounter targets which 'had tail gunners' that not a single Allied bomber was destroyed, or it seems engaged, by an enemy fighter.

As the consequence of this 'insufficient fighter cover', as Rommel calls it, the *Afrika Korps* suffered a whole series of attacks throughout 1 September, without any interference on the part of the Luftwaffe. Seven of von Vaerst's staff officers died, while Rommel was almost added to the casualty list when he arrived on a visit to the front line. The blows falling on the German supply vehicles were still more damaging, for Montgomery had ordered that these were to be 'the principal target of both the Air Force and the Army'. And as a final confirmation of the Luftwaffe's failure, the morning of 2 September, as the Official History confirms, saw 'even more British aircraft operating over the Desert than on the previous day'.

Not even Rommel could bear the ordeal any longer. 'Our offensive,' he states, 'no longer had any hope of success.' He now felt convinced that Montgomery was never going to indulge in a battle of manoeuvre, that the conflict if continued could only be one of attrition. He accepted that the British 'command of the air' had become 'virtually complete'. Early on 2 September, he decided, as he subsequently signalled to Berlin, that *Panzerarmee Afrika* would 'fall back slowly under enemy pressure to the starting line, unless the supply and the air situation are fundamentally changed'.[4]

At the time he made his decision, it appears that Rommel had also heard bad news from further afield. On the night of 1st/2nd September, the *Abruzzi* and the *Picci Fassio*, two of the five tankers promised by Cavallero, had been torpedoed by RAF Beauforts – both sank next day. Two more, the *Bianchi* and the *Padenna*, would be sunk by combined air and submarine attacks on 4 September, though on that same day, the *Sportivo* with her 800 tons of petrol would reach Tobruk safely. By that time, in any case, losses or arrivals were irrelevant, for *Panzerarmee Afrika* was already in full retreat.

The loss of the first two tankers, however, would give Rommel the opportunity, rather meanly, of blaming Cavallero for the defeat, insisting that 'the petrol which was an essential condition for the fulfilment of our plan had not arrived'. Yet the fuel carried in Cavallero's tankers had not been intended to supply Rommel during the battle but to replenish the stocks which the battle was likely to consume. Rommel would later go so far as to complain that he had 'only one petrol issue left' by the evening of 1 September, but in his signal to Berlin on the evening of the following day, he stated that he could only continue 'at the full rate of expenditure' until 5 September, which gives a totally different picture. In fact since his fuel losses had been heavier than expected as a result of the constant air attacks, it confirms that he had possessed, as he intended, seven days' supply when the battle began. Indeed Rommel's complaint to Kesselring about Montgomery not attacking would have been pointless if he had not had the fuel to deal with the 'swine' once the attacks began.

Interestingly enough, many German accounts reject Rommel's claims. Von Mellenthin supports him and specifically mentions that lack of petrol 'prevented any large-scale withdrawal' during 2 September, but von Mellenthin is less reliable than usual on this occasion, for, as he admits, he 'can speak only with indirect knowledge of the course of this battle' – he remained throughout at *Panzerarmee Afrika*'s main HQ at Sidi Abd el Rahman, some 10 miles behind the front line on the coast, suffering from a severe attack of dysentery. He was certainly misinformed about the events of 2 September, for in reality *Panzerarmee Afrika* spent this towing as many of its damaged vehicles as possible to safety, including, it appears, all those knocked-out but repairable tanks that had previously been recovered. Rommel was also able to strengthen his flanks against the expected British interference, sending the remainder of Ramcke's Parachute Brigade and the bulk of the Folgore Parachute Division to reinforce the Axis troops facing the New Zealanders, withdrawing part of 90th Light Division westward to provide a reserve, and ordering twenty-five of Ariete's tanks to the area east of Himeimat to guard against any moves by 7th Armoured Division.

Field Marshal Kesselring by contrast points out flatly in his *Memoirs* that Rommel – as we have seen – had originally had sufficient fuel to enable him to continue the battle for almost a week. He concludes therefore that 'lack of petrol supplies could not be blamed' for the defeat – though his belief that it was a 'cast-iron determination to follow through that was lacking' does less than justice to either Rommel or his opponent.

Still more convincing is the judgement of Rommel's chief German subordinate during the battle. Paul Carell reports that Major General von Vaerst explained to him that there was certainly a fuel shortage but to attribute the defeat to this was a 'fallacy'. Carell also interviewed other senior 'surviving witnesses' and confirms that the argument that Rommel's failure arose from his petrol problems 'cannot be supported'. 'Possibly,' adds Carell doubtfully, 'a more favourable fuel position for the *Afrika Korps* and the resultant improved mobility and manoeuvrability could once more have turned the tables against the obstinate British defence. *Possibly*. But it cannot be denied that the British air supremacy was also a decisive factor in the battle.'

This last point is surely a crucial one. Rommel's difficulty was not that he did not possess the fuel he needed but that to bring it to his fighting soldiers in the front line his petrol lorries had to pass through perilous restricted gaps in minefields under continuous air attacks from a dominant Desert Air Force. This difficulty, it may be added, could not have been solved even if all Cavallero's tankers had arrived safely. In effect Rommel admits this, for he notes that:

> Whoever enjoys command of the air is in a position to inflict such heavy damage on the opponent's supply columns that serious shortages must soon make themselves felt. By maintaining a constant watch on the roads leading to the front he can put a complete stop to daylight supply traffic and force his enemy to drive only by night, thus causing him to lose irreplaceable time. But an assured flow of supplies is essential; without it an army becomes immobilised and incapable of action.

It was a lesson of which Montgomery was already well aware. He continued to add to Rommel's misfortunes on 2 September, ordering Horrocks to 'shoot up, harry and destroy the enemy's motor transport'. Highly effective harrying operations were carried out that morning by 7th Armoured Division, particularly by the Stuart tanks of 4th/8th Hussars from 4th Light Armoured Brigade (a composite regiment made up from two under-strength units), which attacked supply columns east of Himeimat destroying no less than fifty-seven vehicles. By the end of the day, however, enemy armour and anti-tank guns had taken up positions which blocked any subsequent efforts of this kind.[5]

Nothing, though, could stop the incessant raids by the Desert Air Force. Aircraft of every type – Bostons, Baltimores, American Mitchells, Kitty-bombers, Hurribombers – were savaging Rommel's transports, paying special attention to his petrol lorries. The Hurricane IIBs of No. 7 Squadron SAAF which were equipped with 'sticky-bombs', designed so as not to glance off the armoured sides of tanks, showed no reluctance to test their weapons against 'soft-skinned' vehicles. The anti-tank Hurricane IIDs of No. 6 Squadron RAF, though destroying at least nine of their favourite targets in the course of the battle, were also not averse to increasing the miseries of the Axis supply columns. Once more the vaunted German 'aces' imposed virtually no check on Coningham's activities, their lack of success spurring Kesselring to issue a Special Order next day, 'exhorting Luftwaffe pilots' as the Official History puts it, 'to protect their sorely oppressed comrades of the *Panzerarmee*'.

The Axis bombers also continued their strikes on 2 September, but, it seems, more for the purpose of keeping Eighth Army occupied than with any intention of inflicting real harm. Perhaps for that reason, the day saw the Junkers Ju 87s making not dive-bombing attacks but high-level raids for which they were quite unsuited. Not that these tactics enabled them to escape cheaply. That afternoon, for instance, the Hurricanes of 127 and 274 Squadrons scattered a Stuka formation, shooting down six of its fourteen machines without loss and forcing the remainder to jettison their bombs harmlessly.

By midday on 3 September, all Axis forces were in full and final retreat. Despite the attacks on his supply routes on the previous day, by 4th/8th Hussars as well as the Desert Air Force, Rommel had got enough petrol, as Kesselring acidly notes, 'to bring all the units back', while Paul Carell confirms that 'very few vehicles were abandoned' for lack of fuel.

Montgomery's intention now was to inflict as much damage as possible before the enemy retirement could be completed. 7th Armoured Division proved unable to 'tap in', as Montgomery called it, at Himeimat since the Axis strength in this area was too great, but the Eighth Army's main hopes rested on a proposed advance southwards towards Himeimat from 2nd New Zealand Division's positions on Alam Nayil. To this was given the code name Operation BERESFORD.

Montgomery's plan was a simple one. Having transferred 2nd South African Brigade to the Ruweisat Ridge, he was able to send 5th Indian Brigade to join Freyberg, who also received a heavy reinforcement of artillery. 5th Indian Brigade and 132nd (British) Brigade which was already serving under Freyberg, were to secure the existing New Zealand defences, while 5th and 6th New Zealand Brigades moved some three miles southward to capture the Axis positions on the northern edge of the Munassib Depression. Then the reserve 151st (British) Brigade would also come under Freyberg's command to help push the advance further south.

Unfortunately Freyberg, who remembered only too well the casualties his New Zealanders had suffered during Auchinleck's July actions, was not at all co-operative. Most of 2 September was wasted in 'indiscipline at the top'. Freyberg urged the use of 5th Indian Brigade as the attacking force. Horrocks appears reluctantly to have agreed, but when Montgomery learned of this suggestion, he promptly vetoed it, partly because he wanted the attack made by troops with knowledge of the ground, partly because he did not feel that one brigade would be strong enough.

Thereupon Freyberg retorted that in that case 132nd Brigade should be added to the New Zealand Brigades for the assault. Neither Montgomery nor Horrocks approved, for both rightly considered that the inexperienced 132nd Brigade was not ready for offensive operations. Freyberg, however, insisted that if he was to shoulder responsibility for the attack, he must be allowed to choose the units to execute it. Unwillingly, perhaps unwisely, the commanders of Eighth Army and of XIII Corps finally consented.

Operation BERESFORD at last got under way at 2230 on 3 September, with Kippenberger's 5th New Zealand Brigade advancing on the left or eastern flank, 6th New Zealand Brigade on the right, and 132nd Brigade in the centre. All met with fierce resistance from the Italian X Corps – particularly the Folgore Division's parachutists – backed up by the Ramcke Brigade and detachments from 90th Light Division. In spite of this, Kippenberger's men, at a cost of 124 casualties, secured all their objectives, after which the 28th Maori Battalion pushed on still further, destroying a considerable number of enemy transports. Unhappily a supporting squadron from 50th Royal Tanks also went too far, losing twelve Valentines in a minefield.

Elsewhere nothing whatever went right. 6th New Zealand Brigade had been ordered to divert attention from and secure the right flank of 132nd Brigade. It succeeded in doing neither, being thrown back with 159 casualties, including Brigadier Clifton who was taken prisoner.

Total disaster befell 132nd Brigade, consisting of 2nd Battalion, The Buffs[6] and 4th and 5th Battalions, Royal West Kent Regiment, backed by a squadron of Valentines from 46th Royal Tanks. There was a good deal of confusion, inevitable in a unit called on to participate in its first attack at short notice. It was not until midnight therefore, that it eventually moved forward.

By that time, the Axis troops had received ample warning from the New Zealand operations on the flanks. The brigade was met with heavy fire, some 'soft-skinned' vehicles which had been brought forward too early – contrary to the New Zealanders' advice – were set alight, providing illumination for the benefit of the defenders, and the advance was halted well short of its objectives. Brigadier Robertson was severely injured, while in all 697 officers and men were killed, wounded or captured – over two-fifths of the total Allied casualties for the entire battle.

Although several counter-attacks on Freyberg's new positions were beaten off, principally by his artillery, Operation BERESFORD had clearly failed. It had also provided one further proof of the correctness of Montgomery's belief that Eighth Army should not be allowed 'to rush into the attack'. It did perhaps help to hasten the retreat of the *Afrika Korps* during 4 September, but Freyberg, feeling increasingly exposed, determined nonetheless to retire to his original defences on the night of 4th/5th September – a decision later approved by a disappointed Montgomery. The withdrawal was carried out successfully though not without further losses.

Thereafter Rommel's retirement was scarcely impeded by the Allied ground troops, though Coningham's men continued to exact their toll. In these closing stages of the battle moreover, the Luftwaffe also suffered cruel losses. On 6 September, *Oberfeldwebel* (Flight Sergeant) Günther Steinhausen, an 'ace' with forty victories to his credit, all during campaigns in the Desert, was killed in combat with the Hurricanes of No. 127 Squadron. Next day, *Leutnant* Hans-Arnold Stahlschmidt, credited with fifty-nine victories in the Desert, was killed in an encounter with the Spitfires of No. 601 Squadron. The Luftwaffe's leading pilot in North Africa, Marseille, with an official 'score' of 158 Allied aircraft, all but seven of them in the Desert, did not long survive his comrades. He died on 30 September, when a fractured oil pipe set his 109 on fire. He baled out, collided with the tail unit and was so injured as to be unable to open his parachute. All three of these pilots came from I Gruppe of *Jagdgeschwader* (Fighter Wing) 27. Their deaths so demoralized this unit that it had to be withdrawn to Sicily, whence it did not return to North Africa for almost a month – one more indication of the Luftwaffe's folly in allowing individual success to become all-important.

Meanwhile at 0700 on 7 September, Montgomery had 'decided to call off the battle'. His action left the twin British minefields in the south and also the peak of Himeimat in German hands. Lieutenant General Horrocks, whose birthday this was, at first disapproved of his leader's ruling, since from Himeimat the enemy 'could observe everything that went on in the southern part of my sector'. He soon learned, however, that Montgomery was again thinking 'one battle ahead'. He had decided to launch his own main offensive on the northern part of the front but to deceive Rommel into believing it would take place in the south. He therefore had no objection to the Germans spotting his bogus preparations. 'Leave them in possession of Himeimat,' he instructed Horrocks. 'That is where I want them to be.'

So all Rommel had gained by his great efforts was a pair of minefields and a hill, the occupation of which would help to bring about his ruin at a later date. These scarcely justified his losses: 1,859 Germans and 1,051 Italians killed, wounded or captured; 33 German and 22 Italian guns, 38 German and 11 Italian tanks, 298 German and 97 Italian 'soft-skinned' vehicles destroyed; 76 more German tanks plus large numbers of transports damaged but recovered; 41 aircraft, all but 5 of them German, shot down.

Allied aircraft losses were heavier; they totalled sixty-eight though some of these were later salvaged and almost half the airmen had escaped with their lives. The British on paper also lost more tanks, sixty-seven in all, but since Eighth Army remained master of the field nearly half of these were later repaired, including thirteen of the thirty-one Grants that had been knocked out. Only fifteen anti-tank guns had been disabled, while losses of 'soft-skinned' transports were negligible. The human casualties were considerably less than those of the Axis: 110 officers and 1,640 other ranks were dead, injured or prisoners – 39 Indians, 65 South Africans, 257 Australians, 405 New Zealanders, 984 British.

That Eighth Army's gains were immense was clearly appreciated by all those who were in that army at the time. It is very sad therefore that many later commentators should have tended either to ignore the battle altogether, or worse still to belittle it, even to the extent of depriving it of its usual title and reducing it to the 'Second Battle of Alamein', making Montgomery's offensive in October 1942 the third action of that name.

It is difficult to be patient with such an attitude. It is absurd to alter the recognized name of a battle – one might as well call Blenheim the Battle of the River Nebel. In this particular case, it is doubly absurd because no soldier who fought in these actions ever referred to Alam Halfa as 'Second Alamein' or indeed to the October offensive as 'Third Alamein'. For that matter, precious few ever called the latter 'Second Alamein', as has become fashionable, either. To them it was simply 'Alamein'. It is also ignorant, for while the bulk of the fighting in both July and October occurred near El Alamein on the northern part of the front line, Alam Halfa began in the south and the crucial encounter took place beyond the British forward defences, over 15 miles south-east of Alamein as the aeroplane flew and over 50 miles away as the panzers had to travel; no one would think of calling Waterloo the Second Battle of Quatre Bras but in fact this would be less unreasonable as the fields of Waterloo and Quatre Bras are less than 10 miles apart. It is also misleading for, as Liddell Hart points out, 'the crucial significance of Alam Halfa' is 'symbolised in the fact that . . . it has been given a separate and distinct name'.

It may be that the significance of Alam Halfa is overlooked because its most important gains were intangible. The chief of these was confidence. At Alam Halfa, Eighth Army had halted, not an enemy whose men were exhausted, whose tanks were pitifully few in number and whose air support was virtually non-existent, but one who had just received considerable reinforcements of men and equipment, whose troops were fresh and rested, whose air force provided close support and who had better tanks, more 88s and more single-engined fighter aircraft than at any previous time, with the result that 'the strength of the two sides was nearer to an even balance than it was either before or later'. The men of Eighth Army had every reason to feel proud. Indeed Alam Halfa provided the answer to all the criticisms that had been made of them. As Alan Moorehead relates, in August 1942, Eighth Army 'was ready for anything' but badly lacked 'a clearly defined purpose and a leader'. Once it 'got both in Montgomery' it 'did amazing things'.

Eighth Army's leader had also gained in confidence. No doubt Montgomery was an aggressively self-assured character under any circumstances, but he was only human, 'although sometimes seeking to disguise the fact', as General Fraser amusingly remarks in *And We Shall Shock Them*, and it is often forgotten that he had not seen action since Britain's disastrous defeats in the summer of 1940. He therefore 'had the unavowed task of personally learning from experience how to command in the conditions of the desert war'.

So it must have been immensely reassuring to Montgomery to find that he had not only been able to win a vitally important victory but to win it, as has been seen, as a result of the decisions which he personally had taken and of the alterations which he had deliberately made to his predecessor's intentions, from the 'essence of the defensive plan' – 'fluidity and mobility' – downwards. The confidence which this gave to him was colossal. It never left him. In the future it would sometimes make him arrogant, insensitive, offensive. At the time it was vitally needed.

'Alam Halfa,' summarizes General Fraser, 'was not a brilliant nor an original battle. It was, simply, the first of a long sequence of occasions on which Montgomery showed both his subordinates and the enemy who was master.' That Alam Halfa was a personal triumph for Montgomery was always accepted by the enemy. The action, says von Mellenthin, 'revealed a great improvement in British tactical methods. Montgomery's conduct of the battle can be assessed as a very able if cautious performance, in the best traditions of British generalship and strongly reminiscent of some of Wellington's victories.' 'Rommel lost,' states Paul Carell, 'above all to a new military commander, who, even as a newcomer was confident of victory . . . Montgomery.'

What was really important, though, was that this view was also held by Eighth Army. At last a leader had said what would happen, then made good his words in action. 'Alam Halfa,' says General Jackson, 'was a far-reaching psychological victory for the British; not so much over the Axis as over themselves. Montgomery had shown that he knew what he was about and how to do it'. 'The psychological effect of this victory was terrific,' proclaims Lieutenant General Horrocks. Montgomery 'had won it in exactly the manner in which he had said beforehand he would win it. Everyone felt that a new dynamic force had entered into the tired, rather stale, old body of the Eighth Army.' The fact that they liked their general only strengthened the soldiers' faith in him. 'Montgomery's certainty that he was master of his trade,' relates Ronald Lewin, 'seeped through to his men in a thousand ways, but he was also known affectionately throughout his army as a person – rather odd, wearing hats covered with regimental badges and given to issuing Godly Messages of the Day, but unmistakable, unforgettable and unbeatable.'

This would have vital consequences for Eighth Army's next major task. As the Battle of Alamein ground on day after day, seemingly without result, seemingly without end, the troops recalled that their leader had warned them of this but had promised them ultimate victory – and they were sustained by the memory of how at Alam Halfa also they had been promised victory and the promise had been fulfilled. 'From that tight-reined success at Alam Halfa,' declares Williams,[7] 'sprang the morale needed for victory at Alamein not too many weeks later.' 'In winning it [Alam Halfa],' says Montgomery in *El Alamein to the River Sangro*, 'we paved the way for success at El Alamein and the subsequent advance to Tunisia.'

Nor should it be forgotten that confidence did not flow in only one direction. Though Montgomery still had reservations about the state of his army's training, he was rightly delighted with its achievements at Alam Halfa. Nigel Hamilton records how on 5 September, Montgomery issued a message to his troops: 'All formations and units, both armoured and unarmoured, have contributed towards this striking victory, and have been magnificently supported by the RAF. I congratulate all ranks of Eighth Army on the devotion to duty and good fighting qualities which have resulted in such a heavy defeat of the enemy and which will have far-reaching results.' Montgomery summed up his feelings even better in his *Memoirs*: 'I had taken command of truly magnificent material; it did not take me long to see that.'

Alam Halfa, then, marked the moment when a partnership, based on mutual trust, was formed between the Eighth Army Commander and the men under his command. 'For the British Army' says General Fraser, 'it was a moment to savour. For Rommel it was the beginning of the end in Africa.'

It was a judgement confirmed by the enemy. 'With the failure of this offensive,' reports Rommel, 'our last chance of gaining the Suez Canal had gone.'

'When it failed,' says Kesselring, 'I realized that the fate of the North African campaign was sealed.' According to von Mellenthin, Alam Halfa was 'the turning point of the desert war and the first of the long series of defeats on every front which foreshadowed the collapse of Germany'. 'Alam Halfa' states Paul Carell, 'ended that period of the African war which had been determined by the boldness, cunning and courage of the German C-in-C and his men . . . From now on, Bernard Montgomery dictated events.' And he concludes his account of the battle by declaring that it has thus 'rightly been called the Stalingrad of the Desert'.

Notes

1   The figure '2' was included in the title of several Australian battalions because this was the second time that they had been formed as units in the Australian Army.

2   In an article 'Gee One Eye, Sir: Experiences of an Intelligence Officer' which appears in a collection *Monty at Close Quarters: Recollections of the Man* edited by T.E.B. Howarth. 'Gee One Eye' is an abbreviation for General Staff Officer, Grade One – a lieutenant colonel – Intelligence.

3   'Pak' is short for '*Panzerabwehrkanone*' – that is, 'anti-tank gun'.

4   Quoted in Field Marshal Carver's *El Alamein*.

5   It was in response to the success of 4th/8th Hussars that Rommel transferred the Ariete tanks to this area.

6   The Royal East Kent Regiment was descended from a company of the London Trained Bands that had worn buff-coloured jerkins.

7   In his 'Gee One Eye, Sir' article previously mentioned. All quotations from Williams unless otherwise stated come from this source.

Chapter 6

THE DEVIL'S GARDENS

Yet Stalingrad did not end the German hopes in Russia, for after the remnants of the forces there had surrendered, Hitler was still able to deliver a series of counter-attacks which made steady progress until the Russians won their finest victory in July–August 1943 at the great tank battle of Kursk. In the same way Alam Halfa had achieved only the first part of Eighth Army's task. It had certainly deprived Rommel of his last, as well as his best chance of reaching the Suez Canal while Malta remained unsubdued, but Malta's situation was again becoming desperate – its stocks of both food and petrol would be exhausted by the end of November. If Rommel could hold his ground long enough for the crucial island to be starved into surrender, victory could still be his.

Montgomery, to his credit, was well aware of this danger. In *El Alamein to the River Sangro*, he specifically stresses the importance of the Martuba airfields 'whence the Malta convoys could be safely escorted', while in his *Memoirs*, he refers to 'the need to get the Martuba airfields so as to assist by giving air cover to the last possible convoy to Malta, which was short of food and almost out of aviation fuel. The convoy was due to leave Alexandria about the middle of November.'

The trouble was that Montgomery had considerable doubts as to whether Eighth Army was yet ready for a major offensive against a position which could not be outflanked, especially since a considerable percentage of his troops would be inexperienced. The memories of Auchinleck's five attacks and of Operations BULIMBA and BERESFORD were not encouraging. Furthermore, on 29 September, an attempt by 131st Brigade from 44th Division to capture a salient near the Munassib Depression held by the Folgore Division also proved a failure, at a cost of 392 casualties.

Montgomery therefore set out with ruthless determination to prepare

Eighth Army for the task that lay ahead. Inevitably perhaps, in Nigel Hamilton's words, 'heads began to roll': Ramsden, Renton, 'a host of brigadiers and colonels vanished'. No doubt Montgomery was quite right to remove officers in whom he lacked complete confidence, but to describe his action as cutting out 'dead wood' or 'dry rot', as it has been in some accounts, is scarcely fair to many of those who suffered.

Take for instance the sad case of Brigadier Noel Martin, the Eighth Army's senior artillery officer. He had bitterly resented the dispersal of his guns among battle-groups and 'boxes', but by a cruel irony now found that he was blamed, in part at least, for their misuse – even though the artillery had performed with great success at Alam Halfa. To make matters worse, Brigadier Maxwell, the senior gunner at GHQ, Cairo, hearing of Montgomery's doubts, assured him that Martin was a delightful person and an amateur golfing champion. Montgomery's retort was obvious and immediate, and poor Martin duly 'vanished', as indeed did the well-meaning but misguided Maxwell.

Montgomery was equally ruthless in reorganizing the formations of Eighth Army. In other circumstances this might have reduced morale or made the Army Commander extremely unpopular or both. In fact nothing of the kind occurred, for the simple reason that everyone who had fought in it knew that Alam Halfa had been a personal triumph for Montgomery. The units that were transferred – for example Bosvile's 7th Motor Brigade which left 7th Armoured Division for a re-equipped 1st Armoured Division – may not have been happy about the change, but they accepted that their leader knew what he was doing. Even so, Montgomery's insistence – designed to increase the loyalty of subsidiary formations to their divisions – that Bosvile's men replace the famous 'desert rat' emblem 'on their clothing and on their vehicles' with 1st Armoured Division's white rhinoceros, was, says Field Marshal Carver, 'a change that did not come easily to many, and some curious hybrid animals were seen painted on vehicle mudguards for a long time after'.

Changes in personnel and in the construction of divisions were, however, much less important than what the Official History calls 'a programme of rigorous training' that would 'prepare the Army for the offensive which was to drive the enemy from Egypt and Libya'. 'Montgomery,' relates Horrocks, 'was one of the few commanders' who really did effectively 'train the people who worked under him'. Nigel Hamilton points out that as early as 31 August, while Alam Halfa was still at a crucial stage, Montgomery had personally issued training instructions for the future which were to be repeated at length by his corps and divisional commanders during September.

In these, Montgomery again emphasized the changes he required in Eighth Army. He declared his objections to 'splitting up formations and using isolated groups away from the parent formation and scattered over wide

1. Alam Halfa: the turning point of the desert war. The Eighth Army repels the enemy attacks from its fixed positions.

2. Alexander; Churchill; Montgomery.

3. Leese; Lumsden; Montgomery; Horrocks.

4. Rommel (second from right) confers with his staff.

5. Kesselring (right) visits Luftwaffe units in North Africa.

6. 88mm anti-tank gun. The rings on the barrel denote the number of its
victories.

7. A British Crusader tank is put out of action.

8. South African Boston bombers.

9. Hurricanes of No. 73 Squadron.

10. Grant tanks.

11. British 6-pounder in action.

12. German Mark III Special ablaze

13. German prisoners captured at Alam Halfa. They had so nearly reached the Nile.

14. El Alamein: the Sappers prepare for action.

15. A captured enemy strongpoint.

16. Victory at El Alamein: a wrecked 88mm.

17. Von Thoma salutes his captor.

18. Grant tanks bogged down by heavy rain after Alamein.

19. Eighth Army re-enters Mersa Matruh.

20. Eighth Army scales the Halfaya Pass.

21. A Stuart tank refuelling from a RAF petrol bowser.

22. Anti-tank gun crew in action on the road to Tripoli.

23. The advance continues.

24. Leclerc's Force L passes a burning enemy truck.

25. Anti-tank Hurricane in action.

26. Italian defenders of the Mareth Line.

27. British infantrymen in action at the Mareth Line.

28. Indian machine-gunners in the Gabes Gap.

29. Eighth Army passes through the Gabes Gap.

30. British troops in the final advance on Tunis.

31. The inhabitants of Tunis welcome the victors.

areas'. He urged that 'divisions must be fought *as* divisions and under their own commander with clear-cut tasks and definite objectives', that artillery must be 'centralized', and most important, that there must be a 'concentration of effort' and a 'co-operation of all arms'. He also dealt with the need to study specific matters such as preventing the enemy establishing 'strong anti-tank fronts', neutralizing 'enemy anti-tank guns, especially the enemy 88-gun', and encouraging 'the employment of anti-tank guns on the flanks of the [British] armour'. And he insisted that such techniques should not only be discussed but should be practised in exercises carried out behind the lines and any problems that arose examined and solved.

These exercises duly commenced almost as soon as Alam Halfa was safely over. They were hard, numerous and took place as nearly as possible under battle conditions. Live mines had to be cleared. Live artillery barrages were fired and on one tragic occasion Major Sir Arthur Wilmot and five soldiers of the Black Watch were killed by 'friendly' gunfire. 'Co-operation between infantry and armour,' reports Lucas Phillips 'received special attention.' The Valentines of 23rd Armoured Brigade, for instance, trained with the infantry of XXX Corps whom they were to support in the battle, while the New Zealanders trained with the newly arrived 9th Armoured Brigade which was to come under Freyberg's command.

All these matters obviously took time and were further complicated by the arrival of a considerable amount of improved equipment which, although very welcome, meant more delays while the men were trained in its use and its 'teething troubles' were sorted out. Montgomery had decided that the battle must start on the eve of the full moon, since he wished his original attack to take place on a night in which there would be clear moonlight, to be followed by a number of other moonlit nights. He concluded that the necessary training, reorganization and re-equipment could not possibly be completed by the September full moon, which meant that the battle would have to commence on the night of 23rd/24th October.

It was not a decision which won the approval of Churchill. The Prime Minister was desperately anxious that Eighth Army should gain a victory quickly, not only so as to capture the Martuba airfields in time to provide cover for the Malta convoy, but to discourage the Vichy French from opposing Operation TORCH, now projected for 8 November. Postponement of the offensive until 23 October would leave very little margin for error. Yet Montgomery, his confidence at a peak after his success at Alam Halfa, ignored all pressure to bring the date of his attack forward, and he was wholeheartedly supported by Alexander.

Their desire to ensure that all possible preparations had been made was undoubtedly wise. It is amusing to see how, once the battle was safely won, everyone was quite certain that it could not have been lost. Previously the story had been very different. Grave doubts were felt in London, not only by Churchill but by Brooke. When the latter heard that the offensive had started, he noted in his Diary: 'It may be the turning point of the war leading to further success combined with the North African attacks, or it may mean nothing. If it fails I don't quite know how I shall bear it.' Then, he tells us, he remained for some time sitting at his writing table, 'staring into space'.

Some of Montgomery's own chief subordinates were also worried, and their anxieties would be justified by events. Whatever Montgomery may have claimed later, few victorious actions can ever have gone less 'according to plan' than did the Battle of El Alamein. Indeed, as Liddell Hart points out, Montgomery's attitude 'has tended to obscure and diminish the credit due to him for his adaptability and versatility'. 'The battle,' declares the Official History,[1] 'was anything but a walk-over.' Those who disagree call attention to Eighth Army's advantages in men and material – but a simple comparison of numbers omits a whole variety of important factors.

Of course Eighth Army had grown very considerably since Alam Halfa, for the old XIII and XXX Corps had been joined by Montgomery's mobile reserve force, the reformed X Corps. XXX Corps, which was now commanded by Lieutenant General Sir Oliver Leese, who like Horrocks had been specially chosen by Montgomery, held the northern part of the Alamein defences. It contained from north to south, 9th Australian Division, 51st Highland Division – which had been moved up to the front line shortly after Alam Halfa – 2nd New Zealand Division,[2] 1st South African Division and Tuker's 4th Indian Division which had taken over from 5th Indian Division, bringing with it its 7th Indian Brigade to replace 9th Indian Brigade, but acquiring 5th and 161st Indian Brigades and the divisional artillery from its predecessor. The Valentines of 23rd Armoured Brigade provided close support, while 9th Armoured Brigade under the red-haired, quick-tempered and completely fearless Brigadier John Currie, was, as already stated, directly under the command of the New Zealand Division.

XIII Corps under Horrocks held the southern part of the Allied position. As infantry units it contained from north to south 50th and 44th Divisions and Koenig's Fighting Frenchmen. Supporting them was 7th Armoured Division, now under Harding, another of Montgomery's personal choices. 22nd Armoured Brigade was back with the division, which also still contained 4th Light Armoured Brigade now led by Brigadier Mark Roddick who had been second-in-command to Roberts in 22nd Armoured during Alam Halfa. The Royal Scots Greys who had done so well in that battle had also left 22nd Armoured to accompany Roddick to his new command.

The main armoured strength was to be found in X Corps which was commanded by Lumsden, now a lieutenant general. Under him came Gatehouses's 10th Armoured Division, its 8th Armoured Brigade having been joined by the newly arrived 24th Armoured Brigade and by 133rd Brigade from 44th Division, its infantrymen hastily provided with lorries and retrained to operate as part of an armoured division. Under Lumsden also came the revived 1st Armoured Division now led by Major General Raymond Briggs – this contained 2nd Armoured Brigade under Brigadier Fisher and Bosvile's 7th Motor Brigade.

Opposed to these forces in the enemy's front line were the Italian XXI Corps facing Leese and the Italian X Corps facing Horrocks. Or perhaps they should be called German–Italian Corps,[3] for both contained soldiers from each of the Axis countries, deliberately inter-mixed by Rommel in the belief that this would stiffen resistance. The former contained the Italian Trento and Bologna Divisions, 164th Light and part of the Ramcke Parachute Brigade. The latter was made up of the Italian Brescia, Folgore and newly returned Pavia Divisions, the remaining German parachutists and the so-called 'Battlegroup Kiel', a German unit under Major General Krause equipped with captured Stuart tanks. The main Axis armour – 15th and 21st Panzer, Ariete and Littorio – was held back behind the front line, while 90th Light and Trieste were in reserve to the west of Sidi Abd el Rahman.

In both armies, several of the divisions were well below strength. The New Zealanders still had only two infantry brigades. 69th Brigade, reformed from new arrivals in the Middle East, had rejoined 151st Brigade in 50th Division but Major General Nichols could not muster a third British brigade, receiving instead the newly formed 1st Greek Independent Brigade, made up of exiles from their conquered homeland and led by Colonel Katsotas. 44th Division was even worse off: 132nd Brigade had been returned to it but was much depleted after the mauling it had received at Alam Halfa, 131st Brigade had suffered severely during the abortive attack on 29 September, and 133rd Brigade had left for 10th Armoured Division. Yet the weaknesses of the German and Italian formations, especially the latter, were far greater. So much was this the case that while on paper Eighth Army could find only seven Infantry Divisions to its enemy's eight and three Armoured divisions to its enemy's four, its 'fighting strength', according to the Official History, was 195,000 compared with 104,000 for *Panzerarmee Afrika*: 50,000 Germans, 54,000 Italians.[4]

In numbers of tanks, Eighth Army's advantage was still greater. Those fit for action at the start of the battle totalled 1,029: 252 Shermans, 170 Grants, 249 Crusaders, 119 Stuarts and 194 Valentines. *Panzerarmee Afrika* could muster only 249 German tanks of which only 221 were gun-armed, though they included 88 Mark III Specials and 30 Mark IV Specials, and 278 medium and 20 light Italian tanks – a few reinforcements that arrived during the course of the battle would later be added.

Moreover the quality of the British tanks had also improved sharply.

Seventy-eight of the Crusaders were later models which carried a 6-pounder gun instead of the type's usual 2-pounder. Even more important, the long-awaited Shermans were, as can be seen, reaching Eighth Army in large numbers. These had 50mm of armour on the front of the hull and on the turret – 76mm indeed on the front of the turret – and 38mm on the side-plates, and they carried a 75mm gun in the turret instead of in the side-sponson of the Grant. They were in short better tanks than any that had previously served in Eighth Army – though it may be mentioned that they were still inferior to Rommel's mercifully few Mark IV Specials.

Eighth Army's artillery had also grown in strength and quality. There were 908 British field or medium guns as against 200 German and at most 300 Italian; and 1,451 anti-tank guns as against 550 German and 300 Italian. Moreover 849 of Eighth Army's anti-tank weapons were 6-pounders, superior to the 50mms that formed the bulk of Rommel's equipment and about equal to his sixty-eight captured Russian 76mms. Once more though, Rommel had the best of all anti-tank guns, his 88mms, of which there were eighty-six available for the battle.

Coningham's Desert Air Force had increased in size as well, largely because it had received numbers of United States Army Air Force personnel who now flew four squadrons of Mitchells and three of Warhawks. Coningham still had his two Australian Kittyhawk squadrons. There were now nine South African squadrons, two with Boston light bombers, one with Baltimores, two with Kittyhawks, one with Tomahawks and three with Hurricanes: the veteran No. 1 Squadron SAAF in the fighter role, No. 40 Squadron SAAF in the reconnaissance role and No. 7 Squadron SAAF which had converted to anti-tank Hurricane IIDs. The RAF, as was fitting, manned the largest number of squadrons, three of Baltimores, three of Spitfires, three of Kittyhawks and ten of the extraordinarily versatile Hurricanes, among which may be mentioned No. 208 Squadron with its reconnaissance machines, No. 73 Squadron with its night-fighters, No. 6 Squadron with its 'tank-busters' and No. 335 Squadron which had been formed from Greek personnel.

In all Coningham controlled some 750 aircraft of which about 530 were serviceable, and as at Alam Halfa, he was supported by two squadrons of Beaufighters, six of Wellingtons and two of Fleet Air Arm Albacores which did not come under his direct command. A further two Hurricane squadrons were to be found defending the rear areas. The Axis air arm contained about 275 German aircraft, mainly 109s and Junkers Ju 87s and Ju 88s, and some 400 Italian aircraft, the great majority of them fighters; but only just over half of the total strength was serviceable. As at Alam Halfa, the enemy too had support from outside, in its case from the bombers based in Crete.

As if these disadvantages were not enough, Rommel was haunted by past mistakes and misfortunes. His decision to advance deep into Egypt while

Malta remained unsubdued still bore its bitter fruit as the island's aircraft and submarines continued their assaults against his lines of communication. During September, over one-third of the supplies sent to *Panzerarmee Afrika* failed to reach it; during October, the figure was over one-half. Petrol was again desperately low, ammunition was also very restricted and even food supplies had been much reduced – a factor which was partly responsible for the large number of Axis soldiers on the 'sick list'.

And Rommel's defeat at Alam Halfa had not only dented his men's confidence but had deprived them – and him – of several trusted senior officers. Von Vaerst remained at the head of 15th Panzer, but Major General Heinz von Randow had taken von Bismarck's place in command of 21st Panzer and Major General Graf Theodor von Sponeck that of Kleemann in command of 90th Light. Finally, to replace the wounded Nehring as the overall leader of the *Afrika Korps* came Lieutenant General Wilhelm Ritter von Thoma. A tall, lean man who was, in the words of Paul Carell, 'the epitome of courage and gallantry' and whose twenty battle-wounds in two World Wars were worthy of comparison with those of Freyberg,[5] he made a welcome addition to any force – except that although he had fought with distinction in Spain, Poland, France and Russia, he had had no experience of warfare in the Desert.

At the same time it is only right to remember that much of Eighth Army had had little experience of warfare of any sort. The original 51st Division had been forced to surrender at St Valery during the Battle of France – to Rommel, as had not been forgotten – and its present successor had seen no action. Alam Halfa had been 44th Division's first battle and its experiences then and thereafter had not been happy ones: 69th Brigade had not seen combat since it had been reformed in mid-September; 9th and 24th Armoured Brigades were totally inexperienced new arrivals; and 8th Armoured Brigade had been in action as a formation only in its unsatisfactory clash with von Vaerst during Alam Halfa.

In addition, the new equipment reaching Eighth Army greatly increased the problems of inexperience – 8th, 9th and 24th Armoured Brigades for instance all received their new Shermans too late to gain any real practice with them before the battle began. They also found that there was a dearth of spare parts and many important items of equipment, such as compasses, were missing altogether. The Shermans later gained a deserved reputation for reliability but in those early days when neither their crews nor the maintenance units were used to them, it is hardly surprising that, in the tactful words of Lucas Phillips, 'several of them were found to be mechanically shaky'.

In any case, as General Fraser rather unkindly points out, 'reinforcements, whether of men or material, had in the past been no guarantors of victory'. Eighth Army's 'superiority was formidable. It need not, however, have been overwhelming. Battle could still turn on skill in execution.' General Jackson concurs, noting that 'numerical and material superiority alone was not necessarily enough to ensure victory, as Gazala had shown' – and even more so, Auchinleck's five attacks in July, when his superiority had been vastly greater than that now enjoyed by Montgomery. Furthermore another factor had now come into play. As Paul Carell remarks, 'El Alamein saw the climax of the war of mines. No such quantities of mines were laid in any theatre in the Second World War as here.'

By late October, Rommel's front was guarded by half-a-million mines set out in two main belts about two miles apart, between which other mines had been laid to form barriers shaped like the rungs of a ladder so as to 'box in' any force which penetrated the first belt. Also in the areas between the main belts were anti-personnel mines and booby traps of every horrible form that human ingenuity could devise. The whole of this sinister barrier, which the Germans called the 'Devil's Gardens', was between two and four miles in depth.

Within the 'Devil's Gardens', Rommel had placed 'battle outposts' – forward positions, well concealed and usually containing at least one 50mm anti-tank gun. The main infantry defences, though, were sited behind the second belt of mines, and beyond these again was another line, manned by tanks and anti-tank guns, which ran roughly along the Rahman Track, a desert road stretching southwards from Rommel's HQ at Sidi Abd el Rahman.

So protected, any defending force was likely to take fearful toll of its attackers. And the defending force this time was *Panzerarmee Afrika*. No wonder then that Rommel, though he would later complain bitterly that it had been 'a battle without hope' and that 'victory was simply impossible under the terms on which we entered the battle', did at the time hope, almost to the last, that if he could hold out just a little longer, the 'tenacity and stubbornness of our defence' would 'persuade the enemy to call off his attack' as it had persuaded Auchinleck to do in July. Such resolution 'might well have succeeded' reports General Jackson, 'against a less forceful and less professional British Commander'.

Or against less resolute soldiers or ones whose morale had not been inspired by success at Alam Halfa. Montgomery's plan envisaged only a subsidiary operation by XIII Corps in the south. Horrocks was to capture Himeimat and maintain pressure so as to keep as much enemy armour as possible away from the main battle-area. If there appeared little chance of progress, the attack was to be broken off so as to preserve 7th Armoured Division for future operations elsewhere. The limited task of XIII Corps was perhaps inevitable, since both 44th and 50th Divisions were undermanned, while 22nd Armoured Brigade which provided the main strength of 7th Armoured Division, having lost the Royal Scots Greys which had been its 'mobile reserve' at Alam Halfa, now found that 'all our tanks', as the future Major General Roberts remarks, had 'the highest mileage in the Army, so no wonder we were given a minor role'.

The major role was given to XXX and X Corps acting together – a situation that inevitably caused some confusion. The former was to break into the 'Devil's Gardens' on a front of some six miles, using all its divisions except 4th Indian, which, having been stripped of its transport for the benefit of others, was ordered to carry out diversionary raids only. The remaining divisions were to advance for some five miles in the north and three in the south to capture the Miteirya Ridge and a series of high points extending north-west of this to the so-called Kidney Ridge – though the kidney-shaped feature from which this took its name was in fact not a ridge at all but a depression with the ridge running north and east of it.

The assaulting infantry would make their advance straight through the minefields, accepting casualties from anti-personnel mines and relying on the fact that a man walking normally did not as a rule set off an anti-tank mine. To bring up vehicles, anti-tank guns and the supporting tanks of 9th and 23rd Armoured Brigades, lanes would have to be cleared through the minefields by the Royal Engineers. A number of old Matildas from 42nd and 44th Royal Tanks were fitted with heavy chains which revolved so as to strike the ground and explode any mine that was encountered. These 'Scorpions' as they were known were, however, allocated mainly to XIII Corps and at this early stage of their development they did not in any case prove a great success. In most instances reliance had to be placed on the Polish Mine Detector[6] or on the old, dangerous method of prodding the sand with bayonets. This mine-clearing and marking of lanes was a colossal undertaking, necessitating the provision of 88,775 lamps and 120 miles of marking tape, mostly to XXX Corps.

Once the infantry had secured their bridgehead, the engineers of X Corps would clear further gaps through the minefields in two fairly wide areas known as 'corridors' which were to be reserved for the use of that Corps alone. Through these would advance Lumsden's tanks, 1st Armoured Division passing through the northern 'corridor', 10th Armoured Division through the southern. The armour would then move forward to sever Rommel's supply lines, taking up positions on 'ground of its own choosing'. This was a great improvement on the plan for CRUSADER for instead of seeking the elusive enemy armour, it compelled this to attack in order to regain the vital ground lost. In addition it meant that the British armour could fight on the defensive instead of dashing upon the enemy anti-tank guns. Once more, though, it left a good deal of initiative in the hands of the enemy, and it repeated the old idea that the Axis armour should be destroyed first and the Axis infantry 'mopped up' at leisure.

It was thus beneficial that by 6 October, Montgomery had concluded that in any case the armour had not been sufficiently trained for the task envisaged for it. He decided therefore that the tanks would initially continue westward for some two miles beyond the infantry but they would then halt, forming a protective shield for XXX Corps while this Corps engaged the enemy infantry in the battle of attrition – a procedure which Montgomery called 'crumbling'. He was convinced that the enemy armour could not allow this to happen but would have to intervene to save the Axis infantrymen and then, and later, he proved a shrewd judge of Rommel's impulsive character, rightly believing that he would attack with his panzers against the British armour in its defensive positions – as had happened at Alam Halfa. As General Jackson points out, this was 'a radical change of policy' but one which happily necessitated no 'major revision of existing plans'.

It was not, however, a change which reassured the armoured commanders, especially Lumsden and Gatehouse. Their fear was that in either case the tanks would suffer fearful losses as they emerged from restricted passageways guarded by enemy anti-tank guns. The lessons of the past made their doubts valid, but the expression of these had the unfortunate result of making the Dominion divisional commanders, with the memories of Auchinleck's July offensive only too horribly fresh in their minds, question whether the armour had the will or the capacity to carry out its task.

Montgomery remained ruthlessly resolute. The tanks, he declared, 'must and shall' break out. If necessary, if the infantry had not cleared paths for them, they were to fight their own way into the open. Montgomery anticipated that the break-in would be followed by a 'dog-fight', a 'killing match' lasting at least a week. Since the infantry would have to play the major role during this period, he could not afford heavy infantry losses in the earlier phase, particularly in the Dominion divisions which could not expect reinforcements. By contrast he could afford to lose tanks, though not too many of their trained crews. His attitude did much to reassure his infantry commanders, but Lumsden and Gatehouse remained unhappy. For the moment though, it should be said that, to their great credit, both disguised their fears and outwardly showed nothing but enthusiasm for the plan.

'The Army Commander,' relates the Official History, 'now felt free to devote most of his energy directly to his troops. He was out and about, seeing and being seen, sizing up his subordinate leaders, talking to officers and men and arousing their interest and enthusiasm, and generally inspiring confidence and raising the spirits of the whole Army to fighting pitch.' How well he succeeded is made clear by Horrocks who describes Montgomery's explanation of his plan to his senior officers – lieutenant colonels and upwards – on 19 and 20 October, as 'electrifying', 'clear and full of confidence'. Lieutenant Colonel Victor Buller Turner, CO of 2nd Battalion, The Rifle

Brigade, of whom we shall hear more shortly, would refer to it as 'absolutely thrilling'.[7] As for the men in the ranks, the plan, says Horrocks, 'was explained to every soldier taking part in the battle, and there is no doubt that the Eighth Army entered the Battle of Alamein in a state of great enthusiasm, almost exaltation. They had been told by their commander that this was the turning-point of the war, and they believed him.'

It is worth noting that Montgomery made no 'election promises'. On the contrary, he insisted that Eighth Army, in General Jackson's words, must 'face up to the fact that there was no short cut to victory. The Germans had to be fought to the limit of human endurance.' He emphasized that 'spectacular results' could not be expected 'too soon'; that the 'whole affair' would last twelve days. Privately he advised his staff officers that Eighth Army would suffer 13,000 casualties. Even the code name chosen for the offensive had a grimly appropriate implication for a battle among minefields: Operation LIGHTFOOT.

Also being planned at this time was Operation BERTRAM, the deception scheme co-ordinated by the then Lieutenant Colonel Richardson to disguise the time and place of the attack from the enemy. Tanks and guns were concealed by having the shapes of special dummy lorries called 'sunshades' fitted over them. Supply dumps being built up in the north were concealed as far as possible, often by being stacked in such a way that from the air they resembled vehicles. By contrast in the south, where Eighth Army's preparations could easily be observed – as was intended – from the heights of Himeimat, dumps and artillery positions, some of them false ones, were deliberately badly camouflaged, movement of vehicles was encouraged and a bogus water pipeline, complete with pumping stations and water-towers, was laid, moving steadily towards the southern part of the front at a rate of progress that suggested it would be completed early in November.

These carefully considered moves had an undoubted effect. Rommel 'believed,' says Field Marshal Carver, 'that Eighth Army would attack simultaneously at several points and then try to develop the most favourable into a breakthrough'. For this reason and because of his petrol shortages, he split up his armour, as indeed, contrary to legend, he had done so often in the past, placing 15th Panzer and Littorio behind the infantry lines in the north and 21st Panzer and Ariete behind those in the south.

Nor was German Intelligence at all certain of the date of Eighth Army's offensive. In consequence on 23 September, after making the dispositions previously described, Rommel returned to Germany for a well-deserved, much-needed rest, promising that he would return if the Allies launched a major attack.[8] Rommel's successor was General Georg Stumme, a highly experienced practitioner of armoured warfare who had commanded a corps in Russia, but again was new to conditions in the Desert. On the evening of

23 October, he gave the final tribute to the success of Operation BERTRAM in a routine report to Hitler: 'Enemy situation unchanged'.

At 2140 on that same evening, 474 Allied guns commenced a tremendous bombardment of the Axis batteries. This inflicted considerable damage on its targets and greatly heartened the Allied soldiers, but its concentrated fury also carried a deeper message. It gave notice to friend and foe alike that the days of 'mobile artillery battle groups' were gone for ever.

High above the barrage, another practical demonstration of the change in attitude which the change in command had brought about was taking place. The Allied airmen, in particular the Desert Air Force, were by now not just supporting but virtually part of Eighth Army. The first squadron in action, as at Alam Halfa, was No. 73, but whereas at Alam Halfa it had been on the defensive in a defensive battle, now it, like Eighth Army, was taking the offensive. Its Hurricanes were out looking for trouble, strafing targets of opportunity, troop positions, vehicles, supply dumps, often well behind enemy lines. Tedder's six squadrons of Wellingtons were also in action, some provided with special equipment with which to jam Axis wireless signals but most joining in the attack on the enemy defences, dropping 125 tons of bombs – a contribution that passed almost unnoticed amid the thunder of the British guns below.

The barrage lasted until 2155. There followed a grim pause for a further five minutes, then the fire switched to the Axis infantry positions, rolling slowly forward across the area of the assault. Part of the 62nd Infantry Regiment of the Italian Trento Division was so heavily hit that it abandoned its forward defences, much to the benefit of 26th Australian Brigade which was to advance in this particular area.

Behind the moving curtain of steel, the infantrymen from the Australian, New Zealand, South African and 51st Highland Divisions pushed forward into the 'Devil's Gardens'. Wimberley's Scotsmen were led not only by their officers but by their kilted pipers, among them nineteen-year-old Piper Duncan McIntyre of 5th Black Watch who, hit three times, finally collapsed but continued to play until he died.

By midnight, all four divisions had completed the initial stage of their advance to positions which lay about a mile inside the Axis minefields and were known collectively as 'Red Line'. So far casualties had been light. But when at 0100, fresh infantry units advanced towards 'Blue Line', their final objectives, the picture changed. They encountered denser minefields, heavier defences and an Axis artillery which was now recovering from its ordeal. Amidst the clouds of dust churned up by the shells of both sides, it became increasingly difficult to keep direction. Each battalion therefore was led by a 'navigating officer' who went ahead, compass in hand, counting his paces, behind whom white tape was laid to mark the line of advance. This was not

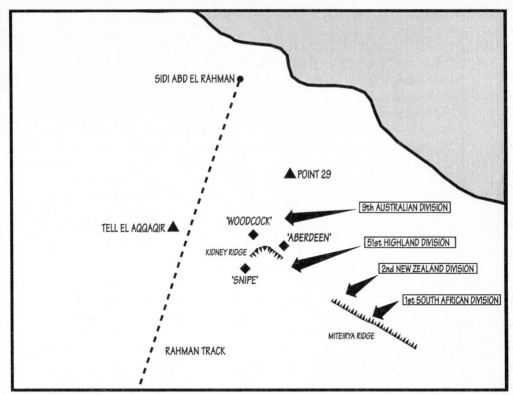

Map 5A: Alamein, the break-in.

Map 5B: Alamein, the break-out.

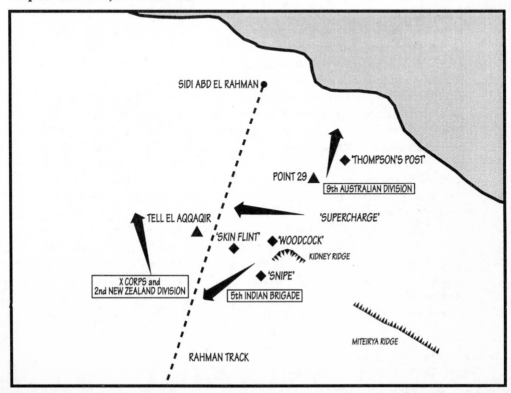

a task for the faint-hearted – in 7th Black Watch six 'navigating officers' were killed or wounded that night.

Nonetheless, despite all the problems, despite all the hideous perils of the 'Devil's Gardens', XXX Corps had captured about 80 per cent of its objectives by the early morning of 24 October. 24th Australian Brigade had made only a feint attack to the north, but 26th Brigade had reached 'Blue Line' and 20th Brigade was about 500 yards short. The New Zealanders had gained the whole of their section of Miteirya Ridge, though they were unable to exploit to the south-west of it as planned. 3rd South African Brigade in the extreme south had also captured part of the Ridge, while 2nd South African Brigade, between 3rd Brigade and the New Zealanders, was also about 500 yards short.

The main difficulties had been encountered by 51st Highland Division. On the extreme left, two companies of 7th Black Watch under Captain Cathcart, though reduced in strength to about forty men, had reached 'Blue Line', but a series of strong fortifications had prevented the remainder of Wimberley's men from getting nearer than some 1,500 yards to the east of this. The division had also suffered the greatest number of casualties, about 1,000, while the New Zealand casualties were 800 and the Australian and South African 350 each.

In return XXX Corps had taken about 1,000 prisoners from Trento and the German 164th Light Division, and had killed the enemy commander. The bombardment and the bombing had so shattered the Axis communications that, soon after dawn, Stumme set out for the front to check up on the situation for himself. He was accompanied only by an Intelligence officer, Colonel Büchting, and the driver of his staff car, Corporal Wolf, and not realizing the depth of the Allied advance, he drove into an area held by Australian troops. These promptly opened fire on the car, just at the moment apparently that Stumme was getting out of it. Büchting was hit in the head and died soon afterwards, and Wolf swung the car round to make off at high speed, unaware of the fact that his general was holding on to the outside. Stumme suffered from high blood pressure and perhaps not surprisingly he had a fatal heart attack. His body was found next day. This incident caused further confusion at the Headquarters of *Panzerarmee Afrika*. It was some time before von Thoma took temporary command and noon before Hitler contacted Rommel to request that he return immediately to the Desert.

Unfortunately the British armour had not enjoyed a similar success. The supporting tanks of 9th and 23rd Armoured Brigades were up with their infantrymen, though both had suffered losses to mines, but Lumsden's X Corps had been unable to pass through the infantry positions as planned. 1st Armoured Division, advancing behind 51st Highland, was held up by fire from unsubdued Axis strongpoints. 10th Armoured's sappers under

Lieutenant Colonel McMeekan, himself wounded by a bursting shell, not only came under fire but found the minefields they had to clear were thick with booby traps. Nonetheless they had cleared four routes to the Miteirya Ridge by dawn. Custance's 8th Armoured Brigade moved up these but when the first regiment, the Nottinghamshire Yeomanry, attempted to cross the Ridge, it encountered another minefield on the crest and also came under heavy fire from anti-tank guns which knocked out eight Grants and eight Crusaders. Accordingly 8th Armoured halted just below the crest, while 24th Armoured under Brigadier Kenchington deployed as best it could in the minefields to the east of it.

Nor did matters go well with the diversionary attack by XIII Corps in the south. Here the attackers had to penetrate the two British minefields, code-named 'January' and 'February', which had been retained by Rommel after the Battle of Alam Halfa. Harding's 7th Armoured Division was given this task, supported by 131st Brigade which consisted of three battalions of the Queen's Royal Regiment from West Surrey. At the same time, two battalions of the Fighting French under Colonel Amilakvari were to seize a position west of Mount Himeimat, onto which they would then move later.

As it happened everything possible went wrong. The initial infantry attack by 1/7th Queens, despite very heavy casualties, broke through 'January', but then the enemy, mainly the Ramcke and Folgore parachutists, counter-attacked, killing Lieutenant Colonel Burton and taking most of his men prisoner. The sappers under Lieutenant Colonel Corbett-Winder cleared four gaps through 'January', earning the personal thanks of Horrocks, but they were unable to make a similar clearance through 'February' for 22nd Armoured Brigade which was left perilously situated between the two mine-fields. To complete the sad story, the tanks of the German 'Battlegroup Kiel', evading the Crusaders supporting the Fighting French, fell on Amilakvari's men, killing a large number of them including their leader.

XIII Corps made no attempt to continue its advance during the daylight hours of the 24th, but elsewhere there was plenty of action, not least in the air. With the dawn, the Desert Air Force was out in strength; the RAF Baltimores, the South African Bostons, the Hurricane and Kittyhawk fighter-bombers all engaged the Axis army. The German 88s had to turn their barrels skywards to deal with this threat, as a result of which they gave away their positions to the Allied ground forces who were able to take advantage of this on several occasions. In the south, the cannon-armed Hurricane IIDs of No. 6 Squadron RAF and No. 7 Squadron SAAF were in constant action, gaining belated revenge for the misfortunes of the Fighting French by putting 'Battlegroup Kiel' out of action.

In the north, during the day and the following night, both the Australians and the South Africans completed the capture of their original objectives;

while in the course of a conference with Leese, Lumsden and Freyberg which began at 0915, Montgomery directed 51st Highland and 1st Armoured Divisions to reach their planned positions and the New Zealanders and 10th Armoured to 'crumble' to the south. He made it clear that he would be prepared to accept large tank losses if necessary but he would not tolerate 'any more hanging back'. 'This action,' he tells us in his *Memoirs*, 'produced immediate results.'

In accordance with the Army Commander's instructions, 2nd Seaforths delivered a spirited attack at 1500. This gained most of 51st Division's remaining objectives, though some were not taken until the night of the 25th/26th, and the last enemy stronghold code-named 'Aberdeen', situated on the eastern end of Kidney Ridge, finally surrendered only at dawn on the 27th. Fisher's 2nd Armoured Brigade followed up the infantrymen and by about 1600 it had reached the front line, though it was unable to advance further as Montgomery had intended.

Not that it mattered too much at this stage, for now the enemy, in Montgomery's words, did 'exactly what I wanted': 15th Panzer and Littorio counter-attacked. 2nd Armoured Brigade, aided by the anti-tank guns of the infantry units, held firm, and the enemy retreated having lost twenty-six tanks. Fisher had lost thirty-one, but Eighth Army could afford this rate of exchange, while *Panzerarmee Afrika* could not.

The events of the night of 24th/25th October would quickly dampen Montgomery's pleasure. In the south, the remaining battalions of 131st Brigade, 1/5th and 1/6th Queens, broke through the 'February' minefield, though with heavy losses, but all attempts to get the tanks through the gaps which the infantry had cleared behind them were thwarted by violent anti-tank fire; Harding, who was inspecting their progress, had a narrow escape when a shell burst beside his jeep, killing his ADC Captain Cosgrave who was driving it. The armour remained between 'January' and 'February' until the following night, when it was withdrawn to the east, and at the same time, 131st Brigade fell back between the minefields, suffering further losses in the process. Also that night, 69th Brigade from 50th Division delivered an attack in the Munassib Depression but it too failed with heavy casualties in a maze of anti-personnel mines. This concluded major operations on the southern front, but at least XIII Corps had performed its main task. 21st Panzer and Ariete were still kept in the south, well away from the real break-in zone.

The chief problems on the night of the 24th/25th, however, concerned 10th Armoured Division. Gatehouse had postponed his attack until darkness had fallen, but when 8th Armoured Brigade began its advance at 2200, it was illuminated by enemy aircraft dropping parachute flares. A bombing attack followed which hit the supporting vehicles of the Nottinghamshire

Yeomanry, setting twenty-two petrol or ammunition lorries ablaze. The enemy artillery promptly opened fire also, halting both the Nottinghamshire Yeomanry and 3rd Royal Tanks which was following it. Custance's third regiment, the Staffordshire Yeomanry, was able to proceed through the minefields, followed by the other regiments later, while by about 0500 on the 25th, Kenchington's 24th Armoured Brigade, after many difficulties, also forced its way through the minefields to link up with 2nd Armoured Brigade on its right.

Unfortunately, prior to this, Custance had suggested to Gatehouse that the advance beyond the Miteirya ridge should be abandoned. Gatehouse, after vainly trying to contact Lumsden by wireless, returned to his Main Headquarters from which he spoke to his Corps Commander on the field telephone, strongly recommending that the operation be halted. At 0230, Lumsden in turn passed on the message to de Guingand, adding that he was inclined to agree. De Guingand spoke to Leese whom he found had been told by Freyberg that 10th Armoured was not 'properly set up for the attack' and therefore was also doubtful whether the armour could carry out its mission. The Chief of Staff rightly decided that Montgomery must be consulted; he asked both Leese and Lumsden to attend a conference with the Army Commander at 0330.

'There was a certain "atmosphere" present,' reports de Guingand of this meeting – and not just because 'a positive inferno caused by enemy aircraft was taking place outside'. 'Montgomery listened to what his Corps Commanders had to say,' relates General Jackson. 'Both believed that the battle had gone so wrong that it should be broken off to avoid further profitless expenditure of life and resources.'

Notes

1   Volume IV: *The Destruction of the Axis Forces in Africa* by Major General I.S.O. Playfair and Brigadier C.J.C. Molony with Captain F.C. Flynn RN and Group Captain T.P. Gleave.
2   Officially the New Zealanders were part of X Corps but in practice they were controlled by XXX Corps throughout the battle.
3   Oddly enough *Panzerarmee Afrika* had the words 'German–Italian' officially added to its title on 25 October, while the battle was being fought. They were rarely used in practice apart from in formal pronouncements.
4   The statistics for this battle vary widely, not to say wildly, in different accounts. Those recorded here are the ones given in the Official History.
5   Freyberg, whom Churchill called 'the salamander' because he 'thrived in the fire', received no less than twenty-seven wounds in the First World War, plus three more in the Second.

6   So named because it was the invention of two Free Polish officers, Captain Kosacki and Lieutenant Kalinowski.

7   Quoted in Lucas Phillips: *Alamein*.

8   Von Mellenthin, by now seriously ill, had already been sent back to Germany on 9 September. He did not return to North Africa, thereby depriving us hereafter of the benefit of his experiences.

Chapter 7

THE HAMMERING OF THE PANZERS

At this tense, critical moment, Montgomery, according to de Guingand, remained 'cool and calm'. He gave his orders 'very quietly' but he made it quite clear that his basic intentions were unchanged, though he agreed that, from 8th Armoured Brigade, only the Staffordshire Yeomanry should proceed beyond the Miteirya Ridge for the time being; and he warned Lumsden that if necessary he would appoint new leaders for the armour who would ensure that his commands were carried out.

The only time that Montgomery became roused was when, at Lumsden's request, he contacted Gatehouse on the field telephone and, he relates in his *Memoirs*, 'discovered to my horror that he himself was some 16,000 yards (nearly 10 miles) behind his leading armoured brigades. I spoke to him in no uncertain voice, and ordered him to go forward at once and take charge of his battle; he was to fight his way out, and lead his division from in front and not from behind.'

In reality, while it is difficult not to admire what Liddell Hart calls Montgomery's 'unflinching determination' and Horrocks his 'steely determination when things go badly, which is the hallmark of a great commander', he was scarcely fair to Gatehouse who had only remained at his Main Headquarters so that he could more easily be contacted as Lumsden had asked; Gatehouse indeed was the very last man to 'lead his division from behind'. Nor were his anxieties unfounded. In the early dawn of 25 October, the Staffordshire Yeomanry came under heavy fire from 88s losing ten tanks, after which Gatehouse, contrary to his orders, withdrew them behind the Ridge. Currie's 9th Armoured Brigade and Kenchington's 24th Armoured Brigade were equally unable to make progress, while further north Fisher's 2nd Armoured Brigade also lost ten tanks to 88mm fire. The fact was that despite all the propaganda then or later about the value of the Shermans, the

Axis anti-tank guns, especially the 88s, were still the most deadly weapons on the battlefield, particularly now when the Allied armour had to move through minefields, of which more were hurriedly being laid by the enemy beyond the Miteirya Ridge.[1]

Thus Montgomery's orders had little material effect and in consequence many commentators, including his biographer, have tended to belittle the importance of this conference. By contrast de Guingand considers it to have been the first of his 'stepping stones to victory'.

There can be no doubt that this description is correct. In the first place, Montgomery's resolution had the same effect as Auchinleck's much more loudly praised intervention when Cunningham had wavered during CRUSADER – it did not win the battle but it did prevent it from being abandoned prematurely. Yet of the two, Montgomery's action was by far the more commendable. Not only was it more difficult for him to take a detached view of events because he was closer to the scene, but while Auchinleck had been sustained by the insistence of both Cunningham's corps commanders that the fight should continue, both Montgomery's corps commanders believed that the battle should be broken off. It was also far more important that Alamein should not be abandoned prematurely – the implications for TORCH and even more for Malta would surely have been catastrophic.

Moreover there are other gains than purely material ones. Ever since he had taken over command, Montgomery had been resolved to build up effective co-operation between the different branches of his army. It was because he felt that there was no such resolve in X Corps that he was particularly critical of its commander – though here again he was by no means fair to Lumsden who personally did genuinely believe in co-operation. It does seem, however, that not all of Lumsden's subordinates shared his attitude and the value of the conference on the night of 24th/25th October was that it demonstrated Montgomery's insistence that the needs of the armour must be subsidiary to those of the Army as a whole. 'The message got through,' reports Ronald Lewin, and 'for the rest of the battle, perhaps for the rest of the campaign, there was no more of that divisive spirit . . . which in the past had so often prevented the British armour from behaving as though it were a part of the army.' This was a credit to all concerned. It should be emphasized that to no one was it more welcome than to Lieutenant General Lumsden.

Montgomery's firmness, though, was by no means his only virtue. 'Within the chosen limits of his planning,' declares Liddell Hart, 'he [Montgomery] showed consummate ability in varying the direction of his thrusts and developing a tactical leverage to work the opponent off balance.' This 'readiness to vary his aim according to circumstances, on this and later occasions,' Liddell Hart adds, 'was a better tonic to the troops and a greater tribute to his generalship' than any attempts to ensure that his battle went exactly 'according to plan'.

By midday on 25 October, Montgomery had realized that attempts to exploit to the south-west of Miteirya Ridge were likely to prove too costly – thereby belatedly confirming the opinions of his armoured commanders. He therefore abandoned these and withdrew 10th Armoured Division to reorganize – apart from Kenchington's 24th Armoured Brigade which he now transferred to the command of Briggs. At the same time he maintained his principal dual aims of 'crumbling' the enemy infantry, and meeting the counter-attacks of the enemy armour when this tried to intervene, with his own tanks and anti-tank guns. He therefore ordered that XXX Corps should complete the capture of its original objectives, while 26th Australian Brigade 'crumbled' northward and 1st Armoured Division continued to push westward in the area of the Kidney Ridge.

During 25 October, the enemy armour did make persistent counter-attacks, but these were first hampered by the Allied airmen, then finally repelled by 2nd and 24th Armoured Brigades, fighting in defensive positions of their own choosing and supported by the anti-tank gunners of 7th Battalion, The Rifle Brigade which formed part of Bosvile's 7th Motor Brigade, and by those of 2/13th and 2/17th Battalions of 20th Australian Brigade. The achievements of the Australians were particularly commendable for they were still largely equipped with the older 2-pounder guns – a fact which strongly suggests that the failures under earlier regimes had been due less to inadequate weapons than to inadequate use of those weapons.

Then during the night of 25th/26th October, the Highland Division, as mentioned earlier, and though its total casualties increased to somewhere in the region of 2,100, completed the conquest of almost all its remaining initial objectives, while 26th Australian Brigade delivered a brilliant stroke to the north. This was a totally co-ordinated effort by all arms, for 2/48th and 2/24th Battalions – the third, 2/23rd, was kept in reserve – were supported by thirty Valentines from 40th Royal Tanks, seven regiments of field or medium artillery and 115 tons of bombs dropped by Tedder's Wellingtons. The main objective was 'Point 29', the most prominent feature on a spur to the north of the Australian position which it effectively dominated.

Lieutenant Colonel Hammer, CO of 2/48th had learned from patrols and the interrogation of prisoners that there was only one small minefield between his men and Point 29. Two of his companies advanced 1,000 yards to seize this, gaps were quickly cleared by the sappers, and then Hammer's third company mounted on Bren-gun carriers charged forward towards Point 29 under cover of an artillery bombardment, gained another 1,000 yards in nine minutes, took the enemy completely by surprise, and captured the position by 0200 on the 26th. On Hammer's right flank, 2/24th, though with heavier casualties, also made important progress. The enemy had lost some 300 men of whom 173 Germans and 67 Italians were taken prisoner, and Private Gratwick of 2/48th, who had destroyed one enemy strongpoint and attacked another single-handed, had won a posthumous Victoria Cross.

On the evening of the 25th, Field Marshal Rommel had resumed his command of *Panzerarmee Afrika*, but since the counter-attacks that his subordinates had been launching had been in accordance with the tactics decreed by Rommel before his departure, his return made no difference whatever to the nature of the fighting. On the contrary, declaring that his aim was 'to throw the enemy out of our defence line at all costs and to re-occupy our old positions', he merely repeated the assaults on Eighth Army. He thereby continued to play into Montgomery's hands. Throughout 26 October, the Axis armour struck out towards the Kidney Ridge and the newly lost Point 29 but all its moves were broken up, this time more by artillery fire and the raids of the Desert Air Force's light bombers and fighter-bombers than by the British tanks.

By the end of this third day of battle, 15th Panzer's tank losses had increased to a total of seventy-seven and those of Littorio to about fifty. 164th Light had also suffered heavily. 'Rivers of blood' as Rommel rather pathetically – and with some exaggeration – records, had been 'poured out' to no avail. That evening he ordered 21st Panzer, part of Ariete and supporting artillery up from the south, and 90th Light and Trieste forward from their reserve positions. At the same time Kesselring directed his airmen to make a maximum effort to support the major attack which Rommel proposed to deliver on the 27th.

Inevitably therefore 27 October was a day of savage clashes. The Axis pilots certainly did their best to assist their ground troops, even the obsolete Italian CR 42 biplanes, eight of which were lost, seeing combat. A major Stuka raid was completely dispersed by the Hurricanes of 33 and 213 Squadrons, though they lost three of their own machines in the process, and everywhere the Desert Air Force held its opponents in check. Meanwhile Coningham's light bombers were equally effective, an attempt by 90th Light to engage the Australians on Point 29 being thwarted by air attacks and a very heavy artillery barrage before it could even come to grips with the defenders.

Fiercest of all, though, were the encounters in the Kidney Ridge area for not only did Rommel intend to attack here but so did 1st Armoured Division, urged on, it may be mentioned, by Lumsden. It was arranged that during the night of the 26th/27th, detachments of 7th Motor Brigade would seize low ridges about 2,000 yards west of Kidney Ridge, which the armour would use as bases from which to advance. The attempt on one of these ridges, code-named 'Woodcock', lost its way and failed to reach its objective. Next night, another attempt was made, this time by 4th Royal Sussex from 133rd Brigade. This battalion was also unable to reach 'Woodcock' and before it could dig in on unsuitable ground it was attacked at dawn on the 28th by enemy armour and overrun with the loss of forty-seven killed, including Lieutenant Colonel Murphy, and 342 taken prisoner.

In stark contrast was the action fought on 7th Motor Brigade's other target, an unnamed ridge which went by the undramatic code name of 'Snipe'. During the night of 26th/27th October, this was taken by 2nd Battalion, The Rifle Brigade, commanded by Lieutenant Colonel Victor Buller Turner, the officer who had felt so inspired by Montgomery's 'absolutely thrilling' explanation of his plan. Turner controlled less than 300 men in all, the most important part of his force being his anti-tank company under Major Thomas Bird with its thirteen 6-pounder guns, to which had been added half-a-dozen others from Lieutenant Alan Baer's 239th Anti-Tank Battery of 76th Anti-Tank Regiment, Royal Artillery. The 6-pounders first proved their worth at about 0400 on the 27th, when a Mark IV Special moved into the battalion's position, only to be sent up in flames by a hit from the gun commanded by Sergeant Brown.

It was only the start of a day of frenzied action for the defenders of 'Snipe'. As dawn broke, they sighted the tanks of 15th Panzer and Littorio Divisions under the overall command of Colonel Teege of the former's 8th Panzer Regiment moving in their direction. At once they opened fire, totally destroying eleven tanks or guns and temporarily knocking out five more. 'Bursts of unrestrained cheers,' says Lucas Phillips, 'ran through the garrison at the thrill of this dramatic success. A ripple of exaltation filled all ranks. From that moment they felt themselves to be on top of the enemy.'[2] Shortly afterwards, 'a single German soldier who had been lying concealed in the very centre,' of the 'Snipe' position, 'was seen to leap up and run at full speed westward. He was unarmed.' Not a shot was fired at him and he made good his escape.

The enemy naturally retaliated, shelling the garrison from long range. Throughout the day, the anti-tank guns were gradually put out of action and their men killed or wounded. A number of unofficial crews were hastily banded together to serve the remaining guns, a particularly effective one being formed by Lieutenant Holt-Wilson, Sergeant Ayris and Rifleman Chard, a very tough character who, Lucas Phillips informs us, was 'often in trouble when not fighting'.

At about 0730, 47th Royal Tanks, the leading regiment of 24th Armoured Brigade, moved up as intended but mistaking Turner's men for the enemy, it too opened fire on them. Lieutenant Wintour drove over in a Bren-gun carrier and managed to halt the 'friendly' bombardment, and at about 0830, 47th Royal Tanks joined the 'Snipe' garrison – only to come under attack from enemy guns which destroyed seven Shermans and forced the remainder to retreat. Further south, 41st Royal Tanks was also checked and fell back with the loss of twelve of its number.

The Riflemen on 'Snipe', however, continued their resistance. At 0900, an attack by Italian infantry was beaten off. About an hour later, so was one by the Littorio Division. 15th Panzer, moving south of 'Snipe' to attack 24th Armoured Brigade, was next engaged by both Turner and Kenchington, eight German tanks in all being put out of action. Exasperated, at 1300, the Littorio Division delivered a full-scale assault on 'Snipe' from the south, preceded by a heavy bombardment which caused numerous casualties.

Only one 6-pounder could be brought to bear against this onslaught, that of Sergeant Charles Calistan, who was now alone, the other members of his detachment having been wounded. Turner and Lieutenant Jack Toms ran to join him. With their aid Calistan destroyed five Italian tanks but there were three more still advancing and the gun had only two rounds of ammunition left. Toms raced to his jeep, 100 yards away, loaded it with ammunition from a gun that was out of action and drove back, all under fire. Ten yards from Calistan, the jeep was set ablaze. Turner, followed by Corporals Francis and Barnett, hurried to help Toms. The ammunition was unloaded and carried to the gun, Turner being severely wounded in the head in the process. Calistan, who had calmly remained at his post, took careful aim and destroyed all three Italian tanks, one after the other.

All through the afternoon, the Riflemen continued to be shelled, Bird and Toms among others being wounded. Then at 1600, a new foe appeared. 21st Panzer had been heavily bombed on its way up from the south and it was again bombed as it tried to form up for Rommel's great assault on the Allied lines. Part of this fell on 10th Hussars of Fisher's 2nd Armoured Brigade which threw it back, claiming thirteen tanks destroyed. Moreover, as the Germans advanced they presented broadside targets to the 'Snipe' garrison which took full advantage of them. The panzers then turned on their tormentors, knocking out several guns. A Mark IV Special, its huge gun 'hideously menacing', closed to within 100 yards of the gun of Sergeant Cullen but his detachment held their ground and their gun and that of Sergeant Binks hit the target simultaneously.

About half-an-hour later, another group from 21st Panzer made a deliberate attack on 'Snipe' from the north. Only the guns of Sergeants Hine and Miles could be brought to bear. Miles was wounded and his men forced to take cover by machine-gun fire from the advancing armour. But Lieutenant Holt-Wilson's crew were able to swing their gun round to face the threat and Sergeant Swann, whose own gun had been knocked out earlier, ran to that of the wounded Miles, loading, aiming and firing single-handed until, says Lucas Phillips, the gun crew 'inspired by his leadership, jumped forward and joined him'. Between them the three 6-pounders set half-a-dozen panzers on fire and the remainder retired. Rommel's planned counter-offensive had failed completely.

At 2315, Turner's men fell back to Eighth Army's main positions. They had suffered some seventy casualties and all except one of the guns that were still serviceable had been so damaged that they had to be abandoned after being rendered unusable. 239th Battery successfully towed out the last remaining 6-pounder – that of Sergeant Ronald Wood.

A Committee of Investigation appointed to assess the Riflemen's achievement a month later, 'concluded' reports Lucas Phillips, 'that the minimum number of tanks burnt and totally destroyed was 32 – 21 German and 11 Italian – plus five self-propelled guns, and that certainly another 15, perhaps 20, tanks had been knocked out and recovered, making a grand total of 57'. Among the wrecks found afterwards were five of Rommel's precious Mark IV Specials. Only a very few of the recovered casualties could have been repaired before the battle ended. The anti-tank gun, not the tank, was clearly the queen of the battlefield. *Panzerarmee Afrika* had long realized this; now the men of Eighth Army knew it as well.

Montgomery, according to Lucas Phillips, was 'delighted', as well he might be. Among the many decorations awarded were DCMs for Calistan, Swann and Chard, a DSO for Bird and a Victoria Cross for Turner, in honour, as the Official History beautifully puts it, of 'his own gallantry in the action and that of all under his command'.

While Rommel was spending 26 and 27 October in furious but unimaginative attacks, Montgomery was once more demonstrating his calm adaptability. He 'realized' states the Official History, 'that the impetus of his offensive was on the wane and he decided to regroup his army to create a reserve with which to restore it' – and also to again vary the direction of his main thrust. During the 26th and 27th, the various preliminary moves were set in train. The operations of XIII Corps were abandoned and it was later decided that 7th Armoured Division, less Roddick's 4th Light Armoured Brigade, should move north on the night of the 31st. 2nd New Zealand Division, including 9th Armoured Brigade, was pulled out of the line, its departure being covered by extending the fronts manned by 1st South African and 4th Indian Divisions. And at a conference with Leese and Lumsden at 0800 on the 28th, Montgomery decided to go onto the defensive in the Kidney Ridge area which would now be held by 10th Armoured Division. 1st Armoured Division retired to rest and reorganize, 24th Armoured Brigade, to its bitter regret, being disbanded and its tanks given to 2nd Armoured Brigade to replenish Fisher's strength. Fighting continued around Kidney Ridge and in the skies above it, but the Desert Air Force proved so successful in attacking enemy concentrations that no major assault took place.

Attention now switched to the north. Montgomery's new plan called for a preliminary thrust northward from Point 29 by the Australians on the night of the 28th/29th; to be followed by the major effort, an advance from the Australian position north-westward down the coast road which would start on the night of the 30th/31st and to which would be given the code name SUPERCHARGE. Montgomery wished this to be led by Freyberg, to whose command he intended to transfer a succession of British infantry brigades in order to sustain the momentum of the assault.

The preliminary attack by Morshead's Australians achieved moderate success. It was well co-ordinated, being supported by artillery and by 40th and 46th Royal Tanks from 23rd Armoured Brigade, but it had to pass through heavily booby-trapped minefields and was opposed by strong fixed defences manned by resolute troops coming mainly from 90th and 164th Light. The Australians inflicted severe casualties on them and although the main German stronghold, which the Australians named 'Thompson's Post', to the north-east of Point 29, held out, 20th Australian Brigade was able to outflank this to the west, threatening to cut off the defenders. Rommel was now becoming seriously alarmed, his anxiety increasing next day when three attacks by 90th Light on the Australians' salient were beaten back by what Rommel had begun to call 'the terrible British artillery'.

In London and Cairo too, a number of important individuals were also becoming seriously alarmed – by Eighth Army's apparent lack of progress. On the morning of the 29th, Alexander, followed later by Tedder, arrived at Montogmery's Headquarters to enquire anxiously as to his future plans. The Army Commander, who 'radiated confidence' according to de Guingand, was able to reassure them. He did, however, under prompting from de Guingand and Williams, agree to launch SUPERCHARGE further to the south – Intelligence reports were making it clear that Rommel, having anticipated the planned break-out in the north, was massing his German troops to meet it, whereas an attack just north of Kidney Ridge would, it seemed, be met by mainly Italian resistance.[3]

Meanwhile the Australians were ordered to continue their northward assaults with the objectives both of making Rommel believe that this was still the crucial point and also of pinning down as many of his men as possible. The night of 29th/30th October was comparatively quiet, as were the daylight hours of the 30th – though in the air the Hurricanes of Nos. 33 and 238 Squadrons successfully dispersed a Stuka raid – but the next night the Australians again thrust forward. Their 26th Brigade failed to take Thompson's Post but, moving north-west of this, it crossed the coastal road and cut off the bulk of 164th Light Division. During the attack, Sergeant William Kibby of 2/48th Battalion, who had displayed constant heroism from the start of the battle, lost his life engaging a machine-gun post single-handed after the remainder of his platoon had already fallen. He was awarded a posthumous Victoria Cross.

Rommel reacted violently. He first ordered a Stuka attack on the Australians but this was broken up by the Kittyhawks of Nos. 112 and 250 Squadrons. Then, ignoring the pleas of Graf von Sponeck commanding 90th Light who urged full-scale infantry attacks on the Australian salient, he insisted on throwing 21st Panzer into the fight, thereby further whittling away his diminishing tank strength. The panzers made three attacks in all. The first was driven back by artillery fire and strikes by the Desert Air Force. The second and third were defeated by 40th Royal Tanks and the Rhodesian 289th Anti-Tank Battery of the 102nd Anti-Tank Regiment, Royal Artillery, transferred to join the Australians from 50th Division.

Still Rommel did not learn his lesson, ordering fresh attacks on the Australians on 1 November. He again planned to begin with a Stuka raid but at 0830, No. 112 Squadron's Kittyhawks fell on the dive-bombers, shooting down seven of them, while the remainder dropped their bombs on their own troops. It appears that this postponed the enemy attack which did not begin until midday, but all afternoon the Germans hurled themselves against the greatly outnumbered 24th Australian Brigade – which had replaced 26th Brigade during the night – and the Rhodesian gunners. Yet despite heavy casualties, which included the deaths of Brigadier Godfrey and the gunners' CO, Major Williamson, the defenders stood firm. In later years,[4] Montgomery, while agreeing that 'all did so well', still singled out for 'special praise', 'that magnificent 9th Australian Division'. Immediately after the battle, Horrocks went to congratulate the Divisional Commander. 'Thank you, General' replied Morshead. 'The boys were interested.'

The enemy did gain some success on the evening of 1 November, forcing 24th Brigade back south of the coastal road, thus enabling the defenders of Thompson's Post to retire safely that night. But by then events in the north had become irrelevant. At Freyberg's request, Montgomery, 'most reluctantly' according to Field Marshal Carver, had postponed SUPERCHARGE for twenty-four hours. The moon rose at 0100 on 2 November. Five minutes later, SUPERCHARGE began.

In essence this was LIGHTFOOT over again on a smaller scale. Once more the attack was accompanied by a 'creeping barrage', on this occasion laid down by the artillery from 2nd New Zealand, 51st Highland and 1st and 10th Armoured Divisions, all under the central control of Freyberg's chief gunner, Brigadier Weir. Once more the Allied airmen took their part, the Hurricanes of No. 73 Squadron ranging ahead, while sixty-eight Wellingtons, accompanied by Albacores to drop flares, bombed targets behind the enemy lines; one raid hit the Advanced Headquarters of the *Afrika Korps*, wrecking its communications and adding to von Thoma's already impressive tally of battle-scars.

Under cover of these bombardments, the infantry attacked, but this time only on a narrow front of 4,000 yards between the base of the Australian salient and the northern point of Kidney Ridge; while to the south of the Ridge a flanking movement by 2nd and 5th Royal Sussex from 133rd Brigade captured 'Woodcock'. The main assault was given to 2nd New Zealand Division supported by the Valentines of 23rd Armoured Brigade although it was not for the most part carried out by New Zealand soldiers. 6th New Zealand Brigade held the start-line in case of counter-attack, while 28th Maori Battalion from 5th New Zealand Brigade captured a strongpoint threatening the right flank of the advance, taking 162 German and 189 Italian prisoners for the loss of 33 killed and 75 wounded, including Lieutenant Colonel Baker. The principal formations used, however, were Brigadier Percy's 151st Brigade from 50th Division – also known as the Durham Brigade since it was composed of 6th, 8th and 9th Battalions, Durham Light Infantry – and Brigadier Murray's 152nd Brigade from 51st Highland Division. It should be noted that these were not independent brigade groups; on the contrary both came under command of 2nd New Zealand Division and were fully integrated with it.

These two brigades were called on to advance 4,000 yards by 0345. This would bring them to about half-a-mile eastward of the Rahman Track, beyond which rose the long, low Aqqaqir Ridge of which the highest point, Tell el Aqqaqir, lay due west of the southern boundary of the break-in. 152nd Brigade had captured all its objectives by the time scheduled, though not without casualties in the face of dogged resistance. Percy's brigade met with more difficulties but it resolutely overcame these and it too had completed its allotted task by 0415.

Once more it was planned that the armour should develop the salient gained by the infantry. First Currie's 9th Armoured Brigade, still under Freyberg's command, would advance a further 2,000 yards, crossing both the Rahman Track and the Aqqaqir Ridge by daylight on 2 November, thereby finally breaking Rommel's last line of defence which, as was mentioned earlier, was situated in this area. Then 1st Armoured Division, in which 8th Armoured Brigade had now joined 2nd Armoured Brigade, would pass through the gap thus created to fall on the rear of the enemy, and would be followed by 7th Armoured Division and perhaps 4th Light Armoured Brigade – which was ordered north on 2 November – later.

Once more the tanks were ordered to fight their own way out if the infantry should be checked and in view of the importance of Currie's attack, Montgomery expressly stated that he would accept 100 per cent casualties if 9th Armoured succeeded in its task. The lion-hearted Currie was willing to take the risk and it is noteworthy that none of the armoured commanders raised any objections to these forthright and ominous instructions.

Currie's brigade had been built up to 121 tanks of which seventy-two were Shermans or Grants and the rest Crusaders, but by this stage of the battle a number of the Shermans in both 9th Armoured Brigade and 1st Armoured Division were very much 'mechanically shaky'. This factor and problems with minefields in practice reduced Currie's tank strength at the time of his attack to ninety-four. Worse still, though the advance had been planned for 0545 on 2 November, one of Currie's regiments, the Warwickshire Yeomanry, had been so delayed by its difficulties that it did not reach the start-line on time. Currie was urged to proceed with his remaining regiments, the 3rd Hussars and the Wiltshire Yeomanry, but, understandably anxious to have his full strength available for such an important operation, he postponed the assault for half-an-hour – much to Freyberg's regret.

It was a fatal delay. Although at first all went well and some 300 prisoners were taken, daylight found 9th Armoured, in the words of Alexander's Official Despatch, 'on the muzzles of the powerful screen of anti-tank guns on the Rahman Track, instead of beyond it as had been planned'. The British tanks charged forward desperately but seventy of them were knocked out, though since the Allies held the battlefield many were later recovered; and 230 officers and men were killed or wounded. Yet their sacrifice had not been in vain. Some thirty-five of Rommel's vital anti-tank guns had also been destroyed. The men of 9th Armoured says General Jackson, 'had fractured Rommel's containing screen, though they did not break it'.

In the confusion, two squadrons of the Royal Dragoons' armoured cars had managed to slip out of the southern flank of the new salient, roaming about far behind the enemy lines causing havoc among his remaining 'soft-skinned' vehicles. Fisher's 2nd Armoured Brigade was also in action by 0800, but it could scarcely be expected to break out since the main enemy defences were still intact and the Germans were already feverishly bringing up 88s to strengthen them. Fortunately Rommel, obsessed with a belief that the major Allied effort would be made in the north, thought at first that SUPER-CHARGE must be a subsidiary movement to divert his attention. Not until dawn on 2 November did he realize the true situation and order von Thoma to counter-attack with every German and Italian tank that he could muster, and it was 1100 before von Thoma was able to oblige.

By that time Eighth Army was ready for him. For two hours, 21st Panzer from the north, 15th Panzer and Littorio supported by Trieste from the west, battered away at the salient, but as at Alam Halfa they were held off by British tanks sited in good defensive positions, backed by artillery and anti-tank guns. 2nd Armoured Brigade bore the brunt of this fighting but Custance's 8th Armoured Brigade also played its part as it came up on Fisher's left flank. 'The British armour,' records Lucas Phillips, 'fought with skill, courage and excellent leadership at all levels, brilliantly supported by "the terrible

British artillery".' Brilliantly supported also by the Desert Air Force. The light bombers made seven attacks on the enemy and two Stuka raids were so disrupted by the Hurricanes of Nos. 33 and 238 and of Nos. 213 and 1 SAAF Squadrons respectively that they dropped their bombs on their own troops.

The integration of all arms of Eighth Army was complete and the result is summarized by Lucas Phillips as 'the hammering of the panzers'. 1st Armoured Division lost only 14 tanks, though 40 more proved 'mechanically shaky', but the Germans lost 70 and the Italians 37. Littorio, in Rommel's own words, was 'practically wiped out', and 15th Panzer was in little better state. And meanwhile Montgomery had determined once more to vary the direction of his thrust so as to break out to the south of his new salient. At 1815, 152nd Brigade attacked 'Skinflint', an area of high ground about a mile to the south-west, under a heavy artillery barrage, duly taking its objective together with 100 prisoners from Trieste. The supporting 50th Royal Tanks lost four Valentines but the infantry had no casualties at all. Moreover the Italians were so shaken that they now surrendered the 'Snipe' strongpoint with sixty more prisoners before it could be attacked – a sad contrast to the previous Eighth Army defence of that famous position.

Though during the night of 2nd/3rd November, a push westward by 7th Motor Brigade was thrown back with considerable losses, Rommel had at last become convinced that he could not hold his ground for much longer. It was a realization that had dire implications for his Italian infantry formations.

A grim background to the loss of Rommel's troops on the ground had been provided by the loss of his supply-ships at sea: the tanker *Proserpina* and the ammunition-ship *Tergestea* on 26 October, the tanker *Louisiana* on the 28th, the ammunition-ship *Tripolino* on 1 November. Yet for Rommel's Italians the shortage of petrol was largely irrelevant. Their problem was not that they had no petrol but that they had no vehicles into which it could be put.

Accordingly Rommel on the morning of 3 November, ordered his non-motorized units to begin their long march back to Fuka, some 60 miles to the west. He ordered Stuka raids to cover their retreat but the first of these at dawn was broken up by the Hurricanes of Nos 33 and 238 Squadrons. At about 1230, an even bigger raid came in, heavily escorted by 109s, but when the Hurricanes of No. 80 Squadron engaged the Stukas, the 109s ignored them, preferring to attack the Hurricanes of No. 127 Squadron while these were at a disadvantage covering No. 80. They shot down no fewer than six Hurricanes but while they were so occupied, No. 80 Squadron ripped into the dive-bombers without interference – enemy records confirm that they destroyed nine of these for the loss of one of their own machines which force-landed.

On the ground Rommel directed his mobile forces, reinforced by the bulk of Ariete which he had brought up to the battle-zone on the previous evening from its futile sojourn in the south, to hold firm for as long as possible while his infantrymen made good their withdrawal. So well did they perform their task that when 153rd Brigade from 51st Highland Division tried to move forward from 'Skinflint' to the Rahman Track some two miles south of Tell el Aqqaqir at 1745, the result was a tragic failure. An air and artillery bombardment had been arranged, only to be cancelled on the pleas of Briggs who wrongly believed that 8th Armoured Brigade had already advanced into this area. As a result, the attack met heavy resistance and was halted with the loss of ninety-four infantry casualties and twenty Valentines of the supporting 8th Royal Tanks destroyed or crippled.

In the meantime at 1530, a signal had arrived from Hitler ordering Rommel 'to stand fast, yield not a yard of ground and throw every gun and every man into the battle', and to show his troops 'no other road than that to victory or death'. Cavallero forwarded a similar message from Mussolini shortly afterwards.

Rommel was dismayed by these instructions, but his later claims that they prevented his army from making an orderly retirement cannot possibly be accepted. Field Marshal Carver declares bluntly that 'it is difficult to see' that Hitler's order 'made much difference, as the attempt to put it into effect does not appear to have succeeded, even if it were seriously made . . . It appears that both in the north and in the south the *Panzerarmee* did in fact continue to withdraw.' Indeed it was scarcely relevant whether the retreat was halted or not so far as the non-motorized Italians were concerned because even had the order from Hitler not arrived, they could never have made good their escape unless the units still in the front line had been able to hold this for a good deal longer than in fact proved to be the case.

Because, ironically enough, after he had received his Führer's signal, Rommel changed the previous orders to his mobile troops to hold their present positions. Instead, as night fell on 3 November, he withdrew his *Afrika Korps* some six miles to the north-west of Tell el Aqqaqir, while Ariete, Trieste and Trento formed up on von Thoma's right and 90th Light fell back to take station on his left. He thus surrendered his line of defences which for so long had defied all efforts to break it. That night, Montgomery launched his last attacks through the southern flank of his salient. At 0645 on 4 November, 154th Brigade, supported by powerful artillery fire, captured Tell el Aqqaqir virtually without resistance. Further south, Brigadier Russell's 5th Indian Brigade from 4th Indian Division, moving out from 'Skinflint', successfully reached the Rahman Track a full four miles south of the Tell by 0900, taking 350 prisoners and numerous anti-tank guns on the way.

Through the gaps thus torn in the enemy's defences poured 1st, 7th and 10th Armoured Divisions, the last-named having regained command of 8th Armoured Brigade. The Trieste and Trento Divisions, already badly mauled, were finally shattered. At about 1300, 22nd Armoured Brigade, passing through Russell's position, fell on Ariete which fought bravely all afternoon but by nightfall had been all but wiped out, 450 prisoners being taken, while Roberts had lost just one Stuart tank and three men wounded. And by about 1300 also, Fisher's 2nd Armoured Brigade had thrown back the *Afrika Korps* and 90th Light as these attempted, valiantly but in vain, to hold Rommel's new line. Von Thoma's own command tank was knocked out and he was taken prisoner by Captain Grant Singer commanding the 10th Hussars Reconnaissance Troop. That evening he dined with Montgomery, rather touchingly inviting his conqueror to come and visit him in Germany when the war was over.

By 1730, regardless of Hitler's orders and Rommel's intentions, *Panzerarmee Afrika* was in full flight. As at Alam Halfa, there was enough petrol to enable the mobile units to escape, and in the south the Ramcke Parachute Brigade which did have transport was also able to get clear, but for the Italian divisions which did not, the Pavia, Brescia, Bologna, Folgore, there was no option but to surrender. Eight Italian generals followed von Thoma into captivity. 'Ring out the bells!' Alexander signalled to Churchill.

The battle, by an uncanny quirk of fate, had lasted for exactly the twelve days that Montgomery had prophesied. Nonetheless it must never be forgotten that it was, in the words of Lucas Phillips, 'a soldier's battle and not merely a general's exercise', which 'owed its triumph' to a number of different factors: 'to the guts and fighting spirit of Montgomery's soldiers, to his own high mastery in the technique of the most unforgiving of all professions, to the sustained support of the Allied pilots in the air, and to the repeated mistakes, which his adversary so shrewdly invited him to make, of Erwin Rommel'.

More sadly, Montgomery had also predicted the price paid for the triumph: over 13,500 casualties, which was less than 8 per cent of the forces involved, but of which about 4,000 were fatal casualties. The Indians and Allied units such as the Fighting French together suffered 4 per cent of the losses, the South Africans 6 per cent, the New Zealanders 10 per cent, the Australians 22 per cent, the British 58 per cent. The airmen lost ninety-seven machines, rather more than their Axis opponents whose losses were eighty-four. Eighth Army also lost 100 guns, but although it has been widely stated that 500 tanks were destroyed, most of these, having suffered only minor damage to tracks or suspension in the minefields, were quickly back in action. Over 300 were repaired while the battle was still in progress and total losses were only 150.

'The enemy losses,' as even the sober Official History reports, 'were tremendous, the German formations being reduced to skeletons and the Italian broken to bits.' Eighth Army took well over 30,000 prisoners, 10,700 of them German. It was officially calculated that 10,000 Axis troops had been killed and 15,000 wounded, but these may be overestimates; Field Marshal Carver considers it 'probable' that about 20,000 were killed or wounded. Rommel had also lost over 1,000 guns and 450 tanks, while the Italians abandoned seventy-five more during the retreat. Most of the Axis soldiers who did escape had lost their fighting equipment.

The victory had immense consequences throughout the world, not least in Russia, for when on 22 November, a counter-offensive trapped the German Sixth Army in Stalingrad, Hitler refused to allow it to cut its way out as it almost certainly could have done any time during the following week, because he was not prepared to countenance a further withdrawal so soon after the one in North Africa. For Britain in general, as for Eighth Army in particular, the extent of the triumph after so many partial or unfulfilled successes was exhilarating. The relief as well as the excitement felt was, as so often, summed up best by Churchill: 'We have a new experience. We have victory – a remarkable and definite victory. The bright gleam has caught the helmets of our soldiers, and warmed and cheered all our hearts.'

Notes

1 When reading criticisms of Gatehouse and Lumsden, it should be remembered that the tanks of XIII Corps, despite the inspiring presence of Horrocks, Harding and Roberts, proved equally incapable of breaking through the Axis defences.
2 Lucas Phillips gives a quite brilliant and extremely detailed description of what he calls 'The Great Stand at "Snipe"' in his *Alamein*. The present account is largely based on this.
3 Ironically this turned out not to be the case because the Italian infantry units, except for the motorized Trieste Division, were further south than was believed.
4 Specifically on 1 October 1967, in an article for the *Sunday Times Magazine*.

Chapter 8

THE RECONQUEST OF EGYPT

At Alam Halfa, Eighth Army had conquered its own doubts and fears and a powerful enemy advance. At Alamein, it had conquered formidable enemy defences. From now onwards its conquests would be of enemy or enemy-occupied territory, though they would also be punctuated by the 'bright gleams' of further victories.

This phase of Eighth Army's achievements began disappointingly with the reconquest of Axis-occupied Egypt. 'Disappointingly' because although the reconquest was duly achieved, it was not accompanied, as had been hoped, by the final destruction of *Panzerarmee Afrika*. So much virulent criticism has been hurled against Eighth Army as a result, that it seems necessary to begin a study of the pursuit from El Alamein by calling for a sense of proportion. The RAF Official History puts the matter into admirable if unintentional perspective by remarking in successive sentences that this advance 'did not quite satisfy our most ardent desires. It swept across the breadth of Africa.' The veterans of previous campaigns would have given much to have suffered such a 'disappointment' earlier.

Because the Battle of El Alamein had been so hard fought for so long, the attention of Eighth Army's leaders had become concentrated more and more on how to win it and less and less on what action to take if and when it was won – and understandably so. Briggs for instance had urged towards the end of the fighting that the ammunition which his supporting vehicles carried – and which Briggs used to such good effect on 2 November, in 'hammering' the panzers – should be replaced by extra fuel for a long pursuit. Much criticism has been aimed at Montgomery for not complying with this suggestion. Yet it should be remembered that though 8th Armoured Brigade had temporarily been added to 2nd Armoured Brigade in his 1st Armoured Division, Briggs could not break through Rommel's last line of defences on

2 or 3 November, only succeeded in passing this after Rommel had ordered a withdrawal, and then still spent much of the 4th in finally defeating the *Afrika Korps*. In the circumstances, it seems that Montgomery was at least prudent to refuse to follow the example of his predecessors who had been so obsessed with the need to pursue a beaten foe that they had neglected to beat him in the first place.

In addition, the pressures on Eighth Army had been immense. 'A successful pursuit after a great battle of attrition is seldom possible,' notes General Jackson understandingly. 'Montgomery had made all his arrangements to exploit his victory which he saw was coming 48 hours earlier, but Eighth Army found itself nearer exhaustion than it realized when the final Axis collapse came. Its staff work was not up to the moment due to the cumulative fatigue and mental stress of the last 12 days.'

How great was the exhaustion and stress can be seen from the fact that many of Eighth Army's officers were coming close to the limits of endurance. Lucas Phillips relates that Major General Wimberley, GOC of 51st Highland Division for one was 'beginning to be mentally and physically worn out', while his chief gunner, Brigadier Elliott was 'by now utterly exhausted'. On 6 November, Brigadier Fisher who had led 2nd Armoured Brigade in so many crucial encounters during the battle had to hand over his command as a result of illness. By the end of the month, de Guingand, who at the battle's close had been awarded an immediate DSO, broke down and had to be flown back to hospital in Cairo.

It was therefore desirable that the pursuit be conducted if possible with fresh troops, but this was not an easy matter to arrange after a twelve-day battle during which Montgomery had deliberately tried to keep his opponents under continuous pressure rather than allow them intervals of rest as had happened in July. Moreover Eighth Army had already carried out a major reorganization so as to provide the fresh troops needed for SUPERCHARGE. De Guingand had tried to create a reserve force, to be commanded by Major General Gairdner, specifically for a pursuit, but, inevitably perhaps, the units allocated to this were thrown into the task of winning the battle first. Major General Tuker, commanding 4th Indian Division, whose 5th Brigade had made the final advance to the Rahman Track, had urged that his two remaining brigades which had played only minor roles in the battle so far, should be used to pursue. He was far from pleased when his ideas were not followed.

Yet Tuker's brigades suffered from two disadvantages. They were infantry brigades which were short of transport vehicles and they were well back behind the minefields of the 'Devil's Gardens'. Accordingly Montgomery, as the Official History declares, 'had decided to exploit with the mobile formations that were already well forward – the X Corps and the New Zealand

Division', the latter being a motorized division which had originally been envisaged as part of X Corps. 'This,' the Official History continues, 'was the quickest thing he [Montgomery] could have done.'

Furthermore some at least of the mobile formations were fresh. 7th Armoured Division had been brought forward from Army Reserve. The New Zealand Division had taken part in SUPERCHARGE but it will be recalled that it had there employed two brigades allocated to it from outside. Freyberg was now commanding 6th New Zealand Brigade which had played only a supporting role in SUPERCHARGE, and 5th New Zealand Brigade which, apart from 28th Maori Battalion, had taken no part in the attack at all; while prior to SUPERCHARGE, both brigades had enjoyed a welcome period of rest. 9th Armoured Brigade which was still under Freyberg was certainly not fresh, but he had been reinforced by another new reserve formation, Roddick's 4th Light Armoured Brigade.

So in practice the pursuing force did contain units which were at least less exhausted than most of those in Eighth Army, and considering all that had gone before this was a feat of organization reflecting the greatest credit on Montgomery and his staff – though it is one that seems never to have been acknowledged. The units brought up from reserve had carried out their task splendidly on 4 November. 7th Armoured Division, as already seen, had annihilated an enemy armoured division without losing a man and at the cost of one Stuart tank. Unfortunately it had been the Italian Ariete, not one of the German divisions. Roddick had also done well, destroying eleven guns and taking 300 prisoners – again, however, all Italian.

It seemed that 5 November might see the final destruction of the German forces also, but this was not to be. Liddell Hart attributes this to Eighth Army's 'old faults of caution, hesitation, slow motion, and narrow manoeuvre'. To blame misleading Intelligence, poor communications, human nature and the accidents of geography appears far less dramatic – but is far more fair.

The basic cause of Eighth Army's failure to round up the remains of *Panzerarmee Afrika* lay with the 'Ultra' Intelligence – surprising as this might appear at first glance. But then it must be appreciated that while 'Ultra' was frequently valuable and occasionally invaluable, it in no way solved all Eighth Army's problems. Indeed had it done so, Eighth Army's 'golden pages' would have begun much earlier and under a different regime.

Brigadier Sir Edgar Williams certainly has no illusions as to 'Ultra's' strengths and weaknesses. He calls it 'a dazzling new experience', but he is never so dazzled as to be blind to its defects. 'Military Intelligence,' he declares, 'is not only spasmodic, it is always out of date: there is a built-in time-lag.' This was especially so in the case of 'Ultra'. The enemy signal had to be detected – and the Germans regularly changed their radio frequencies.

Then it had to be deciphered and translated. Then any problems arising from gaps in the message caused by poor conditions or by errors in deciphering or in translation had to be rectified. Finally the message had to be re-encoded, and only then could it be radioed to the appropriate British Intelligence officer in the field.

As a result, some 'Ultra' interceptions took as long as three days to reach the battlefield. Even when they arrived on the day after the Germans had originally transmitted them, as many did, this was still too late to be of value when fighting was in progress and tactical moves had to be made immediately in response to a rapidly-changing situation. Thus Ronald Lewin, in his book *Ultra Goes to War: The Secret Story*, openly admits that during Alamein 'all the key Intelligence people . . . agree that 'Ultra' had little direct effect.'

Lewin does claim, however, that 'Ultra' could have had a great effect at the conclusion of the encounter. 'The evidence about "Ultra's" deciphering of the Rommel–Hitler exchanges,' he declares, 'must puzzle still further those military critics who, ever since the Second World War, have been unable to understand why Montgomery failed to cut off and destroy Rommel's army after Alamein.' On the contrary, an examination of the signals which were revealed to Montgomery makes it very easy to understand why he failed to cut off and destroy Rommel's army: he was given singularly misleading information by 'Ultra'.[1]

As a matter of interest, Montgomery did not know the full story of 'the Rommel–Hitler exchanges'. Hitler's 'victory or death' signal for instance was, it appears, advised only to Alexander and then not until the afternoon of 4 November 1942. Even if it had reached Montgomery as well, this 'built-in time-lag', so inevitable with 'Ultra', would have robbed it of any importance. By the afternoon of 4 November 1942, Eighth Army had finally broken its foes' resistance and what Hitler had or had not ordered was quite irrelevant.

Far more relevant were two messages sent by Rommel on 2 November, and revealed to Eighth Army on the 3rd. In the more dramatic of these, Rommel declared that 'the strength of the Army is exhausted'; that the escape of his non-motorized units was highly unlikely as they lacked the necessary vehicles and 'a large part of these formations will probably fall into the hands of the enemy who is fully motorized'; that even his mobile troops were 'so closely involved in the battle that only elements will be able to disengage'; and that therefore he expected 'the gradual destruction of the Army'.

Yet during 3 November, all advances by infantry or armour alike were checked and it was clear that, despite its exhaustion, *Panzerarmee Afrika* was going to resist for as long as possible if only to give its non-motorized units a chance of making good their retirement. Montgomery therefore rightly concentrated on terminating that resistance. By the afternoon of the 4th, Eighth Army had at last gained its victory, thereby dooming the Italian divisions, but it was now that the information from 'Ultra' prevented the complete obliteration of the remnants of the German formations as well.

In the signal just quoted, Rommel made the seemingly significant comment that 'the shortage of fuel will not allow of a withdrawal to any great distance.' Then when the second signal of 2 November also reached Eighth Army on the following day, it revealed that Rommel proposed to retire fighting 'step by step' – a decision which appeared inevitable in these circumstances.

So when on 4 November, a further 'Ultra' report was received, indicating that Rommel intended 'to gain some time at the next intermediate position El Daba', before finally retiring to Fuka a further 30 miles to the west, this seemed entirely in accordance with – indeed confirmation of – the information 'Ultra' had previously given. Montgomery therefore, says Nigel Hamilton in his biography,[2] proposed to attack the remaining Axis forces at El Daba immediately, at the moment 'when the enemy was acknowledging defeat, when Axis communications were breaking down', and perhaps even more important before the Axis commanders could grip the situation so as to bring it under some sort of control.

Montgomery's plan called for Freyberg's men, including 4th Light Armoured Brigade, to move 'immediately to Fuka in order to block the enemy's withdrawal to the west', a role for which as the Official History notes approvingly, 'the motorized New Zealand Division was an obvious choice'. While Freyberg prevented further retreat, Lumsden, in Hamilton's rather dramatic words, 'was to use his three armoured divisions' – 1st, 7th and 10th – 'to smash Rommel's remaining armoured and motorized units up against the sea'. This, as Hamilton rightly points out, was 'a far cry from the "cautiousness" which critics have ascribed' to the Eighth Army Commander, and the only trouble was that the armoured divisions were directed on the wrong target, because in reality the 'Ultra' predictions were simply incorrect.

For this, Montgomery cannot fairly be faulted, but he did at this time make another decision which turned out to be very unwise and for which, as Hamilton declares, he 'must bear the blame'. During both Alam Halfa and Alamein, Montgomery had maintained a very tight control over his army, but now, believing that 'the more fluid the fighting, the greater should be the degree of decentralization', he did not personally assume 'direct command of the pursuit'. The lesson 'would not be lost on Montgomery' for the future.

Montgomery's decision appears the more strange in that he had in practice entrusted the pursuit to Lumsden, although that officer's performance during Alamein had not met with his approval. It seems, however, that he felt Lumsden would prove much more effective in a mobile encounter – and with some reason. Horrocks for example describes Lumsden as 'a cavalry officer and a well-known amateur rider before the war', who 'had all the qualities required in a first-class steeplechase jockey, physical fitness, nerve, and the capacity to make up his mind in a split second'. Such a man must have seemed ideally suited to lead the chase of the beaten Axis soldiers and it should be noted in fairness to him that Major Sir William Mather, who was on Montgomery's staff and had been detailed to act as a liaison officer with X Corps, would later tell Nigel Hamilton that Lumsden's 'main aim was to advance as quickly as possible – we had them on the run, his idea was to keep them on the run – and demolish them'.

Unhappily some of Lumsden's subordinates and even Freyberg would not prove active in carrying out his, and Montgomery's, wishes. The cause of this was in part psychological. As Field Marshal Carver notes, the exhilaration that marked the break-out from Alamein was 'tempered by the feeling that having miraculously survived the ever-present dangers of the battle among the mine-fields, it would be folly to fling away one's life too recklessly when victory was at hand'. When it is remembered that a man in a burning tank faced a particularly horrible death and that for their part the New Zealanders had not forgotten how often their comrades had been left 'naked before an armoured attack' during the days of Auchinleck's leadership, it is difficult to blame the pursuing forces too severely for being prudent.

Moreover the pursuers were hampered by the facts of geography. Much of Eighth Army was still on the wrong side of the 'Devil's Gardens' making its slow and painful way through the minefields. Those so handicapped included part of Freyberg's forces, notably 6th New Zealand Brigade, and most of the armoured divisions' supply echelons. Kippenberger remarks with commendable restraint that 'it was all most confused and difficult'; Horrocks considers that it was a 'wonder' that these forces 'ever joined up at all'; even the staid Official History describes the problems as 'appalling'. Nor were the pursuers' difficulties over once the minefields had been passed. The night of 4th/5th November was, says Horrocks, 'very dark', which made 'cross-country movement in the desert a slow and painful business, particularly for tired troops'.

These problems would wreck Eighth Army's plans. 1st and 7th Armoured Divisions were to advance directly on El Daba where it was thought the remnants of *Panzerarmee Afrika* would be making their stand, but they needed to reorganize after their encounters with the *Afrika Korps* and Ariete respectively; they were therefore halted for the night. As far as the forces intended to cut off Rommel's retreat from El Daba were concerned, however, the instructions were very different. Freyberg was ordered to set out for Fuka at 2300 on the 4th, while 10th Armoured Division which was stationed on the left flank of X Corps was directed on Galal midway between El Daba and Fuka, and was urged to move 'all night' to make sure it reached its objective in time.

Sadly neither 2nd New Zealand nor 10th Armoured was able to obey. Freyberg found it so difficult to collect his scattered forces during the hours of darkness that he repeatedly postponed his advance, ultimately to 0530 on 5 November – and then in reality only set off half-an-hour later. In 10th Armoured Division, the tanks of Custance's 8th Armoured Brigade did begin their advance at 1930 on the 4th. By then, though, it was pitch-dark and, explains Field Marshal Carver, 'so great was the confusion and difficulty caused by this, the first attempt of most of them at a night move over un-reconnoitred desert that he [Custance] halted after an hour and decided not to try again until it was light'. As a result we learn from Montgomery's *Memoirs*, 'the pursuit proper began on the 5th November'. If only it could have begun, as was intended, on the evening of the 4th.

The situation was made worse by one further disadvantage. In the past there had been numerous occasions when faulty communications had added to Eighth Army's problems. They now did so again, being in no way helped by Montgomery having unwisely left Freyberg under XXX Corps rather than under Lumsden, to whose command he was only transferred in the afternoon of the 5th. In consequence neither Montgomery nor Lumsden knew that Gatehouse and Freyberg were not moving – indeed as late as midday on the 5th, the former would mistakenly report to Alexander that the 'progress of armoured divisions' had 'continued all night' – while X Corps at this time was not even aware of the exact locations of its 1st and 7th Armoured Divisions.

It was this lack of communication that finally robbed Eighth Army of complete triumph. By 2240 on the 4th, its Intelligence staff had already learned that Rommel, shaken by the extent of his losses, did not intend to fight a delaying action at El Daba after all but to retire all the way to Fuka. By 0245 next morning, this was confirmed by the RAF Wellingtons and Fleet Air Arm Albacores attacking the coast road, which, they reported, was jammed with vehicles all the way from El Daba to Fuka. Attempts were there-fore made to redirect the main attack towards Fuka, but the news that he would face the bulk of the enemy forces there made Freyberg the more deter-mined to wait until his strength had been concentrated before he set out. As for the divisions of X Corps, it seems that Lumsden was never able to contact 1st or 7th Armoured to change their original orders, while, although at 0535 he signalled to Gatehouse that 8th Armoured Brigade should 'take a wider sweep' so as to reach Fuka, the message was apparently misunderstood, for Gatehouse continued to make Galal his objective and only after he had reached it did he intend to turn towards Fuka.

As a result, both 1st and 7th Armoured Divisions missed their prey altogether. The former began its advance at 0730 on the 5th, but saw no action until 0900, by which time it was some three miles south-east of El Daba. Even then the opposition was provided only by a lone 88mm, one shell tragically killing Captain Grant Singer who only the day before had accepted the surrender of von Thoma. The division pressed forward, cutting the coast road west of El Daba which was then taken by 7th Motor Brigade with the miserable haul of 150 prisoners. 7th Armoured Division, advancing on 1st Armoured's left, did not even reach the coast road, Harding halting some five miles south of it when he realized that the main body of the enemy had already escaped.

The other Allied forces at least had more substantial rewards for their trouble. Freyberg's men moved off at 0600, and 4th Light Armoured Brigade began the day well by attacking an enemy column, destroying six German tanks and taking a number of prisoners. By noon, however, Freyberg's advance had been halted by a minefield, covered by artillery fire, and it took three hours before his first troops could pass through it. Maddeningly enough, it was later discovered that the minefield was a dummy one, and as if that was not sufficiently exasperating, a dummy one laid by Eighth Army – apparently by the South Africans – during the retreat to Alamein in June.

Gatehouse's 10th Armoured Division also began its advance at 0600, reaching Galal without opposition. The German troops had already escaped the trap, but at midday, 8th Armoured Brigade encountered the remains of the Italian armour. Liddell Hart underrates the British effort by stating that the destruction of the enemy tanks was achieved only because they 'had run out of fuel'. Field Marshal Carver by contrast makes it clear that the Italians did not run out of anything – they 'ran headlong into the devastating fire of the whole brigade'. By about 1230, Custance's men, backed by the 133rd Motorized Infantry Brigade, had destroyed twenty-eight Italian tanks, four German Mark IIIs, one Mark II and 100 lorries, and had taken 1,000 prisoners. The remaining enemy vehicles, including another eleven tanks, tried to break away to the south but were abandoned later. This was, as Carver relates, 'a most satisfactory haul' and a useful consolation prize for the failure to catch the Germans.

Unhappily it took some time for 10th Armoured Division to reorganize. Still more unhappily Gatehouse then ordered 133rd Brigade eastward to mop up stragglers, and though 8th Armoured Brigade did eventually move towards Fuka, it halted for the night at 2000, still well short of its objective.

Gatehouse, in fact, really does seem to have deserved the accusation of being over-hesitant. Nigel Hamilton quotes General Sir Sidney Kirkman, who had become Eighth Army's Commander, Royal Artillery in place of the hapless Martin, as declaring that: 'There was no *desire* to go on among Gatehouse and his staff.' Yet Kirkman does add understandingly that 10th Armoured Division had 'had a bad time' at Alamein and no doubt its attitude resulted from its experiences during that battle.

Furthermore the 'bad time' had taken more than one form. It will be remembered that the supporting vehicles of 8th Armoured Brigade had suffered heavy losses from air attack on the night of 24th/25th October. The sight of the charred bodies of the drivers and their mates still upright in their cabs had left an indelible impression. Perhaps therefore Gatehouse cannot be blamed too harshly for insisting on 'full fighter cover' for his advance. Equally there can be no doubt that Montgomery was more far-sighted when he over-ruled this decision, stating: 'RAF fighter cover can be dispensed with and all fighters used against the enemy.' By that time, though, it was already early afternoon.

The Desert Air Force has also been the subject of criticism over its failure to check or at least inflict more damage on the retreating Axis forces. It is true that the Allied airmen who had caused such destruction among the enemy 'soft-skinned' vehicles in the cramped conditions of Alam Halfa and Alamein proved much less successful when attacking fleeing transports on an open road. It should be remembered, however, that they, like the soldiers, were by now exhausted after twelve days of intensive action; they were to be seen to much greater advantage in the near future when they had had a chance to recover. The need to provide fighter protection for Gatehouse also restricted their activities. Yet even as it was, the Bostons, Baltimores and Hurribombers delivered a number of successful attacks, particularly in the afternoon when they could be accompanied by an escort, and Rommel, whose Headquarters was twice hit, refers to the Allied air attacks – admittedly with some exaggeration – as 'uninterrupted and very heavy'.

In any event by the time Montgomery overruled Gatehouse's request, it had already become clear that Rommel's remaining German troops were not going to be trapped east of Fuka and the position of their pursuers made it more difficult for them to be trapped west of Fuka either. Many of Montgomery's tank commanders have since stated that he should not have concentrated all his armoured divisions on his attempt to crush his enemy, but should have sent one of them to provide a final blocking-force at Mersa Matruh or Sollum. Ironically Montgomery might well have done this if only he had not been so eager to complete the destruction of his foes – in other words if only he had really been as cautious a commander as his more vocal critics claim.[3]

Yet when the actual performance of the armoured divisions is taken into account, it may be permissible to doubt whether such an action would really have been successful in any case. It is interesting to learn that Field Marshal Carver considers that whatever had been done it is most unlikely that Rommel would have been caught unless he had stopped to fight it out, which he had no intention of doing: 'The man who wants to get away in the desert, and has the vehicles to do so, can usually evade his pursuer, certainly if he is as determined and swift in action and decision as Rommel was.'

In theory the decisions now taken by Montgomery and contained in orders issued by Lumsden at 1340 on 5 November, seemed well suited to corner Rommel west of Fuka. Gatehouse was to put pressure on Fuka from the east, while Freyberg, who was now to come under Lumsden's command, did the same from the south; but Freyberg was to relinquish control of 4th Light Armoured Brigade so that Roddick could speed on to 'Charing Cross', a road junction just south-west of Mersa Matruh where the coast road climbed an escarpment. Briggs was to take his 1st Armoured Division on a wide movement through the desert to Bir Khalda some 40 miles south-east of 'Charing Cross' and about 70 miles from El Daba, travelling all night if necessary so as to be ready to join in the advance on 'Charing Cross' at dawn on 6 November. And finally Harding's 7th Armoured Division would carry out a narrower sweep to capture the landing-grounds near Sidi Haneish about midway between Fuka and Matruh; then head northward for the coast road, again with the aim of 'smashing' Rommel's forces 'up against the sea'.

Yet as so often, practice proved much less satisfactory than theory. Poor communications caused a misunderstanding between Lumsden and Freyberg, which resulted in the latter retaining Roddick under his command and refraining from attacking Fuka in the belief that he was to move on to Sidi Haneish next day – information which Lumsden had intended to be only a statement of possible future policy. Gatehouse, as mentioned earlier, made no progress towards Fuka either and as a result Rommel was not pinned down in his positions there. By 1545, he had already decided to retreat to Matruh. His retirement could not be put into effect until 2300, and was harassed through the night by Wellingtons, Halifaxes and No. 73 Squadron's night-fighter Hurricanes, but he had long disappeared when Gatehouse finally entered Fuka at midday on the 6th, though 10th Armoured Division did add another 300 Italian prisoners to Eighth Army's ever-growing list.

Moreover geography had again given Rommel one great advantage. 'The unbroken coast road,' reports General Jackson, 'lay behind him, along which his mobile troops could make better progress, covered by rearguards, than the British pursuers who had to hook southwards into the desert to outflank his successive delaying positions.' 'Rommel's forces had a main road down which to withdraw,' agrees General Fraser, 'and it would have needed great energy and more than a little luck to move across desert with enough speed to forestall.'

And in practice, Eighth Army was far from lucky. 7th Armoured Division duly set out on its outflanking mission, though its 131st Motorized Infantry Brigade was now trailing some way behind 22nd Armoured Brigade. At about 1500 on 5 November, Roberts encountered the dummy minefield that had so hampered Freyberg and it was about 1800 before his tanks could make their way through it. An hour later, 22nd Armoured was forced to halt entirely. Its tanks were now desperately short of petrol and its supply echelons were still far to the east.

Meanwhile 1st Armoured Division's move had also been delayed by the need to refuel. It did not start off until 1800 on the 5th, but it then pressed on through the night. Unfortunately the difficulties of having to move through the desert instead of down a main road soon became all too apparent. The darkness was described as 'intense', the 'going' was very bad, 7th Motor Brigade fell well behind 2nd Armoured Brigade's tanks and the supporting supply units in particular got hopelessly bogged down in soft sand. As a crowning misfortune, the Shermans revealed another defect which had been concealed by the static nature of the fighting at Alamein: in these difficult conditions they consumed what the Official History calls 'fantastic quantities of fuel'. In consequence at about 0900 on 6 November, 2nd Armoured came to a halt still some 15 miles east of Bir Khalda, and the only Eighth Army units to reach 'Charing Cross' were the valiant South African armoured cars, which were able to secure large numbers of prisoners but could scarcely be expected to block the retreat of Rommel's armoured and motorized divisions on their own.

If 4 November 1942 was, in the words of General Fraser, 'the best moment experienced by the British Army since another November day long ago in 1918', it might be thought from some of the judgements that have been passed, that 5 November 1942 was the British Army's worst day since that time. Certainly it was then that the best chance of rounding up the beaten remnants of Rommel's armoured forces slipped away. Yet this disappointment must not be allowed to mask the fact that on 5 November, the men of Eighth Army inflicted very heavy casualties on their foes, including the final destruction of the Italian armour. They also caused losses to the Axis air forces, for during the day they occupied Landing Grounds 105 and 106, capturing nine brand new Messerschmitt Bf 109s together with some fifty other machines of various types which were damaged but could have been repaired had the enemy only been given a little more time to do so. Moreover their own losses had been minimal. Their predecessors under an earlier regime would have been delighted to have enjoyed a few days as good as 5 November.

Even Rommel's escape on this day was brought about only by a headlong retreat which Eighth Army forced him to execute prematurely and which therefore completed their triumph of the day before. In Rommel's own words, he had hoped to hold Fuka 'long enough for the Italian and German infantry to catch up'. When Eighth Army's pressure forced him out of Fuka late on 5 November, his unmotorized units had no chance of doing anything other than surrender to XIII Corps. It is almost amusing to read the British accounts of Eighth Army's slowness and caution, and then to find Paul Carell for instance, lamenting that:

Montgomery was pressing on with unusual speed, chasing Rommel's troops towards Fuka. His men were marching on a parallel course to the Germans, giving them no time to reorganize or dig in for a defence – not even in Fuka. The British High Command seemed to be fully aware of the disastrous position in which Rommel found himself . . . In any case the boldness of the British pursuit was conspicuous.

It was less conspicuous over the next couple of days, but again there were good reasons for this. 1st Armoured Division spent the morning of 6 November paralysed by lack of fuel. 7th Armoured Division was able to move on but also ran out of petrol again at about midday. It was hastily resupplied and at about 1500 encountered 21st Panzer Division, also immobilized for lack of fuel just south-west of Sidi Haneish. Roberts promptly engaged the enemy, destroying sixteen tanks and a number of guns.

'At the same time as our gunners started firing,' reports Roberts, 'so also did the skies – it started to rain and steadily got heavier and heavier.' All day and all night the rain poured down. 1st and 7th Armoured Divisions were completely immobilized, as were Freyberg and Roddick who were now moving westward over the desert. The ground, says Roberts, 'was like a quagmire'. 'The bottom fell out of the desert,' records Kippenberger; his staff car, he tells us, 'sank down to the axles'. For the rest of 6 November and the whole of the 7th, there was no possibility of an outflanking move cutting off Rommel.

It might have been thought that Eighth Army would have received some sympathy for this outrageous piece of ill-fortune – but not a bit of it. The rain has usually been dismissed as irrelevant, either on the grounds that the best opportunity of trapping Rommel had been missed on the 5th, which does not alter the fact that until the rain came there was still a good chance of trapping him on the 6th; or because it is said that with the advantage of the road behind him, Rommel could always have got back to 'Charing Cross' before the outflanking forces, which may well be true but ignores the fact that to do so he would have been compelled to retire at a considerably greater speed. Liddell Hart even remarks sourly that 'if the pursuit had driven deeper through the desert', to Sollum on the frontier for example, it would have been unlikely to have been affected by the weather, 'for while rain is a likely risk in the coastal belt it is rare in the desert interior'. Apart, however, from Eighth Army having had no reason to anticipate a downpour – 'local showers' only had been forecast – the deeper the pursuers struck into the desert, the more time they would have taken and the more difficulties they would have experienced with the Shermans' consumption of 'fantastic quantities of fuel' and – particularly in the case of 7th Armoured's old tanks – with mechanical problems.

In fact, at the very least, in the words of the Official History: 'Rain was not to blame for everything, but it did wash away an opportunity which had not been firmly grasped.' Certainly it was Rommel's own belief that the 'torrential rain' was highly advantageous to him; he even hoped he might now 'hold on to Mersa Matruh for a few more days and thus gain time for some defences to be constructed' in the frontier area.

With the troops in the desert trapped in rain and mud, Eighth Army's only hope lay with 10th Armoured Division which, like the Germans, had the advantage of moving along the coast road. Unfortunately Gatehouse again failed to rise to the occasion. It was not until midday on 7 November, that he came up to the enemy positions at Matruh. His 133rd Motorized Infantry Brigade was then still well to the rear and his 8th Armoured Brigade was held off by anti-tank guns.

Gatehouse's lack of thrust had an unfortunate consequence. A premature report of the capture of Matruh had reached Eighth Army's Headquarters, and Lieutenant Colonel Mainwaring, the head of the Operations staff, therefore set off to find a new site for the HQ in the Matruh area. At a place called Smugglers Cove, just to the east of the little town, Mainwaring ran into enemy troops and he and his entire party, which included Major Richard Carver, Montgomery's stepson – but no relation to the future Field Marshal Lord Carver – were captured.[4]

Only when Montgomery personally arrived at the front in the late afternoon, appearing, it is reported, 'anxious to get to Matruh' – 'presumably' as Field Marshal Carver remarks, 'a masterly understatement of his state of mind' – was any further action taken. Then Lieutenant Colonel Smith-Dorrien delivered an infantry attack with his 1st Battalion, The Buffs, which was then part of 8th Armoured Brigade. This assault also was beaten back.

General Kirkman, who was on the spot as well, would later be very indignant over Gatehouse's apparent 'lack of desire to do anything', telling Nigel Hamilton that this was 'a case where whatever Monty wanted, his battle was being ruined by Gatehouse . . . It shows how, however good an Army commander's plan is, he can be let down.' In retrospect, though, perhaps it would be fairer to attribute the failure not just to the fault of Gatehouse but also to the courage and determination of the Axis rearguard, the battered but undaunted 90th Light Division.

At about 2100 on the evening of 7 November, Rommel began to withdraw once more, leaving Matruh for Sidi Barrani. At 0830 on the 8th, 1st Armoured Division, having at last been able to resume its advance, assaulted Matruh from the west but found it empty. Montgomery made one final attempt to trap his fleeing foes by sending 7th Armoured Division on a long outflanking move towards the frontier, but this can never really have had much chance of success. Harding was plagued by mechanical breakdowns and shortages of petrol, and on 10 November, as a final touch, more heavy rain fell, bogging down his supply echelons. In practice, after 7 November, Rommel had made good his escape. Not that this brought him any comfort, for next day he received the news of the TORCH landings, a blow which completed the collapse of his confidence.

Also after 7 November, Montgomery took a direct and very tight control of his army, thereby impliedly admitting his error in not having taken personal control of the pursuit. Apart from Harding's unsuccessful mission, he made no further effort to outflank the retreating enemy, but instead maintained an undramatic but relentless advance along the coast. Rommel had at first intended to fight a delaying action at Sidi Barrani, but by the evening of 9 November, his rearguard – the valiant 90th Light once more – had been forced to withdraw a day earlier than Rommel had wished in the face of pressure from 4th Light Armoured Brigade. Mussolini had sent Cavallero to visit Rommel with orders that the frontier area must be held 'as long as possible', but during the night of 10th/11th November, a brilliant attack by Kippenberger's 5th New Zealand Brigade captured Halfaya Pass. 90th Light made another fighting withdrawal, but Kippenberger's men took 600 Italian prisoners.

By the early hours of the 11th then, all Egypt had been reconquered by Eighth Army. On the same day, its leader became a full General and a Knight Commander of the Bath – in recognition, if we may borrow a phrase, of his own ability and achievements and those of all under his command.

Notes

1   These signals are related in *British Intelligence in the Second World War: Its Influence on Strategy and Operations* (Volume II) by Professor F.H. Hinsley and others.

2   Volume II: *Monty, Master of the Battlefield 1942–1944*.

3   Chief of the critics among Montgomery's then subordinates would be Gatehouse. It is a pity to have to record this remembering Gatehouse's own lack of drive in the post-Alamein period, of which examples have been and will continue to be given. It must of course be recalled that he had been understandably embittered by the unjust strictures which Montgomery had made during Alamein – and repeated in his *Memoirs* – to the effect that Gatehouse had 'led his division from behind'. No doubt resentment clouded Gatehouse's judgement.

4   Mainwaring was released from a prisoner-of-war camp in Italy on the surrender of that country in 1943. He eventually found his way to Eighth Army Headquarters, where his arrival, disguised as an Italian peasant, inspired a memorable reunion party. Carver too was able to get back to the Eighth Army lines not long afterwards.

Chapter 9

THE CONQUEST OF LIBYA

Eighth Army's next task was the invasion of Cyrenaica, and in preparing for this its leaders had to bear in mind three main factors. First was the need to capture the airfields in the Cyrenaican 'Bulge', in particular those at Martuba, in time to provide fighter protection for the convoy needed to save Malta. Since this would end Rommel's last chance of ever taking Egypt, all else had to be subordinated to it.

Next came the need to ensure that Eighth Army was not halted at El Agheila but was able to press on towards Tripoli. If the enemy could maintain a hold on French North Africa, as turned out to be the case, and prevent or at least delay an Eighth Army advance into Tripolitania; or better still could hit back once more from El Agheila so that Cyrenaica remained a battleground, then it would become impossible for the Allies to attack southern Europe and knock Italy out of the war during 1943. From the Axis point of view it was obvious that everything feasible should be done to postpone the continuing progress of Eighth Army, since this could have a decisive effect on the outcome of the war.

This factor was very much in the mind of both sides. When von Thoma had dined with Montgomery, he was, reports de Guingand, 'very careful not to give away any future plans', but he made it clear that he 'hoped Rommel would be able to stage a comeback from Agheila'. For his part, Montgomery was well aware how Rommel's counter-offensive after CRUSADER had robbed that victory of its fruits. References to the 'Djebel Stakes' were still being made on all sides with mingled cynicism and dread, and Montgomery was quite determined that past history would not be repeated.

And lastly there was the permanent problem of supplies. As Kesselring notes with some satisfaction, 'even a victorious army cannot keep up a pursuit of thousands of miles in one rush; the stronger the army the greater the difficulty of supply. Previous British pursuits had broken down for the same reason.' Moreover the 'piece of elastic' was under still greater pressure than usual. Montgomery had learned from the errors not only of his predecessors but of his opponent. Whereas Rommel in his dash for the Nile had left his airmen straggling far behind, the Eighth Army Commander, who always believed in the vital necessity for co-operation with the Air Arm and indeed looked on it, sometimes to the airmen's annoyance, as virtually another branch of his command like his engineers or his artillery, was insistent that the Desert Air Force should advance with him. That meant that at the start of the new campaign some 11,500 RAF and AA personnel had to be brought forward, together with the supplies needed for them and for their aircraft, particularly aviation fuel.

So important did Montgomery consider this that he gave 'his' Air Force special priority. It was a wise choice, for the Axis Air Forces, now falling back on their own bases, were able to intervene once more. Fortunately their Allied opponents were ready for them. On 11 November, first day of the Cyrenaican campaign, the Kittyhawks of No. 2 Squadron SAAF attacked fifteen Stukas, and for the loss of two of their own machines, claimed eight destroyed and four 'probables', all of which it appears also went down.

As a result of the supply problems, however, Eighth Army, contrary to popular report, was not able to advance with overwhelming numbers. The New Zealanders were forced to halt in the frontier area. Only 7th Armoured Division, which had now reclaimed 4th Light Armoured Brigade, was able to continue Eighth Army's progress, and it was suffering from a number of shortages, not least of water.

Nonetheless Eighth Army never lost is momentum. Bardia fell to 1st Battalion, The Rifle Brigade, which formed part of 22nd Armoured Brigade on the afternoon of 12 November. On the following night, the Axis rearguard – 90th Light yet again – fell back from Tobruk, the capture of which had once provided *Panzerarmee Afrika* with its greatest moment but which Rommel was now hastily stating 'possessed only symbolic value'. 4th Light Armoured Brigade occupied the fortress without fighting next morning.

With Tobruk secured, Tedder sent a signal urging that Eighth Army dispatch a force across the Cyrenaican 'Bulge' to trap the Axis troops in the same way the Italians had once been. Montgomery did send light units, notably armoured cars, to Msus, which fell on 17 November, but he was not prepared to move any stronger forces across the open desert. Nigel Hamilton feels in retrospect that he should have been, arguing that: 'Monty missed what was to be a unique – because entirely unexpected – opportunity to . . . cut off the retreat of the Panzer Army rearguard at Benghazi. This missed opportunity was the first evidence of excessive caution by the Eighth Army Commander after Alamein.'

By contrast de Guingand, normally so good natured, waxes positively indignant over Tedder 'sitting back in Cairo and not in possession of all the facts'. These were, he relates, that 'administration was becoming very stretched' and Montgomery 'could not afford to embark on ventures of this sort which might overstrain his resources'; that 'the weather was uncertain' and 'rain might well have strangled such a move'; and that only 'very meagre air support' could have been provided. In this connection it may be noted that rain did indeed prove a problem, and the enemy air forces a greater problem, giving Eighth Army's advanced forces 'a rather unpleasant time' until 26 November, when the Desert Air Force could establish its fighters in Msus. Bearing these points in mind, de Guingand believes that it is 'very open to doubt' whether an outflanking force could have 'achieved its object'; on the contrary, such a move, he feels, would merely have given Rommel 'a chance to launch a counter-stroke'.

An additional factor was that Montgomery could not believe that Rommel would linger in the 'Bulge' long enough to provide any chance of his being cut off. The Eighth Army Commander had every reason for this opinion, for after CRUSADER Rommel had paused only at Gazala before retreating in one movement all the way back to El Agheila; and the Axis defeat in CRUSADER did not approach that at El Alamein. Montgomery's strongest motive though, is, curiously enough, not mentioned by de Guingand. He wished to concentrate his strength for an advance along the coast road mainly because he was not prepared to take even the slightest risk that Rommel might, in Nigel Hamilton's words, 'dispute possession of the Martuba airfields'. Their capture was essential and the margin for error was desperately small.

On the other hand Montgomery, so de Guingand tells us, did feel that 'a long-range harassing' of Rommel's supply line *was* very desirable – but that this was 'a job for the RAF'. 'Coningham,' continues de Guingand, 'rose to the occasion,' and the result was a brilliant little operation to which was given the singularly unwarlike code name of CHOCOLATE.

This was carried out by thirty-six Hurricanes from Nos. 213 and 238 Squadrons which together formed No. 243 Wing under Wing Commander John Darwen. On 13 November, they flew to Landing Ground 125 deep in the Cyrenaican desert about 140 miles behind the enemy lines. Thereafter until the 16th, when, with their secret base located, the Hurricanes returned to the airfield at Fuka, they operated almost continuously against the Axis supply lines, totally destroying some 130 vehicles together with the wretched troops manning them, crippling another 170 or so, and also accounting for fifteen enemy aircraft on the ground and two more in the air. Two Hurricanes from No. 213 Squadron were lost to AA fire.

Even before Operation CHOCOLATE had ended, Eighth Army had

gained the greatest strategic prize of its victory at Alamein. After a minor clash in a defile called Ain el Gazala, 4th Light Armoured Brigade captured the Martuba airfields on 15 November. Rain prevented these from coming fully into use until the 19th, but that was just soon enough for the needs of the Allies.

For on the 17th, a convoy, code-named 'Stoneage', left Alexandria for Malta. On the 19th, it entered 'Bomb Alley', but the inevitable enemy air attacks, as Captain S.W. Roskill reports in the Official History of The War at Sea,[1] were 'broken up by the excellent fighter cover sent from the desert airfields'. In the early hours of the 20th, the convoy's four merchantmen, the British *Denbighshire*, the Dutch *Bantam* and the American *Mormacmoon* and *Robin Locksley*, reached Grand Harbour safely. 'The offensive consequences of the relief of Malta,' adds Roskill, 'were immediately reaped.' The island, its striking forces now joined by surface warships, continued, in the understandably less enthusiastic words of Kesselring, to 'cast its shadow over everything'. When Brooke heard that the convoy had arrived, he noted in his Diary simply: 'Thank God!'

Now that Martuba was secured, Montgomery was prepared to give more attention to the prospect of cutting off Rommel's rearguard, particularly after an 'Ultra' interception on 16 November had indicated that Rommel was after all delaying his departure from Benghazi until the 19th. Montgomery therefore ordered that while 4th Light Armoured Brigade – which had captured Derna on the 15th – continued the advance along the coast road, 22nd Armoured Brigade should move across the desert in the wake of the original armoured-car columns; and to replace its now worn-out tanks, Shermans from 1st Armoured Division should be hurried forward on transporters from Sollum. These arrived late in the evening of 17 November, but it was not until mid-morning on the 19th that the re-equipped 22nd Armoured could set out.

By that time it was already too late for the brigade's mission to succeed, and it would probably not have succeeded in any event for the original outflanking columns were hampered by particularly heavy rainfall during 17 and 18 November, though they captured Antelat on the 19th. The rain also effectively ruined an attempt to airlift supplies up to the front line. On the other hand, the Desert Air Force's fighters enjoyed great success against German transport aircraft, Junkers Ju 52s or converted Heinkel He 111s, attempting to assist in the evacuation of Benghazi. During 17 and 18 November, even allowing for exaggerated or duplicated claims, they appear to have destroyed at least fourteen such on the ground and the same number in the air. On the 19th, 90th Light finally moved out of Benghazi; it was occupied by 4th Light Armoured Brigade next day.

Rommel was now definitely committed to reaching El Agheila without further delay. 90th Light fought another skilful delaying action against 22nd

Armoured Brigade at Agedabia during 22 November, before slipping away after dark, and by the following night Rommel's men were once more safely back in 'the strongest position in Libya'.

It had been the longest, most rapid retreat in German military history and it is rather surprising therefore to find that all criticism has been directed not at the defeated but at the victors. Eighth Army at this time has been described as ponderous, lumbering, sluggish, weary, and resembling a 'pachyderm' – by which presumably is meant an elephant.[2] And its remarkable advance has been dismissed as 'a dull and measured affair', 'not one of those mad, head-long, exciting chases' – though remembering all those madly exciting times when the Allies had rushed headlong into the muzzles of anti-tank guns, this may not have been too disadvantageous.

When assessing the Eighth Army's advance, however, it is instructive to compare this with an earlier one which Eighth Army had made in the previous winter. At the start of CRUSADER, Eighth Army had been positioned on the Egyptian frontier, but by the time that Rommel admitted defeat, the front line had moved forward to run roughly south from Tobruk. It took Eighth Army thirty days from 7 December 1941 to 6 January 1942 to reach El Agheila from Tobruk, a distance of some 470 miles by the coast road. It took Eighth Army

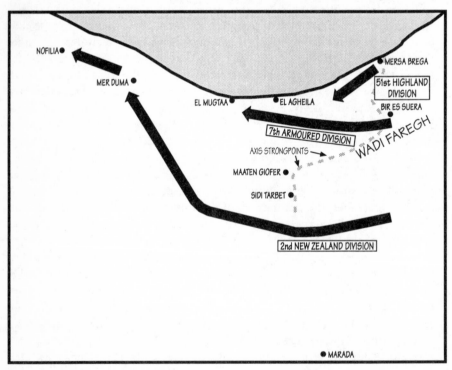

Map 6: The Battle of El Agheila.

nineteen days from 5 to 23 November 1942 to reach El Agheila from El Alamein, a distance of some 840 miles by the coast road. But the critics never describe the advance after CRUSADER as ponderous, lumbering, sluggish, weary, dull, measured, or resembling a 'pachyderm'; they reserve such comments for an advance of nearly twice the distance made in under two-thirds of the time. To say the least, their views would appear to be somewhat inconsistent.

Moreover the advance after Alamein had one further profound difference from that after CRUSADER: it did not end at El Agheila – though the Axis leaders were determined that it should. On 22 November, Hitler had given orders that the position should be held to the last. Two days later, despite Rommel's protests, Kesselring, always an invincible optimist, and Cavallero who had no choice in the matter as he was following the instructions of Mussolini, similarly commanded that El Agheila must be defended. Two days after that, Mussolini requested Rommel to counter-attack Eighth Army. On the 28th, Rommel flew to Germany to appeal against his Führer's decision, but Hitler summarily overruled him.

'Nobody but a Führer or a Duce,' declares Ronald Lewin in his book about the *Afrika Korps*, 'would have dreamed that a stand could be made against a determined and properly planned assault'; but in fact Rommel's situation was far from hopeless. The El Agheila position, says the Official History, was 'very strong naturally because it was almost surrounded by salt marshes, soft sand or ground too broken and rough to give tracked or wheeled vehicles freedom to manoeuvre'. Parallel to the coast the Wadi Faregh, a deep, narrow gorge, protected Rommel's flank, further restricting the movements of an attacker. And reinforcing the natural obstacles was a chain of strongpoints which began at Mersa Brega, a small port lying some 40 miles east of Agheila, and then curved south-westward to Maaten Giofer 25 miles south of Agheila; from which it continued due southwards for 10 miles to Sidi Tarbet. There was an outpost at Marada a further 45 miles to the south; and as a final defence, at El Mugtaa about 17 miles west of Agheila an anti-tank ditch blocked the narrow gap between the sea and the salt marshes.

In addition, all round El Agheila, at El Mugtaa, and between the various defensive posts, lay the minefields, anti-tank and anti-personnel, among which once again were booby traps of every kind. In *El Alamein to the River Sangro*, Montgomery reports that 'the enemy was known to be working hard on the defences, and he used immense quantities of mines', while Nigel Hamilton quotes Major General Wimberley as confirming that 'never again, while I commanded the Highland Division, did we ever meet such a heavily mined area.'

Behind these defences, moreover, the Axis army was beginning to build up its strength again. The Germans had received reinforcements. The Ariete Armoured Division had been reformed and a new Italian Armoured Division, the Centauro, had arrived, as had two fresh Italian infantry divisions, the La Spezia and the Young Fascist. In consequence, Rommel was now commanding sixty to seventy thousand troops, he was well supplied with anti-tank guns and he had fifty-seven gun-armed tanks. In addition, the fact that they were once more behind strong, fixed defences had done much to restore the morale of both Germans and Italians. The Long Range Desert Group, whose men were keeping their enemies under observation, reported that they were 'well disciplined and cheerful', and could not possibly be described any longer as a 'shattered remnant'.[3]

It can of course be argued that Rommel was as usual short of petrol as a result of the efforts of the Malta striking forces, and his Italian infantrymen were almost without vehicles. Yet, as at Alamein, they could have put up a resolute defence from behind their fixed positions, the more so since, as will be seen, Eighth Army at the end of a long supply line did not have anything like the attacking force available that it had had at Alamein. It can also be argued that El Agheila, unlike Alamein, could be outflanked. So indeed it could, but any force attempting such a move would have to make a very wide sweep of over 200 miles through country which turned out in practice to be even more difficult than had been reported and which, despite a fine 'recce' mission by an armoured car patrol under Captain Chrystal of 1st Kings Dragoon Guards, was largely unknown. 'Administrative considerations,' reports de Guingand, 'limited the size of the force' that could be sent on such an outflanking mission and it could also expect to be spotted from the air, as proved to be the case, enabling the enemy to have tanks and anti-tank guns all ready to meet it as it closed in towards the coast.

In short, the defenders could have put up a powerful resistance at El Agheila had it not been for the fact that their leader had lost his will to resist. He felt, says Paul Carell, 'that his defeat at El Alamein was more than a lost battle. He knew that he had lost the North African campaign.' 'He wanted,' declares Kesselring, 'to get back to Tunis; if possible still further away, to Italy and the Alps – wishful thinking that clouded his strategical judgement.' Kesselring indeed considers it was 'certainly a mistake' to 'leave Rommel in his command'.

So low was Rommel's morale that he deliberately played on the fears of Mussolini and Cavallero that the unmotorized Italian divisions would once more be the chief sufferers in the event of defeat. As a result he was able by 6 December to persuade them to let him transport his Italian infantrymen to Buerat some 250 miles further west, though this was not nearly such a good defensive position as El Agheila, being less strong naturally, less well defended artificially, and considerably easier to outflank. Since this action deprived Rommel of the soldiers needed to man his outposts and used up the bulk of that petrol which he rightly claimed to be in short supply, the Axis commander had in practice surrendered the El Agheila position before his enemy could attack it.

Indeed in view of Rommel's state of mind it can well be argued that Montgomery should have delivered his attack on El Agheila as soon as this was possible, instead of pausing to build up his forces in preparation for a planned encounter in mid-December. Yet at the time there seemed to Montgomery to be a number of good reasons why he should make very thorough preparations for his forthcoming offensive.

In part this belief arose from considerations of morale. Williams would tell Nigel Hamilton that there was in Eighth Army 'a tremendous Agheila complex . . . Agheila had become a sort of bogey – because you got as far as Agheila and then back again'. 'The desert veterans,' relates Horrocks, 'reminded us gloomily that twice before we had reached this position, but never got any farther.' Moreover Montgomery was again receiving misleading Intelligence, for the 'Ultra' interceptions revealed that Rommel had been ordered to hold the El Agheila defences but not that he had no intention of doing so. It was not until the evacuation of the Italians on 6 December that Montgomery realized that his foes might withdraw and hurried forward his plans accordingly.

Furthermore Montgomery, at the end of an ever-lengthening supply line, needed a pause in any case so as to reorganize his army, or as de Guingand puts it, 'to get our administration in proper order'. X Corps was pulled back into reserve in the area between Benghazi and Tobruk, thereby ensuring that there could be no successful Axis counter-offensive into Cyrenaica, whatever happened. Leese's XXX Corps, to which 7th Armoured Division had now been transferred, moved forward to undertake the assault, while XIII Corps temporarily ceased to be. 44th (British) Division, which had suffered so severely in the past months, was also disbanded and 9th Australian and 1st South African Divisions returned to their own countries. Tragically, Major General Pienaar, whose determination to hold El Alamein with his division concentrated in fixed defences instead of split up into 'mobile artillery battle groups' had done so much to help preserve Eighth Army, was killed in an aircraft accident on the way home.

At this time also, another Eighth Army veteran left the scene. Horrocks took over the leadership of X Corps, while Lumsden returned to England, supposedly remarking on his arrival that the desert was not big enough to hold two such difficult characters – the quotation is not an exact one – as Montgomery and himself. Though both were undoubtedly strong-minded and self-confident, this comment was fair to neither man. It is difficult not to sympathize with Lumsden but equally difficult not to understand the reasons for Montgomery's actions. In his *Memoirs*, he records that Lumsden had handled the preliminary operations in Cyrenaica 'satisfactorily' and that he considered Lumsden to be 'a good trainer'. Nor does he make any mention of any failure on Lumsden's part during the pursuit from Alamein. He had, though, been very critical of Lumsden's handling of X Corps during Alamein. In particular he believed, unfairly, that Lumsden did not appreciate the need for co-ordination between the different branches of the Army and, more justly, that he lacked experience in putting such co-ordination into practice. For this, it might be added, the real fault lay with Montgomery's predecessors who had never called on Lumsden to do so and whose neglect of the subject had been almost total.

Nonetheless the fact remained that Montgomery anticipated having to fight other major battles in North Africa and he believed, for the reasons stated, that 'command of a corps' in such an action 'was above Lumsden's ceiling'. The luckless Lumsden duly departed. He was later sent to the Far East as Churchill's personal Liaison Officer to the American General MacArthur. On 6 January 1945, he was on board the battleship *New Mexico* watching the landings at Lingayan Gulf in the Philippines, when a Japanese 'kamikaze' suicide aircraft, already in flames, crashed into the bridge. Lumsden was among those killed. 'He was,' says MacArthur in his *Reminiscences*, 'England at its best.'

The loss to Eighth Army of such fine units as the Australians and South Africans emphasizes how far its strength had been reduced. In fact Leese could find only three divisions for his offensive against El Agheila. 51st Highland Division would attack along the coast road, apart from its 153rd Brigade which had been transferred to Harding's 7th Armoured Division – an example of that integration of the army which Montgomery had brought about. Harding also commanded 8th Armoured Brigade which had replaced the exhausted men and machines of 22nd Armoured, and 131st Motorized Infantry Brigade. His task was to attack at Bir es Suera, about 15 miles south of the Highlanders' advance.

These attacks went in on the night of 13th/14th December, but already on the previous night, Freyberg's New Zealanders, accompanied by 4th Light Armoured Brigade now led by Brigadier Harvey, had set off on the lengthy march necessary to outflank the enemy positions. It may be added that Harvey's command had consisted at first only of two armoured car regiments and the Royal Scots Greys with 17 Shermans, 4 Grants and 15 Stuarts. As a result of appeals by Freyberg, nine more Shermans from the Staffordshire Yeomanry in Custance's brigade had joined him just before the battle. Even so this was not a strong force with which to face the *Afrika Korps*, particularly as the Shermans, as usual at this time, proved 'mechanically shaky'.

The force could indeed have proved dangerously weak. Though Rommel had robbed the defence of his Italian infantry, the difficulties caused by the minefields, behind which it must be said the revived Ariete Division and the 90th Light Division offered valiant resistance, were still sufficient to block 51st Highland Division. 7th Armoured Division also found progress extremely difficult and it was not until 15 December that its men, well supported as always by the Desert Air Force, broke through to capture El Agheila.

Meanwhile at 1700 on the 14th, Freyberg's outflanking movement had been detected by the Axis airmen well to the south. Rommel's officers urged him to attack the New Zealanders while they were thus isolated, but *Panzerarmee Afrika*'s leader, having used up his petrol reserves in carrying the Italians to Buerat, felt that he dare not take the risk. In consequence Freyberg pressed on unhindered and by the late afternoon of the 15th, had reached the coast road near Merduma, well to the west of El Mugtaa, though by that time the bad going had reduced his tanks to a total of just seventeen.

These facts throw an interesting light on a comment by Rommel that 'the British commander's planning had contained one mistake' – he should not have 'started bombarding our strong-points and attacking our line until his outflanking force had completed its move and was in a position to advance on the coast road in timed co-ordination with the frontal attack'. In reality, had this happened and had Freyberg been spotted by air reconnaissance as he surely would have been, he would then have been still more isolated nearer to the enemy. He would thus have been in far more danger of an assault by the panzers which he might have had great difficulty in withstanding. When it is added that the New Zealanders did in any event complete their move in time to cut off the defenders, though they were not strong enough to prevent their escape, Rommel's criticism seems not so much ill-founded as irrelevant. But then Rommel, while often generous to defeated opponents, rarely finds much to say in favour of the one whom he could not defeat. Perhaps it helped to console him for Alam Halfa and Alamein.[4]

That night, Rommel determined to withdraw – Kesselring will have noted cynically that as usual he had enough petrol for this. On 16 December, splitting up into small groups, the Germans burst past the New Zealanders to make good their escape. Next day, Freyberg's men caught up with the enemy rearguard at Nofilia but though they engaged immediately, they were held off by heavy artillery fire until darkness fell, under cover of which the Axis soldiers continued their retreat.

The Battle of El Agheila was over. It had not been a large or memorable encounter. No unusual or imaginative tactics had been employed. The Axis casualties had been small: eighteen tanks and twenty-five guns lost and about 450 prisoners taken by Eighth Army. Yet for every man in that Army at the time the victory was an immense one. 'Eighth Army,' as General Jackson declares, 'had at last rounded the corner into Tripolitania.'

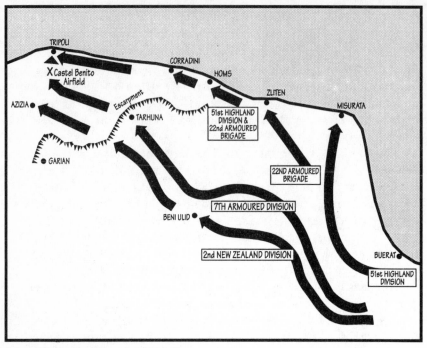

Map 7: The Conquest of Tripoli.

Once again it was 4th Light Armoured Brigade which followed up the retreating enemy. By 21 December, it had reached Sirte, from which the Axis forces only withdrew on Christmas Day, though they had in the meantime suffered losses at the hands of the Desert Air Force, now established on the landing grounds of eastern Tripolitania from which mines and booby traps had hastily been cleared, not without casualties, by the Royal Engineers. Nor were all the enemy losses inflicted from the air. On 24 December, Major General von Randow, the CO of 21st Panzer, was killed by a mine planted by the Special Air Service.[5]

By 29 December, 4th Light Armoured was facing the Axis position at Buerat but the main formations of Eighth Army were held back 40 miles or more to the east, while preparations were made for the coming encounter. These were necessarily thorough, for as Montgomery tells us in *El Alamein to the River Sangro*, 'for administrative reasons, once I struck at Buerat I intended to drive straight through to Tripoli' – a distance of 230 miles.

It was a far more difficult task than some of Eighth Army's critics have allowed. Buerat, though provided, in Rommel's words, with 'every mine we had', was not a particularly strong position. Moreover it could be outflanked far more easily than could El Agheila since the country to the south was much less difficult – though the Wadi Zem Zem running south-west from Buerat would provide a formidable obstacle. It was once Buerat was passed, however, that Eighth Army's difficulties would really begin.

Beyond Buerat the coast road, the Via Balbia, ran north-westward towards Misurata before turning west again to Tripoli. Between Buerat and Misurata movement was restricted to this road which was hemmed in on all sides by rough country and salt marshes. Moreover the enemy could cover any retreat by demolitions, and did – 177 craters, ten destroyed bridges and six anti-tank ditches were later encountered by Eighth Army on the Via Balbia before Tripoli could be reached, not to mention the 'usual' mines and booby traps. If the coast road was ignored and a wide outflanking movement executed, then this would have to cross terrain described by Alan Moorehead as 'so rough that even the desert veterans were left speechless' – it included every conceivable natural obstacle, from miles of soft sand, through appallingly broken ground covered with great boulders, to steep wadis and high cliffs.

After Misurata the difficulties became even worse. About 30 miles east of Tripoli there lay what Nigel Hamilton calls 'the best natural defensive line between Alamein and Tunisia'. De Guingand also refers to this as 'an excellent natural defensive position', while Montgomery describes it as 'an immensely superior defensive position'. This was, in the Eighth Army Commander's words, 'the escarpment running from Homs on the coast through Tarhuna and Garian', which curved in a great arc to protect Tripoli from the east, south-east and south. Montgomery was understandably alarmed in case the defences here which were already rendered formidable enough by nature should be made still more so by his enemies.

Montgomery records indeed that he could 'think of no sound military reason for Rommel's decision' to defend Buerat rather than Homs–Tarhuna. 'I believe,' he adds, 'that Mussolini ordered it.' Mussolini had certainly originally ordered 'resistance to the uttermost, I repeat the uttermost, with all troops of the *Panzerarmee* in the Buerat Line', but by again playing on the fears of Cavallero that the Italian infantry would be cut off, Rommel was once more able to obtain consent for their withdrawal to the Homs–Tarhuna area starting on 4 January 1943. There is no doubt that had he insisted, Rommel would have been permitted to bring all his men, apart perhaps from rear-guards, back to Homs–Tarhuna, for by the time the Eighth Army offensive opened his superiors had come to agree with him that Tripoli was doomed; nonetheless they ordered that the Eighth Army must be delayed for as long as possible to ensure that Tunisia could be made secure. Mussolini who, whatever his other errors, correctly evaluated the strength of the Homs–Tarhuna area, demanded that this be held for at least three weeks. That his instructions were far from being as unrealistic as some critics have claimed, is demonstrated by Rommel's own admission that with 'a somewhat better stock of supplies', he could 'have kept the enemy at bay here' – the Homs–Tarhuna position – 'for a very considerable time'.

There was certainly 'an intense and justifiable longing for better supplies' agrees Kesselring, but, he adds scornfully, 'given leadership even our lamentably small trickle of supplies would have been ample'. He further reports that when he visited the front at the end of December, the Axis troops showed 'no sign of depression, only disgust that they were not being given a chance to fight as they could have done'.

'Not being given a chance' because Rommel again had no intention of carrying out more than a delaying action at either Buerat or Homs–Tarhuna. The soldiers sent back to Homs–Tarhuna, the revived Trieste Division and the bulk of the La Spezia, Young Fascist and Pistoia Divisions,[6] made virtually no attempt to strengthen the defences, though Montgomery admits that 'if the energy expended on Buerat had instead been applied to the Homs–Tarhuna area, I do not think the Eighth Army would have reached Tripoli in January'. The rest of Rommel's forces remained uselessly at Buerat, even though their leader planned to retreat at speed from here as soon as he was engaged – 'fighting,' snarls Kesselring, 'went by the board'.

In practice all that Rommel had done was to disperse his forces. Indeed he would disperse them even wider than the borders of Tripolitania for on 14 January he proved very ready to ease the fears of his superiors for the safety of Tunisia by sending there the 21st Panzer Division. The division's tanks and artillery were, however, handed over to 15th Panzer, now commanded by Major General Boroweitz, though this still left Rommel with only thirty-six tanks plus the fifty-seven inadequate ones in service with the Italian Centauro (Armoured) Division. Rommel also had his Reconnaissance Units, now three in number for the 580th had joined the veteran 3rd and 33rd, 90th Light, 164th Light, the Ramcke Brigade and those Italian units that had not yet retired to Homs or Tarhuna. In support were just over 150 German aircraft and twice that number of Italian, though only 50 per cent of each of these totals were serviceable. The great majority of the German machines were, however, 109s, and these, under the command of Major Joachim Müncheberg, one of Hitler's most capable fighter pilots, inflicted a number of casualties on the Desert Air Force during its preliminary strikes in early January, No. 3 Squadron RAAF losing five Kittyhawks on the 13th, No. 450 Squadron RAAF four, and No. 250 Squadron RAF two.

Despite the disadvantages mentioned, if Rommel had defended the Homs–Tarhuna line resolutely then there is no doubt that he could have thwarted Eighth Army. Montgomery's main problem was less the Axis soldiers and airmen than his supply lines. The 'piece of elastic' was being asked to stretch further than ever before – and on 4 January, nature again intervened dramatically in favour of the enemy.

On that day, in the vivid words of the Eighth Army Commander in his *Memoirs*, 'very heavy gales began to rage in the Mediterranean and these created havoc and destruction at Benghazi. Ships broke loose and charged about the harbour; heavy seas broke up the breakwater and smashed into the inner harbour; much damage was done to tugs, lighters and landing places.' Four large supply-ships were lost, one of which carried 2,000 tons of ammunition; the tonnage received by Benghazi fell from 3,000 tons a day to under 1,000 tons and later as low as 400 tons, and Eighth Army, as its leader records, was 'thrown back on Tobruk'.

Montgomery, usually dismissed by Eighth Army's critics as a cautious, unimaginative commander, acted immediately. X Corps which he had planned to move forward to support his offensive and later to conduct operations west of Tripoli was 'grounded'. Its 1st Armoured Division handed over its tanks to 7th Armoured Division, and the Corps concentrated on providing a transport service, delivering supplies to the front. X Corps in general and its new commander Horrocks in particular were, says de Guingand, 'terribly disappointed, but without grumbling they got down to the task and played their part magnificently'.

Even with their best efforts, however, the supply situation remained so serious that de Guingand calls Montgomery's determination to proceed with his offensive on its original planned date of 15 January, 'a brave decision'. It would be possible to provide supplies for a period of only ten days. If the Eighth Army did not reach Tripoli within that time or at least immediately thereafter, 'the situation,' as de Guingand puts it with some restraint, 'would not be good, for without the use of Tripoli as a supply port, strong forces could not be maintained so far forward. If, therefore, Rommel prevented us capturing the port for, say, two weeks, it might well prove necessary to withdraw the bulk of our forces.' 'The problem was relentless,' agrees the Official History. 'Once the Army and air forces moved they *had* to reach Tripoli without pause in a set time or withdraw for want of supplies.'

Not only did the shortage of supplies render X Corps unable to take part in the offensive, it also resulted in 50th Division, which had originally been detailed as part of the attacking force, having to be left behind at El Agheila. The loss of this formation meant that Leese's XXX Corps again had only three divisions available for what was code-named at the time Operation FIRE-EATER, and would later be called the Battle of Buerat. This, it may be added, much underestimates the task before XXX Corps which was in fact a threefold one: to assault Buerat, to storm the Homs–Tarhuna line and to capture Tripoli.

The divisions which had to perform such a task were the 2nd New Zealand, the 51st Highland, supported by the Valentines of 23rd Armoured Brigade, and the 7th Armoured. Harding at this time had three brigades under him, 131st Brigade of motorized infantry, 4th Light Armoured Brigade now containing only armoured cars for the Royal Scots Greys had been transferred to Freyberg's command, and 8th Armoured Brigade which contained

57 Shermans, 27 Grants, 58 Crusaders and 4 Stuarts. In addition 22nd Armoured Brigade under Roberts was held in 'Army Reserve'.

As always the airmen were there with the Army. A number of squadrons were resting or re-equipping but apart from those bomber units which Tedder employed from bases further afield, the Desert Air Force could still put into action the two veteran South African Boston squadrons, two British and one South African Baltimore bomber squadrons, four squadrons of American Mitchells, a number of photographic reconnaissance units including an entire Hurricane squadron, No. 40 Squadron SAAF, and an entire Baltimore squadron, No. 60 Squadron SAAF, four squadrons now of Spitfires, No. 1 Squadron SAAF having been re-equipped soon after Alamein, three squadrons of US Warhawks, eight squadrons of Kittyhawks – three British, three South African, two Australian – and last but certainly not least the night-fighter Hurricanes of No. 73 Squadron RAF.

Coningham's fighters and fighter-bombers were much in evidence when Operation FIRE-EATER began on 15 January 1943. Montgomery's plan called for two widely separated thrusts, the first one being launched by Leese at 0715 as an outflanking movement south of the enemy position. This attack was delivered by 2nd New Zealand Division with 4th Light Armoured Brigade on its left and the bulk of 7th Armoured Division on its right. The attackers encountered strong resistance from 15th Panzer but by evening had destroyed fifteen German tanks, were across the Wadi Zem Zem, and had in fact turned Rommel's defences.

Meanwhile at 2230, 51st Highland Division attacked down the Via Balbia. Remembering how his control of events after Alamein had been thwarted by poor communications, and considering that the distance between the separate thrusts was too great to allow them to be controlled by one Corps Commander, Montgomery took personal charge of this advance. 51st Highland Division encountered deep minefields and since the Highlanders had suffered heavy casualties at and after Alamein, Montgomery ordered that they proceed with caution – at first. Nonetheless Wimberley's steady advance, coupled with the threat of being outflanked, was enough to ensure Rommel's retirement. By dawn on the 16th, the whole Buerat position was in Eighth Army's hands.

Now that the fixed defences had been passed it was vital that Eighth Army should reach Homs and Tarhuna before its enemies could prepare adequate defences there. Montgomery promptly cancelled all orders for caution, calling instead for 'great resolution and determination'. Despite the mines, demolitions and booby traps on the coast road and the appalling going facing Leese's advance, the men of Eighth Army met the challenge. By the evening of the 17th, Leese had captured Beni Ulid, south-east of Tarhuna and due south of Homs, while 51st Highland Division had advanced to within some twelve miles of Misurata.

That night the Desert Air Force's light bombers effectively hit the main Axis air base at Castel Benito, just south of Tripoli, an operation which they repeated on the night of the 18th/19th. During the intervening daylight hours, the Allied fighters and fighter-bombers were also out in strength, playing their part in the capture of Misurata by 51st Highland Division, followed in the late evening by that of Zliten, midway between Misurata and Homs, by 22nd Armoured Brigade. The enemy fell back to Homs and Tarhuna, and the crisis of the battle was at hand.

Montgomery was well aware of this. During the night he summoned Wimberley to his Tactical Headquarters which was now with 22nd Armoured, and warned him of 'the need for speed now on the coastal route' in view of the serious shortage of supplies and the consequent need to take Tripoli within ten days of the start of the offensive. Over the next forty-eight hours, Montgomery would continue to badger his unfortunate subordinate, his rebukes showing little consideration for the Highlanders' very real problems but being justified perhaps by the urgency of the situation.

On 19 January, Wimberley closed up to the Homs defences, while away on Eighth Army's left flank, 7th Armoured Division was attacking the pass at Tarhuna – a narrow defile between two high ridges – and 2nd New Zealand Division and 4th Light Armoured Brigade were pushing south of Tarhuna towards Garian. Unhappily during the attack on Tarhuna, Harding, who was standing on top of a Grant tank directing operations, was blown off it and badly wounded in the left arm and leg by a bursting shell. His senior staff officer, the future Field Marshal Carver, was able to arrange for Harding's hasty removal to hospital in a light aeroplane and, on Harding's own previous recommendation, his place at the head of 7th Armoured was taken by Roberts. He, however, could only arrive next day and in the meantime progress on the Tarhuna front came to a halt.

In practice this did not matter greatly, for Rommel, alarmed by Harding's pressure, had already transferred 15th Panzer, 164th Light, the Ramcke Brigade and his Reconnaissance Units to Tarhuna, leaving only 90th Light to hold Homs. Thereupon Montgomery, as at Alamein, switched the direction of his main thrust, reinforcing 51st Highland Division with 22nd Armoured Brigade and sternly commanding Wimberley to attack day and night until victory had been achieved. The Scots certainly did their best. Homs was taken on the afternoon of the 20th, and Corradini 12 miles to the west, despite bitter resistance by 90th Light, fell next day. On the 21st also, a detachment of the 1/7th Queens Royal Regiment from 131st Brigade under Major William Griffiths was able to move round to the west of Tarhuna, and that night, concerned over the threat this development posed and appreciating that it was in any case no longer possible to halt Montgomery's coastal thrust, Rommel abandoned the Tarhuna pass to fall back towards Tripoli.

On the 22nd therefore, all the Allied forces continued their advance. That of 51st Highland Division and 22nd Armoured Brigade along the coast road was delayed temporarily during the afternoon by demolitions guarded by rearguards from 90th Light, but Wimberley, as ordered, renewed his pressure successfully during the hours of darkness. Meanwhile on the left flank, 2nd New Zealand Division and 4th Light Armoured Brigade captured Azizia to the south-west of Tripoli, while 7th Armoured Division struck out towards Castel Benito, where on the previous day the Kittyhawks of Nos. 250 and 260 Squadrons had performed the unusual but important task of destroying tractors which were attempting to plough up the airfield so as to prevent its future use by the Allies. South of Castel Benito, the enemy checked this pursuit for a time from behind a double anti-tank ditch, but a night attack by 1/6th Queens, led by Lieutenant Colonel Roy Kaulback, took the position by storm. Eighth Army's twin thrusts were closing in on Tripoli and despite the protests of Cavallero, Rommel decided it was pointless to try to hold the city a moment longer.

'In the swaying battle of the desert,' declares Alan Moorehead, 'Tripoli had for two and a half years appeared as a mirage that grew strong and now faded away again, and was for ever just beyond the Eighth Army's reach.' He compares its capture to that of Paris by the Germans and Singapore by the Japanese and the re-entry into Stalingrad by the Russians. Yet none of these had had to wait so long for their moment of triumph. 'So many had died,' says Moorehead, 'or been withdrawn through wounds at a time when the struggle looked futile and endless. So many had recovered hope only to lose it again. So many had aged and grown sick and weak.'

Now at last it had all proved worthwhile. At 0530 on 23 January 1943, the 11th Hussars from 7th Armoured Division thrusting north from Castel Benito entered the capital of Libya, just ahead of the 50th Battalion of the Royal Tank Regiment from 23rd Armoured Brigade pushing westward along the Via Balbia with the men of the 1st Gordon Highlanders riding on its Valentines. Montgomery and Leese met and shook hands and, just three months from the start of the great offensive at El Alamein, the soldiers of Eighth Army were able to stand in the main square and gaze with delight at the plumes of white water from the fountains of Tripoli.

Notes

1   Volume II: *The Period of Balance*.
2   In fact a 'pachyderm' is defined as a member of any species of 'hoofed quadrupeds that do not chew cud'. An elephant is certainly a pachyderm. So is a racehorse.
3   Their reports may be found in *The Phantom Major* by Virginia Cowles, an account of the exploits of David Stirling, founder of the SAS Regiment.

4   It is of course typical of those eager to belittle Eighth Army that Rommel's criticisms are always accepted by them at face value despite their often palpable bias. For example Rommel, speaking of the post-Alamein period, sneers that 'bold solutions were completely foreign' to his enemy. Even had it been correct – which as has been and will be seen, it was not – the comment would still come ill from the man who had just retreated for more than 800 miles and intended disobeying his instructions in order to continue to retreat for another similar distance.

5   The SAS made a number of attacks on the coast road during and following the El Agheila action, but on the whole these achieved little success and the raiders suffered heavy casualties.

6   The Pistoia Division had moved to North Africa in August for garrison duties in Tripolitania.

Chapter 10

THE NEW BATTLEGROUND

In the early hours of 8 November 1942, while the Desert Air Force was hastening Rommel's withdrawal, eighteen Hurricane IICs from No. 43 Squadron RAF, the 'Fighting Cocks', were on their way from Gibraltar to the Maison Blanche aerodrome near Algiers. At their head was Wing Commander Pedley who must have been an anxious man for he had only once previously flown a Hurricane and he did not know for certain that he would be able to land at Maison Blanche if he got there – it might still be in hostile hands. In that case, even with their long-range tanks, the RAF fighters could never have returned to Gibraltar. Fortunately, when they reached their destination at about 0900, the troops holding it proved to be American. That evening, Pedley attacked a Junkers Ju 88. He claimed only to have damaged it but enemy records indicate that it failed to return to its base.

Pedley's experiences might serve as a symbol of the fortunes of Operation TORCH, the code name given to the Anglo-American landings in Vichy French North Africa under the overall command of Lieutenant General Dwight Eisenhower. It had been prepared hurriedly. It took place in an atmosphere of uncertainty and justifiable anxiety. It was risky in the extreme. But in the end it proved successful.

This was partly because complete surprise was achieved, for despite the contrary advice of Kesselring and the Italians, the German High Command had been convinced that the target of the troop transports was Tripoli or perhaps Sicily or Sardinia. Even so all the main landings, at Oran and Algiers in the Mediterranean and at Casablanca on the Atlantic coast of French Morocco, suffered from considerable delay and confusion; an attempted parachute raid on the airfields at Oran failed completely; and direct assaults on the harbours of Oran and Algiers resulted only in the death or capture of every man who got ashore. At Algiers resistance had ceased by 1900 on 8

November, but Oran was not taken until midday on the 10th – and then mainly because the French commanders there were aware that negotiations for a general armistice were in progress – while in Morocco, Major General George Patton had at that time still not secured Casablanca or the vital airfield at Port Lyautey some 55 miles to the north.

Luckily Eighth Army's victory at El Alamein cast its 'bright gleam' over the Allied fortunes. In the first place it ended any chance that Hitler might be able to persuade Spanish troops to seize Gibraltar or at least render its harbour and airfield unusable by artillery fire, thereby severing the Allied supply route – a fact which the Führer was sensible enough to realize. In addition, it seems to have had a crucial influence on Admiral Darlan, heir-apparent to the aged Marshal Pétain as Vichy's Head of State, who happened to be in Algiers visiting a son dangerously ill with polio. Since his aversion to the British was notorious and his first angry reaction to the news of Operation TORCH had been to put the US Consul-General in Algiers, Mr Robert Murphy, under arrest, he can scarcely have been a convinced believer in the Allied cause. On the other hand, as Liddell Hart drily remarks, he had 'a shrewder sense of realism than many of his compatriots' and recognized that the tide of the war had turned. He therefore issued a ceasefire order to all French troops in North Africa at 1120 on 10 November.[1]

The British First Army, under Lieutenant General Sir Kenneth Anderson, now began a rapid advance eastward towards Tunis and the port of Bizerta, aided by further seaborne landings at Bougie and Bone and by a parachute drop on the Bone airfield. By the end of November, Anderson's men had approached to within 20 miles of Tunis – but they were not to cover that last short distance for many weary months.

On 9 November, Junkers Ju 52s had arrived in Tunis carrying all the German troops that could be found at short notice: a parachute regiment and Kesselring's personal guard unit. Others followed by air and by sea for though the Malta striking forces were still decimating the Axis convoys to Tripoli, they were not at first able to interfere with the new shorter route to Tunisia. By early December, there were 15,000 German and 9,000 Italian soldiers in that country, forming the Fifth Panzer Army under General Jurgen von Arnim, a harsh, grim man who had formerly been a corps commander in Russia.

It was not only von Arnim of whose services Germany's Eastern Front would be deprived. As Major General Fuller points out in *The Decisive Battles of the Western World*, Hitler's attention had been 'suddenly attracted to events in North Africa'. German reinforcements destined for Russia 'were not sent east, but were sent west into [Vichy] France' – which unhappy country they quickly overran – 'and to Tunisia'. Some 400 operational warplanes and numerous aerial transports were transferred out of Russia to the

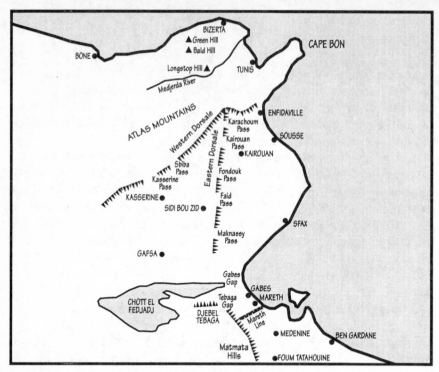

Map 8: The Tunisian battleground.

Mediterranean area. These decisions led directly to an Axis catastrophe, for they greatly assisted the Russian counter-offensive at Stalingrad and subsequently vastly increased the difficulties of supplying the trapped German forces from the air.

Nonetheless Hitler considered he had no choice in the matter. If the Allies could speedily conquer Tunisia, they could attack Tripoli from the west thereby dooming *Panzerarmee Afrika*. Moreover with North Africa secured, they could launch an assault on Italy which Hitler rightly feared would knock his increasingly reluctant ally out of the war. Whatever the risks he had to fight for Tunisia. On 27 November, Field Marshal Kesselring personally hurried to Tunis to forbid any further withdrawals. Four days later, the newly arrived 10th Panzer Division counter-attacked and the battle for Tunisia had begun in earnest. It was a battle in which Eighth Army was to prove in Churchill's words, 'a new favourable factor of decisive importance'.

Eighth Army's new battleground was very different from its old one. The only desert areas in Tunisia were in the southern third of that country which was strategically unimportant. Central Tunisia by contrast was a fertile, fairly well-watered plain which was covered with pretty white villages and groups of olive groves and in spring, as Alan Moorehead recalls delightedly:

> burst into a wild fantasy of colour, and that overworked cliché 'a
> carpet of flowers' became a proven fact. It was just that, a rich deep

Persian carpet woven of bluebells and poppies, of sweet-peas and tulips, of daisies and lillies; and these grew so thickly that for miles you could not see the ground or the grass, only flowers. They made patterns that swept over hill-tops, hilarious shouting bands of colour.

Clustered around the central plain, as though to protect it, were the mountains, their lower slopes covered with forest, broken by fertile but usually steep valleys. In the north was the Atlas range, running all the way from Morocco, to end in the Cape Bon Peninsula, thrusting north-eastward into the Mediterranean just south of Tunis. Through this area moved two rough roads, one near the coast making its way towards Bizerta, the other further inland, at first following the course of the Medjerda River which flowed into the sea midway between Bizerta and Tunis, then swinging away south-eastward to the capital city.

It was along these roads that the men of First Army were attempting to advance but on 7 December, the resistance of the enemy was reinforced by the hostility of the elements. On that day, reports General Jackson, 'the Tunisian winter rains broke, turning the valleys and plains into quagmires of thick yellowish-grey mud of a glutinous consistency which bogged vehicles, beat the power of tank-engines, and made men's lives a constant battle with the all-pervading clay'. On the coast road, no further attempts were made to overcome German resistance at a narrow defile between Djebel Azag and Djebel Adjred – Green and Bald Hills as the British called them – where the advance had been checked at the end of November. In the Medjerda valley, fighting continued throughout December around the sinister double-crested Djebel el Almara – Longstop Hill – but after changing hands several times it was finally secured by the Germans on Christmas Day, and Eisenhower and Anderson abandoned their offensive for the winter.

Having reached the base of the Cape Bon Peninsula, the mountains turned south. A spur doubled back to the east reaching almost to the sea at Enfidaville to form the northern boundary of the central plain. Its western boundary was a longer range called the Eastern Dorsale which ran due south from Cape Bon and in which were a number of important passes – Karachoum, Kairouan, Fondouk, Faid and Maknassy – while an outer guard was provided by the Western Dorsale which proceeded south-westward from Cape Bon.

While Anderson had been fighting in the north, other Allied forces had been moving up to the Eastern Dorsale. The French by this time were wholly committed to the Allied cause and their XIX Corps secured the three northern passes, while Major General Fredendall's II US Corps took the Faid Pass, leaving only the Maknassy Pass, guarded by the Italians, in Axis hands. Unfortunately Kesselring was not prepared to allow this situation to continue and during the latter part of January 1943, Axis counter-attacks regained all the passes and inflicted over 4,500 casualties.

The Allies had been checked in northern Tunisia and again in central Tunisia. Luckily there was one further avenue of advance open to them. On 23 January, Tripoli fell to the Eighth Army. 7th Armoured Division which had now been rejoined by 4th Light Armoured Brigade, was given little time to enjoy this triumph, being ordered by Montgomery to keep Rommel 'on the run' as far as the Tunisian frontier. Following the retreating enemy along the coast road, 7th Armoured took Zavia on 25 January. It was then hampered by bad going and bad weather but on the 31st, it reached Zuara and by 4 February, had crossed the border into Tunisia.

There would be a delay before the main body of Eighth Army could move up to its support, however. The weather continued to be dreadful and, as Montgomery reports in *El Alamein to the River Sangro*, 'for several days the desert became a quagmire and made operations impossible'. Furthermore, as Kesselring rather admiringly points out, 'the British Eighth Army had marched halfway across North Africa – over fifteen hundred miles – had spent the bad winter months on the move and in the desert, and had had to surmount difficulties of every kind'. Nor did those difficulties cease once Tripoli was reached, for the enemy, as Captain Roskill states in his Official History of *The War at Sea*, had 'managed to destroy the port facilities very thoroughly, and to block the entrance completely with six merchantmen' that had been scuttled as well as with other debris including 'many barges filled with concrete'. Air raids and a violent storm did nothing to improve the situation, the first supply ship could only enter the harbour on 2 February, and it was not until the 14th that large quantities of stores began to arrive. Yet when weather conditions improved at last on 15 February, Eighth Army had managed to overcome all difficulties and was ready to resume its victorious advance forthwith.

The natural defences guarding the southern edge of the Tunisian plain were of a type already familiar to Eighth Army in Tripolitania: salt marshes – but those in Tripolitania were as nothing to the vast, trackless wastes of Tunisia's Chott el Fedjadj which blocked any attempt at an outflanking manoeuvre as effectively as did the Qattara Depression at El Alamein. A long tongue of the marsh reached out particularly close to the sea just north of the little town of Gabes, to provide a tight bottleneck called the Gabes Gap, across which was a series of high ridges running from west to east.

To the south-west of the salt lake lay an almost equally impassable sea of sand known as the Grand Erg, while to the south-east the Djebel Tebaga and the Matmata Hills ran parallel to the line of the coast. There was thus a further narrow passage to be negotiated east of the hills at Mareth, and this had been barred by what Ronald Lewin calls the 'French-built, solid defences' of the

Mareth Line. Finally, any movement through the difficult country west of the Matmata Hills would be blocked by the marshes and would have to turn back towards the coast through the tightest bottleneck of them all, the Tebaga Gap.

Eighth Army's first operation in Tunisia was an attack on the Axis stronghold of Ben Gardane on the coast, which was duly taken on 16 February by 7th Armoured Division reinforced by 22nd Armoured Brigade. 51st Highland Division was also moving up to the front line and on the 17th it combined with 7th Armoured to capture the important road centre at Medenine, south-east of the Mareth Line, as well as its four landing grounds. Next day, Foum Tatahouine, to the south of Medenine and on the eastern fringe of the Matmata Hills, also fell. It is again interesting, in view of all the criticisms about Eighth Army's deliberation and slowness, to discover that Rommel records that these conquests were achieved 'rather earlier than we had bargained for'.

Eighth Army's next task was to build up its supply bases in the area of Ben Gardane, ready for an assault on the Mareth Line. XXX Corps was to be responsible for this, while X Corps would be kept in reserve to follow up success and perhaps break through the Gabes Gap on the heels of a retreating enemy.

It was anticipated that this operation would take place by mid-March, but on 22 February, all plans were disrupted. A signal was received from General Alexander, who had arrived at Algiers a week earlier to establish Eighteenth Army Group Headquarters, from which he would exercise tactical control over the entire land battle in Tunisia. In this, Alexander urgently requested that Eighth Army should put increased pressure on the enemy immediately so as to assist the Allies to rectify a grave situation that had arisen elsewhere.

While Eighth Army was waiting at Tripoli in order to build up its strength, *Panzerarmee Afrika* was falling back onto its supply bases in Tunisia. Encouraged by this fact, by his junction with his comrades, and by the prospect of assaulting inexperienced troops instead of his usual formidable Eighth Army opponents, its leader now reverted briefly to the old, aggressive Rommel of the days before El Alamein.

Rommel's first aim was to strike at Gafsa, west of Maknassy, which was the nearest position held by II US Corps and which threatened the rear of his right flank. For this attack he wished to use not only his own armoured units, 15th Panzer and the Italian Centauro, but also his former 21st Panzer Division, now re-equipped and led by Major General Hildebrandt, and 10th Panzer Division under Major General von Broich. Von Arnim opposed this suggestion as he wanted 10th and 21st Panzer to attack westward from Faid towards the American positions at Sidi Bou Zid. Kesselring, attempting to keep the peace between his two difficult subordinates, therefore declared by way of compromise that von Arnim's attack should proceed but thereafter he should release 21st Panzer to Rommel to help the latter's advance.

Von Arnim placed his Chief of Staff, Lieutenant General Heinz Ziegler, in command of the preliminary offensive and on 14 February, that officer struck at Sidi Bou Zid, well supported by Kesselring's dive-bombers. The Americans knew an attack was planned but 'Ultra' interceptions had indicated that it would come in the Fondouk area. Consequently the defenders were taken completely by surprise and 'in three days' says General Jackson, 'Ziegler had destroyed two tank, two artillery and two infantry battalions of Fredendall's II US Corps'.

Rommel's spirits were raised dramatically by Ziegler's success, particularly since it had forced the Americans to evacuate Gafsa, which was occupied without resistance on the 15th. He now proposed that he be given command of all the German armour, with which to strike north-westward beyond the Western Dorsale to the main American bases with their vast supply dumps, the capture of which he felt certain would wreck all chance of an American offensive for the foreseeable future. Kesselring, despite von Arnim's objections, gave his support, and on 19 February, Rommel, disdaining once more to concentrate his armour, advanced down both the two main roads leading through the Western Dorsale, attacking the Sbiba Pass with 21st Panzer and the Kasserine Pass with 15th Panzer and Centauro.

Contrary to later exaggerated accounts, these assaults achieved comparatively limited results. All attempts to seize the passes on the 19th failed and Rommel was forced to abandon his planned breakthrough at Sbiba entirely. Reinforced by units from 10th Panzer, reluctantly and belatedly released by von Arnim, he did manage to capture the Kasserine Pass on the afternoon of the 20th, but he was able to make little further progress next day, and on the day following he was compelled to turn his attention to a new source of anxiety.

For on the 22nd, Alexander's signal for assistance reached Eighth Army. General Richardson records that, knowing Montgomery's insistence on making proper preparations and remaining 'balanced' at all times, 'I would not have been surprised if he had answered that there was nothing he could do. Not a bit of it! His reaction was: "Alex is in trouble; we must do everything we can to help him".'

'It is at such moments,' remarks de Guingand, 'that Montgomery is at his best. He always responds wholeheartedly to an appeal.' 'It was Monty in his most generous mood,' agrees Richardson. 7th Armoured and the Highlanders were ordered up to the Mareth Line at once; the Desert Air Force's Kittybombers stepped up their attacks; and Montgomery sent a cheerful signal to Alexander – which did not reflect his true feelings – that they might be able to get Rommel 'running about' between them 'like a wet hen'.

Alexander replied that he was 'greatly relieved', as well he might have been.

Rommel would later remark only that success at Kasserine was no longer possible and would make no mention of any concern over Eighth Army's activities – but then Rommel rarely gives more credit to his conqueror than is absolutely essential, and what he may have said afterwards is unimportant compared with what he felt at the time his decision was made. On the evening of 22 February, he reported his reasons for abandoning further attacks in the Western Dorsale to Hitler. His signal was intercepted by 'Ultra', and we know therefore that a major motive was 'the situation at Mareth' which 'made it necessary to collect my mobile forces for a swift blow against Eighth Army before it had completed its preparations'.[2]

Certainly Rommel also gave other reasons for his decision, chiefly the arrival of Allied reinforcements, bad weather and difficult terrain. Yet even ignoring the points that his troops had been outnumbered throughout the offensive and that on 22 February the weather and the terrain over which they were fighting were both better than they had been in the immediate past, these arguments were irrelevant. If Rommel wished to collect his mobile forces for a swift blow against Eighth Army, then he could not have continued his operations against the Americans even had no reinforcements reached them, had the weather been perfect and had the terrain been entirely suitable for his purposes. The simple fact was that his mobile forces could not be in two places at once.

Field Marshal Kesselring emphatically confirms that Rommel's main anxiety was with Eighth Army and other factors were little more than excuses. 'On 22nd February 1943,' Kesselring reports, 'I had a long talk with Rommel at his battle HQ near Kasserine and found him in a very dispirited mood. His heart was not in his task and he approached it with little confidence. I was particularly struck by his ill-concealed impatience to get back as quickly and with as much unimpaired strength as possible to the southern defence line.' Nor did Kesselring think that Rommel's anxiety was ill-founded for he approved the decision to break off the Kasserine battle, and indeed promoted Rommel to the command of Army Group Afrika which had been set up to control the activities of both *Panzerarmee Afrika* and von Arnim's Fifth Panzer Army.

The 'Ultra' interception detailing Rommel's intentions reached Montgomery on 25 February. Ronald Lewin in his *Ultra Goes to War: The Secret Story* claims that the code-breakers had thus 'intervened with devastating effect'. In reality the Allies were already aware that Rommel was retreating from the Western Dorsale since they had reoccupied Kasserine Pass without resistance on the previous day; air reconnaissance had revealed the German movement in any event; and Williams would inform Nigel Hamilton that from his knowledge of 'how Rommel would behave', he was absolutely certain that such an attack was coming: 'You didn't need "Ultra" to know that this was going to happen.'

Nor was the news in any way welcome to Montgomery for, despite his cheerful 'wet hen' signal, he was really far from happy about the situation in which Eighth Army was now placed. He 'frankly admitted to me,' says de Guingand, 'that for once, through his action to assist First Army, he now found himself unbalanced.' Half his army – X Corps – was still at Benghazi and his nearest reserve division, 2nd New Zealand, was 200 miles from the front line reorganizing in Tripoli. No wonder that he feared for Eighth Army's forward units and that when the danger had passed he would tell de Guingand that he 'had sweated a bit at times!'

The real credit should therefore be given to Eighth Army's administrative staff who performed the brilliant feat of rushing substantial reinforcements to the front over a single inadequate road, which luckily was well protected by the Desert Air Force. On 28 February, the tanks of 2nd Armoured Brigade arrived at Tripoli from Benghazi on transporters. They were at once sent on to 7th Armoured Division at Ben Gardane, where they were handed over to its 8th Armoured Brigade. The Valentines of 23rd Armoured Brigade were also moved up to the battle-area, as were 2nd New Zealand Division, 201st Guards Brigade and as many additional anti-tank guns as could be found. By the evening of 4 March, a 'period of great anxiety', as Montgomery calls it in *El Alamein to the River Sangro*, had passed.

'Rommel,' adds the Eighth Army Commander, had 'missed his opportunity', yet it should be noted that while 'Ultra' had warned Eighth Army of Rommel's general intentions – and in any case, as already seen, Eighth Army 'didn't need "Ultra" to know that this was going to happen' – it had revealed neither the date nor the direction of Rommel's thrust. Eighth Army's Intelligence staff deduced from more orthodox means – chiefly air reconnaissance – that the date would be after the 3rd and before the 7th of March, but as Nigel Hamilton relates: 'Not until the Axis formations emerged from the mist on 6th March 1943, did Montgomery know for certain the line of the enemy attack.'

For that matter, the line of the enemy attack was not even decided until 3 March. The flurried improvisations on the Axis side, while having the unintentional advantage of concealing the plan from 'Ultra', form indeed a sorry contrast to the calm, sound and extremely thorough preparations made in a very short space of time by Eighth Army. Nor were the attackers helped by disputes between, or belated changes in the identity of, the men who were to lead them.

When Rommel was promoted to the command of Army Group Afrika, he handed over his old *Panzerarmee Afrika*, now renamed First Italian Army, to General Giovanni Messe. Ronald Lewin in his history of the *Afrika Korps*, calls Messe 'an excellent, experienced, if stolid commander', and like many of the later arrivals in North Africa, he had gained that experience in Russia, where he had led an Italian Corps with sufficient ability to be awarded a Knight's Cross by Hitler. Yet this was hardly an easy time for a new man to take over, and his task was made still less easy by his Chief of Staff, Bayerlein, now a major general, retaining direct and complete control over all German units. The *Afrika Korps* was originally entrusted to Ziegler, but on the day before the battle, he was replaced by Lieutenant General Cramer. While that officer was well suited for this post – he was a former commander of 8th Panzer Regiment from 15th Panzer Division – it was an odd decision to remove a leader of Ziegler's calibre on the eve of an encounter which Rommel, in his own words, believed would be of 'decisive importance for the defence of the whole Tunisian bridgehead'.

Rommel's initial desire was for a direct attack from the north-west down the main road from Mareth to Medenine. On 3 March, a reconnaissance in force in this area drove back 51st Division's outposts but also revealed that the defences were very strong, 'heavily mined and covered by many guns'. Rommel's subordinates were also afraid that a tank attack from the north-west would have no room for manoeuvre and so be an easy target for the British artillery and the Desert Air Force. Finally it was felt that paths for the tanks would first have to be cleared through the Germans' own minefields

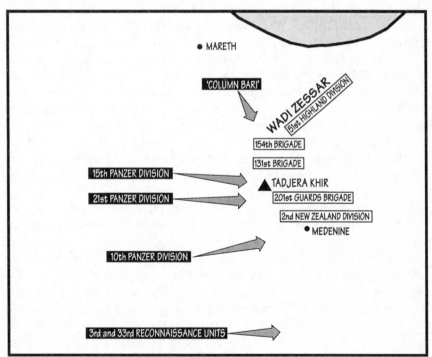

Map 9: The Battle of Medenine.

protecting the Mareth Line and this would prevent any chance of attaining surprise. Faced with this opposition, Rommel reverted to his mood of sulky pessimism. He withdrew from any further role in planning the assault, being content to demand 'the utmost commitment from every soldier' participating therein.

The panzer commanders therefore planned a sweep round Eighth Army's defences in order to attack these from the west and south-west out of the Matmata Hills. By one more irony, this decision did enable them to achieve complete surprise. Montgomery, who at Alam Halfa had agreed with his Intelligence staff's assessment because it fitted in with his belief as to how Rommel would act, and who at Alamein had anticipated that Rommel would deliver those impulsive counter-attacks which proved so beneficial to Eighth Army, had once again correctly predicted Rommel's personal intentions. He was convinced that Rommel would wish to advance down the road from Mareth. Even when his airmen reported movement in the Matmata Hills on the afternoon of the 4th, he considered that this was a feint to divert his attention from the real point of attack.

This error could have had serious consequences, for the Axis onslaught was potentially a formidable one. A subsidiary thrust was to be made down the Mareth-Medenine road by a force called 'Column Bari' under Graf von Sponeck, containing his 90th Light and the Italian Trieste and La Spezia Divisions. The main assault was due to come from the west against a small but steep hill known as Tadjera Khir which dominated Eighth Army's western defences. This assault would be the responsibility of Cramer's *Afrika Korps*, with the sixty tanks of 15th Panzer on the left and the forty-six tanks of 21st Panzer on the right. Meanwhile the thirty-five tanks of 10th Panzer, supported by detachments from 164th Light, would strike from the south-west directly towards Medenine, and 3rd and 33rd Reconnaissance Units, as at Alam Halfa, would provide the extreme right flank of the turning movement; they were to block the road from Medenine to Foum Tatahouine to prevent reinforcements arriving from this direction.

The attack was to be supported by as much artillery as could be brought to bear, including a number of the new six-barrelled 150mm mortars which the Germans called '*Nebelwerfers*' but the British 'Moaning Minnies', and which were vastly superior to anything of a similar type on the Allied side.[3] The Axis air forces would also take part in the attack, and they had about 100 German and sixty Italian warplanes serviceable. Moreover the Stukas, 109s and Macchi MC 202s had now been joined by a *Gruppe* of Messerschmitt Me 210 fighter-bombers, which for the sake of convenience may be described as much improved successors to the Messerschmitt Bf 110s, and a *Gruppe* of the very latest German Focke-Wulf Fw 190 fighters. In addition the Axis cause would be much assisted by the fact that poor weather conditions over the Allied airfields would considerably handicap the Desert Air Force.

As at El Agheila and Buerat, Eighth Army in the coming action – it would be known as the Battle of Medenine – had only Leese's XXX Corps on hand. This again contained three divisions: 51st Highland, 2nd New Zealand and 7th Armoured. Admittedly 7th Armoured was exceptionally strong, for it consisted of 8th Armoured Brigade, 22nd Armoured Brigade, 4th Light Armoured Brigade and 131st Motorized Infantry Brigade, with 201st Guards Brigade also temporarily under command – another example of that integration of the Army which by now was accepted as a matter of course. In consequence, as its critics never tire of pointing out, Eighth Army was still superior in men and material.

Yet such superiority in the past had scarcely guaranteed victory: it should not be forgotten that Rommel had had only 2,500 infantrymen at the start of the Battle of Mersa Matruh while Messe had 10,000 at Medenine; it should not be overlooked that *Panzerarmee Afrika* had won 'Second Ruweisat' with forty-two German tanks of which only eight were of a calibre comparable to any of those used by First Italian Army at Medenine; it should not be ignored that Eighth Army, as General Jackson rather unkindly remarks, had 'about half the equipment which the Americans possessed in Tunisia' – the difference being that it was made up of 'experienced troops'.[4]

What decided Medenine in fact was neither the numbers of nor the weapons in Eighth Army, but the quality of the soldiers behind the weapons and of the commanders who led them. Montgomery, as Liddell Hart remarks, had made 'the most of his ability for planning a well-woven defence' and despite his confidence that the attack would come from the north-west, he had not neglected the defences in other areas either; the hallmark of his preparations was always their thoroughness. He had for instance appreciated the crucial importance of Tadjera Khir, and de Guingand relates a visit to this key hill by Montgomery, Leese and their staffs which might have had tragic consequences. The position was well within range of German heavy artillery to the west, and as the party descended it was spotted by the enemy. 'The Army Commander,' says de Guingand, 'was in the middle of a discussion with Leese when a shell landed very close to our path. It had no visible effect on him whatsoever; there was not even a pause in his conversation.'

On 6 March 1943, therefore, the Eighth Army's positions were secure at all points. From the coast the front line moved gradually south-westward along the Wadi Zessar which had been strengthened by 70,000 mines and behind which the bulk of 51st Highland Division had taken its stand, supported by the eighty Valentines of 23rd Armoured Brigade. Then the defences turned south, continuing for 16 miles in all along the western edge of the ridge which carried the Mareth–Medenine road, the angle between the northern- and western-facing defences being strongly held by 51st Highland

Division's 154th Brigade plus a number of additional anti-tank guns. On the left of the Highlanders was 131st Brigade, then 201st Guards Brigade holding Tadjera Khir, and finally 2nd New Zealand Division guarding the approaches to Medenine.

The defenders' main weapons were their anti-tank guns, some 460 of them, mostly 6-pounders though there were still a number of 2-pounders in this total and also a few brand-new and extremely formidable 17-pounders which went by the innocuous name of 'Pheasants'. Moreover, so confident were the men of Eighth Army and so far had the fear of the panzers evaporated, that for the first time the anti-tank guns, in the words of the Official History, were 'sited to kill tanks and not to "protect" infantry, field-guns or anything else'. Not that the artillery was negligible either for Eighth Army had 350 field or medium guns which, as General Jackson tells us, were 'centralized under XXX Corps' control to ensure concentration of fire on important targets'.

'We always thought,' declares Kippenberger, 'this Medenine position was our masterpiece in the art of laying out a defensive position under desert conditions.' It was 'admirably thought out' agrees the more sedate Official History. So much so that the 300 tanks in 7th Armoured Division – as well as those in 23rd Armoured Brigade – saw hardly any action, though for the record 8th Armoured Brigade was stationed behind 51st Highland Division, 22nd Armoured behind Tadjera Khir, and 4th Light Armoured behind the New Zealanders.

So good in fact was Eighth Army's defensive technique that the battle appears in retrospect as very unexciting, the issue never in doubt. Of course it all seemed rather different at the time. At 0900 on 6 March, the enemy attacked from three directions. The diversionary move by 'Column Bari' was easily repelled with heavy losses. The thrust by 10th Panzer towards Medenine was neither particularly resolute nor well organized and was halted by the anti-tank guns of 28th Maori Battalion which destroyed five panzers at point-blank range and drove the rest into hasty retreat. But in the centre around the crucial Tadjera Khir hill, the Axis armed forces proved worthy of their reputation.

Here the attackers were Eighth Army's old foes 15th and 21st Panzer Divisions, which advanced with great determination, their tanks in the lead, their supporting infantry regiments close behind. They closed to within some 400 yards of the defences, but then the British artillery went into action, concentrating as ordered not on the panzers but on the German infantrymen, who were forced to seek shelter, leaving the tanks to continue on their own.

This they duly did, probing persistently for weak spots but failing utterly to find any. 21st Panzer attacked the Guards Brigade. Brigadier Julian Gascoigne had held back 6th Battalion, the Grenadier Guards as a reserve, and 3rd Battalion, the Coldstream Guards was scarcely engaged, but 2nd

Battalion, the Scots Guards was quickly in action, destroying three tanks. The remaining ones fought back, knocking out some of the British guns, but the Scots Guards hit tank after tank, claiming to have destroyed fifteen during the day. On their left, the Coldstreams' anti-tank platoon was at last able to join in the fight, setting a panzer ablaze with the first shot fired.

An even heavier attack was delivered by 15th Panzer on 131st Brigade, commanded by Brigadier Lashmer 'Bolo' Whistler, whom Montgomery would call 'perhaps the best fighting brigadier in the British Army'. The main blows fell on 1/7th Queens in the centre of the brigade's position, its anti-tank gunners claiming the destruction of twenty-seven panzers in a series of clashes throughout the morning. So determined and so continuous was the enemy assault that Whistler asked for assistance and 22nd Armoured Brigade moved up a squadron of Shermans in close support; these put seven more enemy tanks out of action.

By midday, the Axis commanders had had enough and retired to reorganize. At 1530, they renewed their advance from the same three directions as before, but this time it was their infantrymen who came forward first, the tanks lagging well behind them. Again all the attacks were broken, mainly by artillery fire, and though an attempted counter-attack by 7th Argyll and Sutherland Highlanders of 154th Brigade was halted by German mortars, by 2030, the Axis soldiers were withdrawing on all fronts and the battle was over. This was not immediately apparent since a number of movements on the part of the enemy were reported during the night – they attracted heavy artillery fire and kept the defenders on the alert for further encounters. In reality, as it subsequently transpired, these movements were merely attempts by the Germans to recover their knocked-out panzers. They failed in this mission but achieved an unexpected bonus by masking the retirement of their main forces. By dawn on 7 March, they had all fallen back into their own defences in the Mareth Line.

'The Battle of Medenine,' declares de Guingand, 'was a little classic all of its own. It was the perfectly fought defensive battle.' The Axis soldiers had not even penetrated Eighth Army's front-line defences as at Alam Halfa. There had been no flaws like the misfortunes of Operations BULIMBA and BERESFORD to mar the brilliance of the whole encounter. Before it began Montgomery had sent a message to his troops, urging them to 'show him [Rommel] what the famous Eighth Army can do' – and that they, and especially the infantry and the anti-tank gunners, had certainly done!

Eighth Army's losses had been minimal: not a single tank, hardly any guns, and 130 killed or wounded, 'all ranks'. The enemy had lost 635 dead, wounded or prisoners, over two-thirds of them Germans. Rommel would later admit to '40 tanks totally destroyed', but Paul Carell, who gained his information from senior German officers including Bayerlein and Ziegler, records that 'fifty-five burnt-out German tanks' were left behind when the panzers retreated, while de Guingand states that 'Rommel lost fifty-two of his tanks which were counted on the battlefield.'

It was Rommel's final battlefield in North Africa. On 9 March, he handed over Army Group Afrika to von Arnim and returned to Germany, a sick, disillusioned man, his exhaustion shown clearly by the unsightly boils which covered his face. It is much to the credit of his army that Rommel's departure, in Ronald Lewin's words, 'made no essential difference to its performance in action'. Indeed his absence may have been a blessing as Rommel's 'mood of depression' had by now become 'acute' and his pessimistic outlook can hardly have had a beneficial effect on morale. Certainly after he had left, *Panzerarmee Afrika*, now Messe's First Italian Army, would come very close indeed to an achievement that had never been attained by Rommel: the defeat of an Eighth Army commanded by Montgomery.

Notes

1   Whatever Darlan's motives, he did not live long enough to gain any personal benefit from his actions. On Christmas Eve, he was shot dead by a youthful anti-Vichy fanatic named Bonnier de la Chapelle, who in turn was hastily court-martialled and shot two days later.

2   Rommel's signal is quoted in Professor Hinsley's account of *British Intelligence in the Second World War*.

3   '*Nebelwerfer*' literally translated means 'smoke projector', but these mortars could project much more lethal missiles containing just over 75lb of high explosive for a distance of well over 7,000 yards, the six barrels being fired separately over a period of ten seconds. Later a five-barrelled 210mm version also reached North Africa, though luckily the Germans were very short of ammunition for this.

4   It should be pointed out that Jackson was personally serving in First Army during this period, so he cannot be said to have been prejudiced in Eighth Army's favour.

Chapter 11

THE BATTLE OF THE MARETH LINE

'Will you please convey to General Montgomery and the forces under his command my sincere congratulations on their magnificent performance of March 6th.' Eisenhower, who since 11 February, had been a full 'four-star' general, had every reason to express his gratitude to Eighth Army for having ended the series of Allied set-backs with an indisputable success, but for Alexander, to whom this signal was sent, the victory at Medenine was of even greater significance.

As was mentioned earlier, in late February, Alexander had set up the Eighteenth Army Group in Algiers, with which to co-ordinate the actions of all Allied forces in Tunisia. From then onwards, the campaign was, relates General Jackson, 'his concept, carried out under his direction and in his way. He earned his title Lord Alexander of Tunis.' It was Alexander's intention to employ his armies in what he liked to call a 'two-fisted assault'. The Battle of Medenine, however, completed his belief, according to Jackson, that his 'fists were unequal in striking power. Eighth Army – his right – could be relied on to find its mark and inflict serious damage; First Army was less experienced, lacked confidence, and its thumb – II US Corps – was badly bruised.'

This was particularly unfortunate because II US Corps was on paper ideally placed to sever the links between Messe's First Italian Army and Fifth Panzer Army – now under von Vaerst's command – by advancing either eastward through the Faid or Maknassy Passes to the port of Sfax, or south-eastward to attack the Gabes Gap from the rear. In practice, though, Alexander did not feel that it was yet capable of doing either. As a first essential therefore, he proposed, as he states in his Official Despatch, 'to get Eighth Army through the Gabes Gap into the flat country' where it would form a continuous front with the remainder of his Army Group. First Army would assist in this aim but only by drawing Axis troops away from Eighth Army, not by cutting off Messe's retreat.

Alexander's decision provides an eloquent tribute to his faith in Montgomery's men. To reach the 'flat country' of the central Tunisian plain, Eighth Army would not only have to overcome the defences in the Gabes Gap but, as was seen earlier, before it could even reach these, it would have to get past the Mareth Line, once designed to protect the French from the Italians but now, ironically, protecting an army that included Italians from an army that included a contingent of Fighting French. And Alexander's own opinion, declares Jackson, was that 'the combination of the Mareth Line and the Gabes Gap gave Messe a stronger position than Rommel had defended at El Alamein'.

Furthermore, as at El Alamein, Eighth Army had to carry out its task quickly. In Russia, the Germans, recovering with astonishing rapidity from the disaster at Stalingrad, were again embarking on an offensive which would culminate in their recapture of Kharkov on 15 March. The Western Allies were in consequence beset with demands that they should relieve the pressure on the Russians by an invasion of Italy. It had already been appreciated that if meaningful progress was to be made in that mountainous country before the approach of winter, the preliminary move – the occupation of Sicily – must take place in July. To prepare for this adequately, it was essential that the Axis bridgehead in Tunisia should be eliminated without delay.

No wonder therefore that when Lieutenant General Bedell Smith, Eisenhower's Chief of Staff, had visited Montgomery in Tripoli towards the end of February, he had been both amazed and delighted to learn that the Eighth Army Commander was confident that his men could reach Sfax by 15 April. As Montgomery relates in his *Memoirs*, Bedell Smith had promised that if this could really be done, then 'General Eisenhower would give me anything I liked to ask for.' It was not a wise offer. Montgomery had immediately requested that a Flying Fortress, complete with its American crew who would remain on the US pay-roll, should be provided for his use for the rest of the war. When Eighth Army duly performed its part of the bargain, its commander promptly claimed his 'prize' and insisted that Eisenhower should 'pay up'.[1]

'Perhaps no other act,' states Nigel Hamilton, 'would so typify Monty's monstrous insensibility to the problems of coalition warfare than this insistence on the payment of an unwritten bet' which would involve the hapless Eisenhower in difficult explanations to the US War Department. Brooke understandably was most displeased by the incident but to their great credit, both Eisenhower and Bedell Smith swallowed any indignation they may have felt in recognition of the achievement which the payment of the 'bet' acknowledged. Indeed the real point of the whole story is surely that when Bedell

Smith made his offer, he simply did not expect that he would ever have to make it good. It is not surprising that he is reported to have said that to serve under Montgomery would be a great privilege for anyone, but to serve over him was hell!

In the series of actions by which Eighth Army would win a Flying Fortress for its leader – and a title for its Army Group Commander – it would deservedly be assisted by the effects of its previous triumphs, particularly its capture of Tripoli. Those who had believed that Tripoli must be held for as long as possible if Tunisia was to be properly secured were about to have their views justified. Despite heavy air attacks the port was now providing a suitable base for Eighth Army, eliminating the long tenuous supply lines which had proved such a handicap in the recent past. As a result, for the first time since Alamein, Eighth Army was able to build up its forces to their full potential.

Thus X Corps was back again in Eighth Army's battle-line. It brought its 1st Armoured Division with it, while 7th Armoured was now placed under its control as well. 4th Indian and 50th (British) Divisions also arrived as re-inforcements for XXX Corps, though neither was at its full strength of three brigades, the latter possessing only 69th and 151st Brigades and the former 5th and 7th Indian Brigades. And then there was 'Force L' – the initial standing for General Philippe Leclerc, who on 1 February had joined Eighth Army at Tripoli at the head of over 3,200 French and colonial troops, volun-teers all, who had marched a thousand miles over the desert from Chad in French Equatorial Africa to place themselves under Montgomery's orders.

Although the Eighth Army Commander was not normally a great admirer of his French allies, he immediately, says General Richardson, 'recognized' Leclerc's 'quality'. Leclerc 'became "one of us"' and was given 'what proved to be a highly critical role in the Mareth battle, which we were already beginning to plan'.

One aspect of that planning had taken place even before Eighth Army captured Tripoli. Back in December 1942, Montgomery, once more looking 'one battle ahead' – in this case rather more than one – had sent the Long Range Desert Group to check on the possibilities of carrying out operations to the west of the Matmata Hills. Its patrols had reported that movement in this area, though difficult, was perfectly feasible, and Lieutenant Nicholas Wilder had discovered south-west of Foum Tatahouine, a 'gap' in the hills which would henceforth bear his name and provide the route by which forces could be moved westward from the coastal area.

These discoveries, though, by no means solved Eighth Army's problems. A force moving through Wilder's Gap and then northward along the edge of the Matmata Hills would still have to make a detour of some 150 miles over extremely difficult, waterless terrain. Then when it reached the northern end of the hills, it would have to turn eastward to the south of the Djebel Tebaga

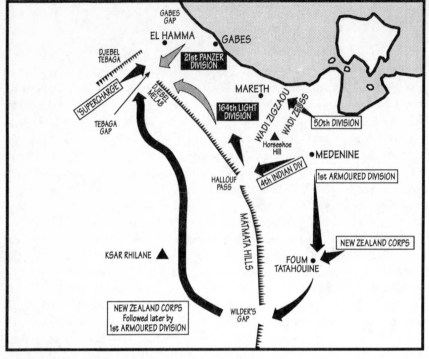

Map 10: The Battle of the Mareth Line.

into a narrow valley which could be a death trap if properly defended. Nonetheless, the knowledge that an outflanking movement was possible gave flexibility to Eighth Army's planning and dictated the 'highly critical role' that Leclerc would be asked to play.

For when 7th Armoured Division headed for Medenine in mid-February 1943, Leclerc's Fighting Frenchmen advanced also, guarding its left flank. Their objective was Wilder's Gap, through which they passed to take up station to the west of the Matmata Hills, thus ensuring that the way would be clear for use by Eighth Army. Then when Alexander called for increased pressure by Eighth Army to help ease the situation at Kasserine, 'Force L' pushed on to the craggy massif of Ksar Rhilane due west of Foum Tatahouine and about a third of the way forward from Wilder's Gap towards the Djebel Tebaga.

At Ksar Rhilane, Leclerc's men were dangerously isolated, and Montgomery, who had already made a personal gift of a new battle-dress for their leader, ensured that they received reinforcements, including a pair of Sherman tanks, sixteen 6-pounder anti-tank guns and the British 159th Light AA Battery. It was a wise decision for on 10 March, in the curiously casual words of the Official History, 'Major von Luck with a group of reconnaissance units, reinforced by tanks, investigated this area.'

It was not a move welcomed by Leclerc but he remained admirably unperturbed, despite also suffering heavy attacks from the Luftwaffe which inflicted losses of men and material. Fortunately, although Eighth Army was too far away to assist, Leclerc as 'one of us' enjoyed the support of Eighth Army's companions in arms of the Desert Air Force. The Kittyhawks of No. 112 Squadron which provided fighter cover suffered heavily, shooting down two 109s but losing seven machines with six of the pilots killed or captured; but the Kittybombers of Nos. 250 and 260 Squadrons made a highly effective attack, and the anti-tank Hurricane IIDs of No. 6 Squadron made repeated highly effective attacks on the German ground forces, destroying or damaging six tanks, five half-tracks, thirteen armoured cars, ten lorries, a gun and a wireless van.

The enemy, not surprisingly, retired. Messages of congratulation, from Tedder, from Montgomery, and, presumably with especial fervour, from Leclerc, poured in for the successful pilots – but it seems scarcely likely that they had any idea of the importance of the precedent which they had just set.

After its experiences at Medenine and Ksar Rhilane, First Italian Army had no further intention of resuming the offensive, but wisely preferred to stand firm behind the fixed fortifications of the Mareth Line. This ran south-westward for 22 miles from the coast to the Matmata Hills. Its main feature was a natural one, the Wadi Zigzaou which varied from sixty to 200 feet in width and was some twenty feet deep. Its sides had been artificially steepened and on its far bank an anti-tank ditch had been cut – all of which factors combined to make it, in de Guingand's words, a most 'horrible obstacle'. Parallel to the Wadi Zigzaou and about halfway between it and the Wadi Zessar, which Eighth Army had defended in the Battle of Medenine, was another useful barrier, the Wadi Zeuss; this formed the outer perimeter of the Axis defences. Between the Wadi Zigzaou and the Wadi Zeuss were numerous strongpoints, the chief of which, in the centre of the position, was at Sidi el Guelaa, or as the British called it for obvious reasons, Horseshoe Hill.

It was beyond the Wadi Zigzaou, however, that the Mareth Line was at its most formidable. Here the original French defences had been greatly strengthened by the Germans and consisted of a maze of mutually supporting artillery posts, connected by trenches, protected by barbed wire, and backed up by fortresses as much as 1,200 yards long by 400 yards deep which were capable of holding a full battalion. The areas around the defences and the bed of the Wadi Zigzaou were densely packed with mines, 100,000 anti-tank and 70,000 anti-personnel, plus innumerable booby traps.[2] And holding the defences were most of Messe's infantrymen: nearest to the coast the Young Fascist Division which contained, says de Guingand, 'the best of the Italian troops' and which had been further strengthened by German detachments; on its right flank the Trieste Division; then in the centre 90th Light; and finally La Spezia and Pistoia.

At the south-western end of the Line, the high, rugged Matmata Hills, the tracks through which had also been mined, provided further protection. They were held by 164th Light. At their northern end were Messe's remaining infantry, some seven battalions of frontier guards, known as the Saharan Group, whose task was to watch the Tebaga Gap. These were not regarded as being of particularly good quality but if it proved necessary, Messe could transfer reinforcements to this area much more easily than his opponents who had to cover far greater distances. In addition, the Tebaga Gap was only four miles wide, was protected by an anti-tank ditch, minefields and a series of strongpoints and, as the RAF Official History records, was 'bristling with enemy guns'. In all First Italian Army contained some 80,000 men, about 450 field or medium guns and 720 anti-tank guns, over 300 of them German and seventy-six of them 88mms.

As for the Axis armour, 15th Panzer was stationed in close support about five miles north of Mareth. It had only thirty-two gun-armed tanks fit for action but fourteen of these were the 'murderous Mark IV Specials', superior to any in Eighth Army, and ten more were Mark III Specials. 10th Panzer had moved north to watch II US Corps but 21st Panzer was in General Reserve at Gabes from which it could direct its seventy tanks to counter a break-through by Eighth Army at either Mareth or Tebaga as required.

Eighth Army, as its critics eagerly relate, had a considerable superiority in numbers: 160,000 men, nearly 750 tanks, nearly 700 field or medium guns and over 1,000 anti-tank guns, three-quarters of which were 6-pounders. In the air, the Allies had an even greater advantage, for whereas their enemies could be supported by only about 100 German and sixty Italian warplanes – and only some two-thirds of these were serviceable – the Desert Air Force was now stronger than ever and equipped for every possible task.

Thus for reconnaissance duties there were now three full squadrons: No. 680 Squadron RAF, upgraded from No. 2 Photographic Reconnaissance Unit, and flying Spitfires and Hurricanes, mainly the former; No. 40 Squadron SAAF which in early March had begun to re-equip and also now possessed more Spitfires than Hurricanes; and No. 60 Squadron SAAF with its Baltimores, plus a pair of precious Mosquitos which had joined it on 4 February in response to a personal request to Churchill made by Montgomery. In the light bomber role, the Desert Air Force still contained its two veteran Boston squadrons, three squadrons of Baltimores and four of Mitchells; while for heavy bombers the Allies had their Wellingtons and Halifaxes operating from further afield.

It was in fighters and fighter-bombers though, that the Desert Air Force had made its greatest advance. The Hurricanes of No. 73 Squadron still shouldered the night-fighter duties, but in the day-fighter role there were now the equivalent of six squadrons equipped with Spitfires, the latest arrivals adding to the wide variety of nationalities fighting in North Africa, namely

No. 417 Squadron from the Royal Canadian Air Force, recently moved to the front from Egypt, and the Polish Fighting Team, a hand-picked volunteer unit attached to No. 145 Squadron but led operationally by Squadron Leader Skalski, a distinguished officer who would later become the first Pole to command a British squadron. There were also no less than sixteen Kittyhawk or Warhawk squadrons, all now used in the fighter-bomber role, while the Hurribombers of No. 241 Squadron would join them on 23 March. And finally there were the anti-tank Hurricane IIDs, the 'winged tin-openers' of No. 6 Squadron RAF.

Nonetheless this superiority in numbers was certainly not sufficient to guarantee success against defences which were naturally far stronger than those at Alamein and had been artificially increased in all the hideous ways previously described. Moreover the Axis commanders now enjoyed the benefits of good Intelligence work. Whereas at Alamein the defenders had been caught completely by surprise, on this occasion intercepted signals had given them advanced warning of Eighth Army's outline plans for the operation in general and they had exact knowledge of one of the preliminary moves, having captured a British artillery officer who was carrying a map setting out full details of the supporting fire plan.

These preliminary operations began on the night of 16th/17th March, when XXX Corps advanced across the Wadi Zeuss. The main movement by 50th and 51st Divisions, assisted by the Valentines of 50th Royal Tanks and by 'Scorpions' to help clear a way through the minefields, was successful in driving the enemy back to the Wadi Zigzaou, while a diversionary raid by 4th Indian Division into the Matmata Hills also inflicted casualties without any corresponding loss. But an assault on Horseshoe Hill by two battalions from 201st Guards Brigade, 6th Grenadiers and 3rd Coldstreams, met with disaster. This was the attack about which the enemy knew all the details, and the position was protected by what Montgomery in *El Alamein to the River Sangro*, rightly calls 'most intensive minefields'. As the Guards struggled through these, they came under very heavy fire and it is greatly to their credit that, covered by a powerful artillery bombardment, they did in fact wrest almost all their objectives from the defenders, a detachment from the redoubtable 90th Light.

Unhappily so many casualties had been suffered in the process, particularly by the Grenadiers, that there was no possibility that the captured positions could be retained. They were heavily shelled by the enemy and all attempts to bring up supporting vehicles through the minefields proved unsuccessful. In the early hours of the 17th, 90th Light counter-attacked, taking over 100 prisoners, and just before dawn, the British troops withdrew over the Wadi Zeuss. The Grenadiers had lost 27 officers and 336 men killed, wounded or captured, among the wounded being their CO, Lieutenant Colonel Clive, whose conduct during the action won him a DSO; the Coldstreams' casualties were 11 officers and 148 other ranks.

It is at least pleasant to be able to record that Montgomery later wrote to Brigadier Gascoigne, apologizing for having underestimated the strength of the defence but offering the consolation that the operation had 'definitely helped the Army plan'. This statement sadly would prove more generous than accurate, though by another irony it might have been true if only Montgomery had taken to heart the warning provided. As it was, the Eighth Army Commander remained in a dangerously over-confident mood and his plan for the assault on the Mareth Line – it went by the belligerent name of Operation PUGILIST – is accordingly open to a good deal of criticism – though not by those who deride Montgomery's very thorough and realistic planning on other occasions as 'over-cautious'.

As in his assault on Tripoli, Montgomery intended to attack in the coastal area and also from the open desert – at both Mareth and Tebaga. The New Zealand Division, as the expert on outflanking operations, was entrusted with the latter task, being suitably reinforced for the purpose – indeed it was officially raised to the status of the 'New Zealand Corps'.[3] Just as 9th Armoured Brigade had formed the New Zealanders' third brigade at Alamein, so their 5th and 6th Infantry Brigades were now joined by Brigadier Harvey's 8th Armoured Brigade with about 100 Shermans and fifty Crusaders. The armoured cars of the 1st King's Dragoon Guards were also added to Freyberg's strength, as were Leclerc's 'Force L', the 111th Field Regiment and 64th Medium Regiment, Royal Artillery with a total of 112 guns, the 57th Anti-Tank Regiment, Royal Artillery with 172 guns, and the 53rd Light AA Regiment.

This considerable force, containing in all some 26,000 men and 6,000 vehicles, had assembled behind Eighth Army's lines near Foum Tatahouine by 18 March. It was supplied with enough food and water to make it self-sufficient for eleven days and carried as much ammunition as could be packed on board its transports. On the evening of the 19th, Freyberg set out and that night passed through Wilder's Gap to head northward for Ksar Rhilane.

It had originally been hoped that the existence of the New Zealand Corps could be kept concealed from the enemy; the intention had been that it would remain stationary and undetected throughout the daylight hours of 20 March, move on again during the night, and make a surprise attack on the Tebaga Gap – which Eighth Army had renamed 'Plum Pass' – on the morning of the 21st. Unfortunately his Intelligence had already warned Messe that a major force would be making for Tebaga, and by the 20th, an 'Ultra' interception had revealed to Eighth Army that its secret was out.

Montgomery therefore ordered Freyberg to abandon deception and race for Tebaga as fast as possible. Ahead of Freyberg's main force, Leclerc's men seized areas of high ground which might threaten the advance, while a detachment of British sappers with 'Force L' prepared crossing-places over the deep dry wadis that lay on Freyberg's route. This was very necessary, for even as it was, Kippenberger complains that the New Zealanders 'never did more difficult and tiring marches'. The tank-transporters were particularly liable to be bogged down, on several occasions having to unload their tanks so that these could tow them onto firmer ground. As the New Zealand Corps moved northwards, the terrain became still more difficult, an attack by American bombers did nothing to assist progress, and Freyberg was eventually forced to halt for the night of the 20th/21st March, some 10 miles short of Tebaga.

Freyberg's open advance, Montgomery tells us, 'would, I hoped, distract attention from the coastal sector'. This is an interesting statement because, with his usual reluctance to admit that all had not gone exactly 'according to plan', Montgomery would later emphasize the flanking manoeuvre and 'play down' the coastal thrust. It is true that he always intended, as with his advance on Tripoli, that if the enemy should concentrate against one of his moves he would reinforce the other, but his use of the flanking operation to 'distract attention' strongly suggests that initially at least he regarded it as very much the less important of the two. Kippenberger, who attended a conference where Montgomery explained his plan to officers down to the rank of lieutenant colonel, also states that his clear understanding was that Montgomery 'expected the frontal attack to be decisive'; while the Official History unhesitatingly calls the offensive against Mareth 'the main attack' as compared with 'the New Zealand Corps' subsidiary flanking manoeuvre'.

That the coastal thrust was more important seems certain when it is appreciated that Operation PUGILIST was intended to do far more than just break through the Mareth Line. It will be recalled how Eighth Army had captured the Buerat position, stormed the Homs–Tarhuna defences before the enemy could organize resistance here, and taken Tripoli, all in one continuous series of encounters. Montgomery now aimed to repeat this success, this time capturing the Mareth Line, storming the Gabes Gap before the enemy could organize resistance here, and taking Sfax, the port of Sousse further to the north, and perhaps even Tunis, all in one continuous series of encounters. Yet to do so, he really needed to break through with his coastal attack. As the Official History points out: 'A successful quick thrust' at Mareth 'would have split open the position and crippled the defence, and so would have given the considerable forces of exploitation, and the outflanking New Zealand Corps their opportunity.'

The trouble was that the 'forces of exploitation' were too 'considerable', while the attackers of the Mareth Line were not strong enough. XXX Corps had three infantry divisions available, yet only 50th Division was detailed for the attack, and although it would be backed up by the fire of thirteen field and three medium regiments, the only armoured formation in support was 50th Royal Tanks, containing just fifty-one Valentines. 51st Highland and 4th Indian Divisions were held in reserve with the intention of launching them through the bridgehead once this had been secured, while X Corps, with 1st and 7th Armoured Divisions under command, was also kept back, 'ready' in the words of its leader, Horrocks, 'to exploit success towards Gabes'.

Both Montgomery and Leese seem in fact to have paid far more attention to the plans for exploiting success than to those for achieving success. As a result, states the Official History, 50th Division's commander, Major General Nichols, 'was left largely to his own devices'. This was hardly a wise or a fair course of action considering that the division had played only a small part at Alamein and had seen little action thereafter; though Nichols did entrust the initial assault mainly to his more experienced brigade, the 151st.[4]

In other words, Montgomery had committed exactly the same error that Auchinleck had made so often during his infamous five attacks in July 1942: he had been so obsessed with the uses to which victory could be put that he had forgotten the need to win the victory first. This might seem the more surprising as Montgomery had steadfastly avoided this mistake in the past and should have been well aware of the strength of the Mareth Line – apart from the warning given by the action at Horseshoe Hill, he had been well served by offensive patrols, by air reconnaissance, in particular that of 'his' two Mosquitos, and by invaluable advice from a number of French officers, including Captain Paul Mezan, a former Garrison Engineer at Mareth.

'Fame, adulation and a growing feeling of infallibility after Medenine,' declares Nigel Hamilton sternly, had 'all contributed' to Montgomery's over-confidence. So no doubt they had, but the main cause of that over-confidence was quite different – it arose from the fact that Eighth Army had once again received misleading Intelligence from 'Ultra'.

Thus 'Ultra' interceptions had revealed that some of the leading enemy commanders, chiefly Rommel and his successor at the head of Army Group Afrika, von Arnim, favoured a withdrawal from Mareth to the Gabes Gap or even as far as Enfidaville. This tended to suggest a lack of resolution which was quite contrary to reality, since in practice Hitler, Kesselring and even Messe had no intention whatever of abandoning the Mareth Line without a struggle. 'Ultra' had also revealed the anxieties of the Italians in particular, which had given Montgomery what Ronald Lewin in his book on this subject, calls 'a well-founded contempt for the defensive will of the Italians' – except that in many cases that contempt was not in fact well-founded.

'It is difficult not to feel,' Lewin concludes, that it was principally 'the authority of "Ultra"' which led Montgomery to believe 'that an abrupt assault by his infantry, supported by generous gunfire, would "bounce" the Young Fascist and Trieste Divisions into a rapid retreat'. It is indeed, and it may again be noticed that the existence of 'Ultra', far from guaranteeing Eighth Army's success, thus proved a handicap which would bring Eighth Army perilously close to failure.

Eighth Army was also hampered by its usual ill-luck with the weather. This all but prevented the Desert Air Force from carrying out the preliminary operations planned for 19 March, and though happily better conditions prevailed on the 20th, when the coastal thrust was due to commence, on subsequent days the elements would again restrict the aerial support at vital moments. Worse still, heavy rain falling on the Matmata Hills had made the Wadi Zigzaou a still more 'horrible obstacle' than the enemy had intended. It now contained a watercourse which in places was thirty feet wide and up to eight feet deep, while the ground underneath the water became soft and treacherous – increasingly difficult for vehicles to cross.

Nonetheless all went well at first. The Royal Air Force Baltimores, the South African Air Force Baltimores and Bostons, and the United States Army Air Force Mitchells kept up raids on the enemy defences all day on the 20th, while after dark, Wellingtons and Halifaxes, accompanied, as at Alamein, by Fleet Air Arm Albacores to drop flares, continued the assaults, and the Hurricanes of No. 73 Squadron, again as at Alamein, roamed ahead to look for targets of opportunity.

Meanwhile at 2230, Eighth Army's artillery opened fire on the Mareth Line and at 2345, 151st Brigade launched its attack. Ronald Lewin, perhaps feeling the need to mitigate the ill-effects of 'Ultra's' misleading information, argues that Eighth Army, 'fresh from the open spaces', was 'not suited mentally or technically for smashing its way into a stronghold', but it is not necessary to look to subsequent events at Tebaga or Wadi Akarit to refute this suggestion. The assaulting units, 8th and 9th Battalions, Durham Light Infantry, burst over the Wadi Zigzaou and by morning, despite fierce resistance, had gained a bridgehead about a mile wide and some 800 yards deep and taken a considerable number of Italian prisoners. On their left, 7th Battalion, Green Howards from 50th Division's other main formation, 69th Brigade, though under heavy fire, stormed a strong forward position threatening the Durhams' flank, and then held it in the face of repeated counter-attacks, Lieutenant Colonel Derek Seagrim, whose outstanding bravery proved an inspiration to his men throughout the action, earning a Victoria Cross.[5]

It was not the seizing of the stronghold that could not be achieved but the provision of adequate support for the men who had seized it. When the Valentines of 50th Battalion, Royal Tank Regiment moved into the Wadi Zigzaou, the first one stuck fast in the water, bringing the whole advance to a halt. The Royal Engineers, working furiously under artillery, mortar and machine-gun fire, managed to construct another route across the wadi and four tanks passed over this. They carried 'fascines', large bundles of wood, tightly bound together, about ten feet long by eight feet high, and these they dropped into the anti-tank ditch on the far side of the wadi and so were able to cross this also. Then came disaster. The next tank to arrive, in the graphic words of General Jackson, 'broke through the thin crust of the wadi floor and sank up to its turret, totally blocking the crossing'. No further vehicles reached the far bank that night or the next day.

Despite the lack of armour, the men of 151st Brigade, with the aid of further supporting attacks by the Desert Air Force's light bombers, retained and consolidated their positions during the 21st. Then at 2330, reinforced by their third battalion, 6th Durhams, and by 5th East Yorkshires from 69th Brigade, they resumed their advance, capturing five major strongpoints and further large numbers of prisoners. Meanwhile, during the day, the selfless efforts of the sappers, whose losses were very heavy, improved the crossing over the wadi sufficiently for it to be able to take vehicles again, though they could not construct more than one passage as had originally been hoped.

Indeed at this point the situation in the coastal area looked considerably brighter than that at Tebaga. During the 21st, Freyberg closed up to the entrance to the pass, while the Desert Air Force's Kittybombers and anti-tank Hurricanes attacked enemy concentrations. That night, Brigadier Gentry's 6th New Zealand Brigade pushed through minefields to rout the Saharan Group and capture a key enemy outpost at Point 201. Gentry urged that 8th Armoured Brigade should break through the Tebaga Gap forthwith but although Brigadier Harvey had no objections, 'nothing resulted' as the Official History relates, 'because Freyberg had not been enthusiastic', preferring to wait until dawn.

By then Messe had already taken action. Early on 22 March, 21st Panzer arrived from the Axis Army Reserve, being closely followed by 164th Light which Messe had transferred from the Matmata Hills. Freyberg has been accused of missing a great opportunity, but it should be noted that even if he had passed through the Tebaga Gap he would have had to face the full might of 21st Panzer in the open, and the New Zealanders, understandably enough, were still very conscious of the perils inherent in such an encounter. Yet whatever Freyberg's justification, the fact was that the defence of the pass had now come into the hands of 164th Light's commander, Major General von Liebenstein, and a typically resolute German resistance henceforth barred the New Zealand Corps from any further noticeable progress.

By contrast, at Mareth, Eighth Army, for all Lewin's comments, had in fact successfully 'smashed its way' into the 'stronghold' by dawn on 22 March, and the defenders had again suffered during the night from the attentions of the Albacores lighting the way for their Wellingtons and Halifaxes. Moreover the gallant sacrifices of the sappers had by this time cleared the way for reinforcements. Though an enemy counter-attack was a virtual certainty, it appeared that at worst Eighth Army would face an Alamein-style 'dogfight' which Montgomery rather welcomed if anything. Yet just when success seemed assured, a series of ill-judged or unlucky steps were taken which would deprive Eighth Army's soldiers of the rewards earned by their valour.

For a start, Major General Nichols, who was not nicknamed 'Crasher' for nothing, had personally crossed the wadi to encourage and hearten his men in the front line – the best place no doubt for a brave and honourable soldier but not for a divisional commander whose Headquarters was left undirected and as a result lost control of the battle.[6] The burden of command thus in practice fell on Brigadier Beak and though he was an officer of immense personal courage – the holder of a Victoria Cross – this was the first occasion on which he had directed 151st Brigade in action.

No doubt it was lack of experience which caused Beak to neglect preparations 'to receive a counter-attack with 6-pounder guns ready . . . in spite of repeated enquiries from above whether this was being done', as Montgomery later complained to Alexander.[7] Instead he employed the early hours of 22 March in bringing up the remaining Valentines of 50th Royal Tanks. Forty-two of these did pass over the wadi but they so damaged the crossing that no other vehicles, wheeled or tracked, could use it. More heavy rain then fell, making conditions still worse and preventing even the Royal Engineers from rectifying the situation. On the 22nd, Montgomery personally ordered that '6-pounder guns and machine-guns must be manhandled across the wadi at once' – but by then it was too late.

For at 1340, the tanks of 15th Panzer Division's 8th Panzer Regiment did counter-attack, backed up by the division's 115th Motorized Infantry Regiment, units of 90th Light – and the elements. Once more Eighth Army was cruelly unlucky with the weather for more heavy rain at the critical moment handicapped the British artillery and even more the Allied airmen. By one further irony, at almost this precise time near El Hamma, which lies to the north-east of the Tebaga Gap, the Hurricane IIDs of No. 6 Squadron were destroying nine tanks from 21st Panzer; but at Mareth, the Desert Air Force's light bombers which might have delivered, and were preparing for, a much more powerful blow against 15th Panzer, were grounded by the downpour.

The Valentines of 50th Royal Tanks did everything possible to resist the enemy onslaught but in vain. Much stress has been laid on the fact that only eight of them had been uprated to carry a 6-pounder, which meant that all the others were out-gunned by Messe's 10 Mark III Specials and even the eight were outgunned by the long-barrelled 75mms carried by Messe's fourteen Mark IV Specials. The British armour was thus far more genuinely inferior to that of the enemy than on most earlier occasions on which a similar excuse is put forward. Yet it was the absence of those anti-tank guns which had broken the panzers' attacks at Alam Halfa, at Alamein and most recently at Medenine, that really crippled the defence. No one was more aware of this than the armour's CO, Lieutenant Colonel Cairns, who throughout the morning of the 22nd had been pleading that anti-tank guns be sent forward – but the Wadi Zigzaou remained impassable.

By contrast the Germans did have anti-tank guns available, which as usual were handled more boldly and more brilliantly than their armour. These knocked out three Valentines before the panzers fired a shot. Throughout the day, 50th Royal Tanks kept up the fight but by nightfall, thirty Valentines had been destroyed, Cairns was dead, and his successor in command, Major Maclaren, had withdrawn the remains of his force to the edge of the wadi.

The British infantrymen were also in trouble. Three of the captured strong-points were lost again, and casualties mounted. At midnight, the Germans put in a new attack and 50th Division was once more driven back. At 0200 on 23 March, Montgomery was aroused from sleep to be told by Leese that Eighth Army's bridgehead had been virtually eliminated.

Notes

1   The Flying Fortress, plus its crew, arrived on 16 April and, says Montgomery, 'made me a thoroughly mobile general'. It was 'written off' in an accident in Sicily on 28 July, and the Americans generously provided a Dakota aircraft as a more practical replacement.

2   After the failure of Eighth Army's preliminary attack on Horseshoe Hill, which will be related shortly, it proved necessary to remove 700 mines in order to recover the bodies of some 70 casualties.

3   No subordinate divisional commander was appointed, however, and Freyberg continued to exercise direct control.

4   Although 50th Division as such had performed only a minor role at Alamein, its 151st Brigade had taken a vital and successful part in SUPERCHARGE under the command of the 2nd New Zealand Division.

5   Alas he was never to learn of the award, for he was killed on 6 April, leading a similarly gallant assault on the defences of the Gabes Gap.

6   Nichols would pay dearly for his misguided, if gallant conduct, for Montgomery would shortly replace him with Kirkman who was therefore promoted to major general.

7   Quoted in Nigel Hamilton's *Monty: Master of the Battlefield 1942–1944*.

Chapter 12

THE LEFT HOOK

On hearing this news, Montgomery's cool self-confidence deserted him for once – and paradoxically this fact is a supreme tribute to his generalship. At Alamein, when Montgomery had been awakened to hear pleas by his subordinates that his attack be called off, he had curtly refused. Almost any other commander, recalling this earlier incident, would have been tempted to think that once more all that was needed was a bit of resolution, and have insisted that 50th Division keep up its pressure. It is very much to Montgomery's credit that he realized instinctively that this time the situation was very different.

The point was that this time Montgomery was personally worried by the situation, particularly the failure to bring the 6-pounder anti-tank guns into the front line – hence the 'repeated enquiries from above whether this was being done'. For the moment he ordered Leese to hold fast in the bridgehead to the best of his ability but he clearly recognized that this could only be a temporary expedient, and at 0900, he called another conference at which he told Leese that the coastal thrust would be abandoned. During 23 March, the light bombers of the Desert Air Force made no less than ten raids against enemy positions, but these were designed to protect the British troops from further molestation, not to assist a renewed advance. That night, under cover of a heavy artillery barrage, the surviving tanks and infantrymen fell back over the Wadi Zigzaou. 151st Brigade alone had suffered some 600 casualties.

Montgomery's anxieties had already prompted him to ask Alexander whether II US Corps – now commanded by Patton – could assist him by striking at First Italian Army from the rear. As was mentioned earlier, the Americans were ideally placed to trap Messe's men either by breaking through the Maknassy Pass or by advancing from Gafsa which they had reoccupied without resistance on 17 March. Alexander did request Patton to push forward strongly in both these areas, but his doubts whether this would prove effective were quickly realized. Patton's 88,000 men were opposed by only some 1,000 Germans and 7,000 Italians, backed by the forty tanks of 10th Panzer and the obsolete Italian armour with the Centauro Division; yet a series of attacks starting on 22 March all met with failure, though at least they prevented the Axis forces resisting them from adding to the numbers facing Eighth Army.

The American assaults also greatly alarmed von Arnim, who appears to have inherited Rommel's pessimism as well as his post at the head of Army Group Afrika. Fearing that First Italian Army might be cut off as Montgomery envisaged, von Arnim issued instructions that the defenders at Mareth should begin to withdraw on the night of 25th/26th March, covered by von Liebenstein's troops at Tebaga, and be back in the defences of the Gabes Gap by the 28th.

These orders would later lead Patton, whose arrogance was certainly no less than that of any other officer of any nation, to claim that it was really he who had 'won Mareth' for Eighth Army; but his contention overlooks the point that von Arnim's views were rejected by his superiors and in particular by the unquenchable Kesselring. On the afternoon of 24 March, by which time of course 50th Division had already retired across the Wadi Zigzaou, Kesselring arrived at Messe's HQ. Here, as the Official History makes clear, he firmly 'pronounced against withdrawal'. Next day, he also 'visited the Tebaga sector and reported to von Arnim that von Liebenstein was not in immediate danger'. In addition Messe, 'encouraged by Kesselring', sent a written report to von Arnim recommending that the retirement to the Gabes Gap 'be postponed' and Tebaga 'reinforced'. Von Arnim provisionally ordered that the retirement should be delayed until the night of the 26th/27th March, but Messe's actions on the 25th scarcely indicate any intention to withdraw at all; on the contrary he now sent 15th Panzer to an area south of El Hamma, ready to reinforce 21st Panzer and 164th Light at Tebaga should the need arise. During the 25th also, Patton's final attacks were broken, thereby proving that von Arnim's fears had been groundless.

The danger to First Italian Army would in fact come not from II US Corps but from Eighth Army. When Montgomery held his conference at 0900 on 23 March, he had, as General Richardson relates, 'recovered his "poise"'. His orders to de Guingand, Leese and Horrocks, all of whom were summoned to attend, were to set in motion what Ronald Lewin would call 'the brilliant outflanking move by the New Zealanders and 1st Armoured Division which levered General Messe's army back into Tunisia'. In Eighth Army it would become known simply – and very appropriately in a battle code-named PUGILIST – as 'The Left Hook'.

In fact two moves were set in train. One was by forces from X Corps, chiefly

1st Armoured Division under Major General Raymond Briggs, through Wilder's Gap to join Freyberg. The other was by Tuker's 4th Indian Division from XXX Corps due westward into the Matmata Hills, taking advantage of the withdrawal of 164th Light to Tebaga. Its tasks were first to clear the Hallouf Pass the use of which would provide a much shorter route by which to get supplies to the forces at Tebaga, and then to head northward through the hills with the object of outflanking the Mareth Line in this area also, thereby putting still more pressure on its defenders.

When Montgomery had first learned of 50th Division's repulse at 0200 on the 23rd, he had spent more than an hour discussing with de Guingand the prospects of strengthening the New Zealand Corps. Consequently when the 0900 conference broke up, the Chief of Staff was able to begin at once to put the necessary steps in hand. There were, however, a considerable number of these, chiefly the provision of transporters for the tanks of 2nd Armoured Brigade, now once more commanded by Brigadier Fisher, which formed the cutting edge of 1st Armoured Division, and the arrangement of anti-aircraft protection. In addition, as after Alamein, there was the confusing circumstance of two different corps trying to advance over the same area.

As a result, neither 1st Armoured nor 4th Indian Division could set off until late on the 23rd. 7th Indian Brigade which was ordered to attack the Hallouf Pass from the south-west was then able to embark on its mission without further delay, but 5th Indian Brigade, the task of which was to clear the pass from the east, and 1st Armoured Division both arrived at Medenine at the same moment on converging lines of march, causing a tremendous 'traffic jam' which cost a good deal of valuable time.

Fortunately little real harm was done except to strained nerves. On 26 March, 4th Indian Division secured Hallouf Pass, though in practice the route through this was scarcely needed. Lieutenant Colonel Robert Scott had already led his 4th Battalion, 6th Rajputana Rifles northward through the hills, and the remainder of 5th Indian Brigade now followed, and was in turn followed by 7th Indian Brigade which had been much hampered by extensive minefields. Enemy resistance proved understandably slight for on 27 March, a general Axis retreat was ordered as a result of dramatic events elsewhere – ironically 4th Indian Division would probably have met with far greater opposition had it not been delayed by the 'traffic jam'. But the natural obstacles and the mines proved a more than sufficient handicap on their own and it was not until the morning of 28 March that Tuker's men emerged from the hills and successfully outflanked the Mareth Line – only to find that it had already been abandoned.

In any case the exploits of 4th Indian Division were minor compared with those of 1st Armoured Division – which, it may be added, was not the only part of X Corps to be involved in the coming action. Late on 24 March,

Horrocks, with the Headquarters staff of that corps, arrived at Tebaga. The official reason given for his presence was that now that 1st Armoured was being added to Freyberg's forces, the number of troops employed would need a corps HQ to handle them. The real reason, though, was that Montgomery had shrewdly assessed that, in the words of General Fraser, 'Freyberg had to be pushed hard, for he needed to husband New Zealand manpower and he was disinclined to take risks.' Horrocks, thrusting and enthusiastic, was, Montgomery felt, just the man for this task, though for reasons of tact, it was agreed that all messages would be sent to both Freyberg and Horrocks jointly as equal commanders.

Unfortunately this combined control made it difficult for Horrocks to overcome Freyberg's anxieties. That officer favoured a further outflanking move by 1st Armoured around the western end of the Djebel Tebaga while the New Zealanders contained the enemy in the pass. This would not only take another ten days but would mean that the two formations would be separated by an impassable mountain range. Possibly a series of 'set-piece' attacks might be made at Tebaga instead, but Freyberg estimated that these would take from five to seven days. Finally an all-out attack could be launched on the Tebaga Gap but it would probably prove costly and even this would result in further delays while the artillery and ammunition necessary to support it were brought forward.

Montgomery not only rejected the first two alternatives out of hand but made it quite clear that there was to be no delay in putting the third into effect. 'I want to speed up your thrust as much as possible,' he signalled brusquely to his two generals, 'and I think we can do a great deal to help you by heavy air bombing all night and day. To take full advantage of this you would have to do an afternoon attack with the sun behind you.'[1]

The suggestion of an attack when the afternoon sun was shining into the eyes of the defenders – much used by the Germans but never before possible for Eighth Army since this was the first time it had attacked from west to east – was also greatly favoured by Briggs, and it would accordingly be adopted by Horrocks and Freyberg. Yet they found it impossible to meet Montgomery's wish that their blow – to raise morale it was given the same code name of SUPERCHARGE as the decisive attack at Alamein – should be delivered on 25 March. It was just not possible for 1st Armoured Division to arrive before the 26th.

More alarmingly, it was clearly equally impossible to provide the additional weight of artillery which Freyberg rightly thought necessary, for several days after that. Fortunately, however, an alternative could be found. After de Guingand had left the conference on the morning of 23 March, he had held hurried consultations with the leader of the Desert Air Force. Coningham, who had been promoted to Air Marshal, was now in Algiers as the head of

North-West African Tactical Air Force, of which his former command, the Desert Air Force, formed only part. Consequently it was to his successor that de Guingand turned for aid.

Air Vice-Marshal Harry Broadhurst had begun the War as the CO of No. 111 Squadron which two years earlier had been the first RAF unit to receive Hurricanes. On 29 November 1939, he had shot down a Heinkel He 111 to gain his squadron's first victory. Promoted to Wing Commander, he had seen further action in the Battle of France, the Battle of Britain and the subsequent cross-Channel sweeps over occupied Europe, raising his total of enemy aircraft destroyed to twelve. In May 1942, he had become a Group Captain, but his rank had not prevented him from flying four sorties in a borrowed Spitfire during the raid on Dieppe on 19 August. In November, now an acting Air Commodore, he had joined the Desert Air Force as Coningham's Senior Air Staff Officer, and in February 1943, had succeeded him in command, with a further promotion to acting Air Vice-Marshal, the youngest in the RAF. De Guingand describes him as 'a delightful man to work with, and full of initiative and new ideas. He was also prepared to accept risks.'

This was just as well in view of de Guingand's proposals. In the past, the men of the Desert Air Force had of course co-operated splendidly with Eighth Army but mainly by attacking enemy positions, lines of communication or 'thin-skinned' vehicles. They were now asked to participate directly in the actual Army assault on the Tebaga Gap. Moreover, apart from the anti-tank Hurricanes, the Allied fighters and fighter-bombers had not normally come down to very low levels to make their attacks, but de Guingand felt that they should do so on this occasion because 'the cannons of the fighters might prove more deadly and disrupting to the enemy than the fighter-bombers with their bombs dropped from comparatively high altitudes.'

This was quite a favour to ask, for although the Official History proclaims that 'the technique had long been worked out by the Desert Air Force', it had certainly never been put into effect. In consequence the 'chief memories' of those who participated in the action at Tebaga, as Horrocks recalls, would be of 'our fighters and bombers screaming in at zero feet, the first time that this had been attempted in the desert'.

Nor were several important Air Force officers at all eager that the technique should be put into effect. Coningham was so concerned that he sent his Senior Air Staff Officer, Air Commodore Beamish, to warn Broadhurst that to use his Air Force in this way could result in very severe losses and the ruin of his career. There was every excuse for this view, since the sides of the Djebel Tebaga and the Djebel Melab which formed the northern point of the Matmata Hills were liberally supplied with 88s in the dual role of anti-tank and anti-aircraft guns. Yet by now co-operation between the different branches of Eighth Army had been fully achieved, and Broadhurst was not the man to allow co-operation between the services to lag behind. 'I will do it,' he promised de Guingand. 'You will have the whole boiling match – bombs and cannon. It will be a real low-flying blitz.'

Indeed for the next few days, it was the airmen who would dominate the battle – and not only those of the Desert Air Force. The ever-obliging Alexander had agreed to assist by ensuring that the Allied Air Forces in northern Tunisia should keep the Axis warplanes at bay while Broadhurst directed his whole attention towards the support of Eighth Army. On 23 March, Spitfires from 'Alexander's Air', flown by American pilots, were on patrol near Gabes when they were attacked by 109s headed by the leader of Germany's fighter force in North Africa, Major Müncheberg. That redoubtable pilot shot down the Spitfire of Captain Theodore Sweetland in flames – but it was his last success. Whether Sweetland flew his burning aircraft into the 109, or, as seems more probable, this was hit by flying debris from the Spitfire, is not known for certain, but Müncheberg crashed beside his 135th victim, and his loss undoubtedly weakened Luftwaffe morale just at the moment when the Desert Air Force began its preliminary onslaught in preparation for the breakthrough at Tebaga.

Also on the 23rd, Bostons, Baltimores and Mitchells attacked enemy positions, while the Hurribombers of No. 241 Squadron and the Kittybombers of Nos. 2 and 5 Squadrons SAAF and of No. 450 Squadron RAAF, all struck at 'thin-skinned' Axis transports near Tebaga, destroying a large number of these. Next day, the Hurribombers and Kittybombers, now joined by the anti-tank Hurricanes of No. 6 Squadron, resumed their attacks, and 164th Light lost thirty-two vehicles. The following night, the Wellingtons and Halifaxes, guided by Albacores, continued the offensive and the night-fighter Hurricanes of No. 73 Squadron were also in action, Pilot Officer Chandler shooting down a Junkers Ju 88. On the 25th, the Bostons of Nos. 12 and 24 Squadrons SAAF and the Baltimores of No. 21 Squadron SAAF, escorted by Kittyhawks from No. 260 Squadron and Spitfires from No. 145, again bombed targets in the Tebaga area, the Spitfires of No. 1 Squadron SAAF flew offensive patrols, and No. 6's Hurricane IIDs hit eleven tanks but lost six aircraft to AA fire, though amazingly not one of the pilots was injured and all returned safely in due course.

This was perhaps not an encouraging omen for the planned 'blitz' at Tebaga, but, after another night of bombing, the Desert Air Force made ready for its greatest test on the 26th. That morning, a bad dust storm prevented operations, but by 1330 the worst was over and Broadhurst's men confirmed they would be able to carry out their tasks. Arrangements were hurriedly completed whereby the exact locations of friend and foe could be given to the pilots by means of smoke or shell bursts, and Wing Commander Darwen, who had so brilliantly carried out Operation CHOCOLATE, was sent up to the front in an armoured car to radio directions to the fighter-bombers as the need arose – a technique which would develop rapidly and with outstanding success later in North-Western Europe, Italy and Burma.

There still remained the problem of whether 1st Armoured Division could arrive in time. 'Superhuman effort,' declares Montgomery, was 'expended in getting the transport across the difficult country'. The drivers of the tank-transporters, many of whom had manned long-distance lorries in peacetime, met every challenge successfully. They 'never stopped moving,' reports de Guingand, 'until they got to their destination'. The last vehicles arrived just half-an-hour before the attack was due to start. The ammunition lorries drove right up to the gun positions to unload their shells, heedless of the risk from enemy artillery, and some of the tanks are said to have come straight off their transporters to form up on their start-line. Ten had been lost during the approach march but Fisher's 2nd Armoured Brigade still contained 67 Shermans, 13 Grants and 60 Crusaders, 22 of which had been uprated to carry 6-pounders.

At 1530 on 26 March, the new Operation SUPERCHARGE began, as the Bostons of Nos. 12 and 24 Squadrons SAAF, the Baltimores of No. 21 Squadron SAAF and No. 55 Squadron RAF and the Mitchells of Nos. 83 and 434 Squadrons USAAF, coming in at very low altitude from an unexpected direction, bombed Axis positions, knocking out a number of guns and disrupting the enemy's communications systems. Close behind came the anti-tank Hurricanes of No. 6 Squadron RAF and the Kittyhawks of No. 250 Squadron RAF and No. 3 Squadron RAAF – and from then onwards the assaults of the fighters and fighter-bombers in support of Eighth Army were continuous. In just over two hours, the Desert Air Force flew 412 sorties and despite the fears expressed earlier, only one Baltimore from No. 21 Squadron SAAF and thirteen single-engined aircraft were lost – though a few more force-landed at Allied bases – and six of the pilots returned safely to their units while others survived as prisoners of war.

Under cover of the confusion which these strikes caused, the New Zealand infantry and 8th Armoured Brigade whose previous preparations had been concealed by the dust storm, moved forward: 3rd Royal Tanks followed by 6th New Zealand Brigade on the left; the Staffordshire and Nottinghamshire Yeomanry followed by 5th New Zealand Brigade on the right. Their orders were to advance 4,500 yards to a wadi, the Wadi Hernel, capturing the high ground on either flank in the process. They would be supported by the full artillery strength of the New Zealand Corps, plus two field regiments and one medium regiment which had come up from X Corps. Even so the officers of 8th Armoured referred to the attack among themselves as 'the Balaclava do', while Horrocks admits that 'they thought they were being launched on a second Balaclava, but there was no hesitation.'

Behind this initial wave came 1st Armoured Division, with 2nd Armoured Brigade in the van. Its duty was to pass through the positions gained and proceed for a further 3,000 yards. It would then halt until 2315, when the moon was due to rise, after which it would press on to El Hamma, while the New Zealanders dealt with any enemy still remaining in the Gap before rejoining it. Freyberg, who had not forgotten what had happened on earlier occasions, was still anxious. 'If we punch the hole,' he asked Horrocks, 'will the tanks really go through?' 'Yes, they will,' retorted the eager X Corps Commander, 'and I am going with them.'

At 1600, the artillery barrage opened, and at 1623, as at Alamein, it began to move forward, the tanks and infantry following closely behind it. The Axis soldiers, already shaken and disorganized by the air attacks, and handicapped by having the setting sun in their faces, offered only weak resistance at first. On the left flank, 3rd Royal Tanks, despite difficulties with mines, reached the Wadi Hernel, knocking out several guns in the process. Here Major Barker's 'C' Squadron was engaged by 21st Panzer, losing five Shermans, but the attack was beaten off and the Germans lost four Mark IV Specials. The Staffordshire Yeomanry also reached its objective for the loss of six Shermans, and indeed pressed on beyond it to seize another wadi, the Wadi Aisoub.

Only on the extreme right did the attackers meet real problems. Anti-tank guns on Point 209, a hill too steep to be climbed by the armour, destroyed three of the Nottinghamshire Yeomanry's Shermans and delayed the advance for a time. 28th Maori Battalion attacked the hill, but the savage fighting there would continue for many hours to come.

Nonetheless by 1800, the enemy defences had been torn open and 2nd Armoured Brigade, with Fisher urging: 'Speed up, straight through, no halting', was taking full advantage of the hole that had been punched. It reached the area planned at about 1930, and though clouds hid the moon, delaying a further move until about midnight, the British armour then continued its advance, and by 0210 on 27 March, von Liebenstein was ordering all his forces to fall back to El Hamma. Some units of 21st Panzer, which had been cut off by 2nd Armoured's progress, attacked it from behind but were repulsed by anti-tank guns including some of the new 17-pounder 'Pheasants'. At dawn, 15th Panzer also tried to intervene from the flank but was thrown back in disorder by the 10th Hussars, whose CO, Lieutenant Colonel Wingfield, was later awarded a DSO.

The breakthrough at Tebaga had cost Eighth Army about 600 casualties but 2,500 prisoners, all of them German, had been taken, and the Battle of the Mareth Line had been won. Isolated pockets of resistance still held out but were remorselessly subdued, the last of them being at Point 209 which fell on the evening of the 27th, after a final gallant assault led by Second

Lieutenant Ngarimu who won a Victoria Cross – posthumously, for he was shot dead in the moment of victory.

It seemed at one time that the 'Left Hook' might be able to trap the whole of Messe's First Italian Army, but it was not to be. Early on the morning of the 27th, von Liebenstein managed to gather together enough anti-tank guns to check the British armour in a defile three miles south of El Hamma. This anti-tank screen was reinforced as the day wore on and more dust storms imposed a further handicap on Horrocks who was not able to overcome the defences and was reluctant to outflank them before the New Zealanders caught up with him, which they did only in the early hours of the 28th.

Meanwhile the Axis troops in the Mareth Line were pouring back along the coastal road, covered by 90th Light, the last units of which moved out on the night of the 27th/28th. Next day, XXX Corps, attempting to pursue, was delayed by the 'usual' mines and booby traps, while further dust storms continued to hamper X Corps and the New Zealanders. On the 29th, 1st Armoured division at last captured El Hamma and the New Zealanders and both 4th Indian and 51st Highland Divisions from XXX Corps moved into the town of Gabes – but by then the survivors of First Italian Army were already falling back into the safety of the defences north of the town. Eighth Army had captured at least 7,000 prisoners, the majority of them Italians, and about the same number of Axis soldiers, Germans or Italians, had been killed or wounded. 15th and 21st Panzer and 164th Light had all been terribly mauled and the last-named had lost almost all its heavy weapons and vehicles. The Italian divisions had also suffered badly and only 90th Light had retired in good order. Moreover it seems that the enemy's confidence had again been shaken.

For the men of Eighth Army on the other hand, the battle, in particular the 'Left Hook', had increased still further their confidence in their leaders, their supporting Air Force and themselves – and with reason. 'It showed,' declared Captain Liddell Hart,

> Montgomery's capacity for flexibility in varying his thrust-point, and creating fresh leverage when checked – even better than at Alamein – although, as was his habit, he subsequently tended to obscure the credit due to him for such flexibility, the hallmark of generalship, by talking as if everything had gone 'according to plan' from the outset. In many respects Mareth was his finest battle performance in the war.[2]

General Fraser similarly considers that 'the battle demonstrated Montgomery's excellent flexibility of mind. It also once again showed his strength and will-power' – though he too deplores Montgomery's 'proneness to exaggerated claims for the nature of his successes, untouched by error or miscalculation'. De Guingand and Eighth Army's staff in general, Horrocks, Freyberg, Briggs and their subordinate commanders all did well, while Broadhurst, who was prepared to risk the wrath of his superiors and possibly his career in the cause of inter-service co-operation, is surely entitled to especial credit.

Yet none of them would deny that the greatest praise belongs elsewhere. 'Most of all,' reports Fraser, 'it (the battle) demonstrated the excellence of British troops who, from the preliminary operations on 17th March, through to 1st Armoured Division's rapid move [when movement became possible] and dashing assault on 26 March, showed a skill and energy which gave its true lustre to the day.' And it was not only the excellence of the ground troops that was demonstrated. 'Never before,' relates de Guingand, 'had our Desert Air Force given us such superb, such gallant and such intimate support.' 'Brilliant and brave work by the pilots,' declares Montgomery in his *Memoirs*, 'completely stunned the enemy.'

On 30 March, the advanced forces of Eighth Army reached the Gabes Gap which Montgomery had originally hoped to break through 'on the run' as he had the Homs–Tarhuna position. Sadly the chances of doing so without very heavy casualties had been wrecked by the initial repulse on the Mareth Line as even the eager Horrocks was quickly forced to conclude. Montgomery therefore proceeded to make preparations for another 'set-piece' battle. He has been strongly criticized for his 'caution', but not by the men whose lives were saved thereby.

For the Gabes Gap seemed designed by nature for a successful defence. It was some 15 miles in width, stretching from the sea to the salt marshes of the Chott el Fedjadj, which could be neither outflanked nor crossed. Rising abruptly from the edge of the marsh was a ridge, about 500 feet high and a mile wide, which ran north-eastward to the centre of the position where it doubled in width to form the feature called the Djebel Fatnassa, and in height to the peak of Ras Zouai, which Eighth Army knew as Point 275.

Beyond the eastern outcrop of the Djebel Fatnassa, a flat-topped hill named El Meida, there was a two-mile gap until the ridge rose once more as the Djebel Roumana, again 500 feet high and too steep to be crossed by tracked or wheeled vehicles. Then came a further small gap before the coastal sector, nearly four miles long, was reached. This was protected by the Wadi Akarit, from which Eighth Army, somewhat misleadingly, would name the coming battle; like the Wadi Zigzaou at Mareth it had been deepened, widened and mined to make it a daunting obstacle. The gaps on each side of the Djebel Roumana had been blocked as well, in their cases by wide anti-tank ditches. Both the wadi and the ditches contained considerable amounts of water after the recent rains, and while the enemy had paid less attention to the defences at Gabes than to those at Mareth, the approaches to them had been guarded

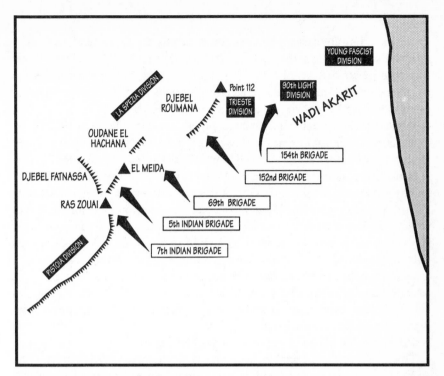

Map 11: The Battle of Wadi Akarit.

by 4,000 mines. Messe's supporting artillery included twenty-eight 88mms detailed for use solely as anti-tank guns and thirty-five more in the dual-purpose role; and although we are told that the defenders were short of ammunition, it can only be said that no one in Eighth Army appears to have noticed this deficiency.

Montgomery's first intention was that 51st Highland Division should cross the upper reaches of the Wadi Akarit and the anti-tank ditch to the west of it, while 4th Indian Division secured the Highlanders' flank by taking the Djebel Roumana. X Corps would follow up, using both 1st Armoured Division and the New Zealanders who had been demoted from their status as a corps on 31 March, and were attached to X Corps for this battle. 7th Armoured Division would remain in reserve.

Remembering what had happened at the Wadi Zigzaou, neither Tuker nor Wimberley was greatly enamoured of this plan. In addition the former had learned from night patrols, splendidly organized by the 1st Battalion, Royal Sussex Regiment, that the defenders of the Djebel Fatnassa had overestimated the difficulties of its forward slopes and had therefore sited most of their heavy weapons so as to fire east and west rather than straight ahead. Furthermore they were too few in number to hold such a large area – indeed the whole length of the front from the salt-marshes as far as the first anti-tank ditch, including Fatnassa, had been entrusted to the Pistoia Division, stiffened by what was left of von Liebenstein's shattered 164th Light. Tuker therefore persuaded first Leese, then Montgomery, that the battle should commence with a night attack on Fatnassa by 4th Indian Division, unsupported by artillery fire so as to achieve surprise. This attack has understandably attracted much high praise but the adulation heaped on Tuker and his division is in many ways unfortunate since it has distracted attention from other at least equally important aspects of the battle.

In the first place while 4th Indian Division achieved surprise because of the enemy's over-confidence in the difficulties presented by the Djebel Fatnassa, Eighth Army as a whole also achieved a more important surprise for a different reason. At the time he originally issued his plan – that is before Tuker suggested the assault on Fatnassa – Montgomery had already, in the words of Liddell Hart, taken 'the bold decision' that 'rather than wait a further week for a moon-light period', he would begin the battle 'in the dark, relying on the advantage of security to outweigh the risk of confusion'. De Guingand confirms this, stating that: 'As time was important, the Army Commander decided to attack on a dark night – with no moon. We had not attempted this before and so he hoped to obtain a measure of surprise.'

This hope, as the Official History makes clear, was happily fulfilled. The Axis leaders had not envisaged an encounter before the period of the full moon. In consequence when Eighth Army's attack began on the night of 5th/6th April, it found the Italians – though not, to their great credit, the Germans – completely unprepared. Moreover von Arnim had placed both 10th and 21st Panzer in General Reserve on 5 April. Though he ordered them to the Gabes Gap on the 6th, they were too late to take part in the battle, as a result of which only 15th Panzer was on hand to support Messe's German and Italian infantry.

The redirection of Tuker's men to Fatnassa also meant that 51st Highland Division was now compelled to carry out not only its own tasks but those previously intended for 4th Indian as well. Its 154th Brigade, covered on its right by diversionary actions on the part of 201st Guards Brigade, would strike across the anti-tank ditch to the east of the Djebel Roumana, a move that would be opposed by the Trieste Division, detachments from 90th Light, and possibly the Young Fascist Division which guarded the Wadi Akarit. 152nd Brigade in the meantime would attack at right-angles to 154th against the Djebel Roumana, defended by part of the La Spezia Division. 153rd Brigade, not surprisingly, was kept back as a reserve in case of trouble.

This would still leave a gap between Wimberley and Tuker, so to fill it Montgomery ordered up 50th Division from Mareth. The losses suffered by 151st Brigade meant that only 69th Brigade could come forward and because of the short notice given, there was no chance of bringing up 50th Division's artillery in support. 69th Brigade's task was to cross the anti-tank ditch to the west of the Djebel Roumana, defended by the rest of La Spezia. 152nd, 154th and 69th Brigades were all opposed by more enemy soldiers, more artificial defences and more heavy weapons than were the British and Indian troops commanded by Tuker. They were also to inflict greater losses on the enemy – after the battle both the Trieste and La Spezia Divisions had been so mauled that they retreated in disorder whereas Messe was able to detail Pistoia to form part of his rearguard along with his German divisions.

Not that 4th Indian Division did not play its own part brilliantly. As darkness fell on 5 April – and the night-fighter Hurricanes of No. 73 Squadron yet again set out to seek targets of opportunity – its 7th Brigade commenced its stealthy advance into enemy territory. By midnight, 1/2nd Gurkhas had taken the heights of Ras Zouai in an action made memorable by the Victoria Cross awarded to Subedar Lalbadur Thapa[3] who had captured three machine-gun posts, the last single-handed after his men had been shot down, in a display of what even the restrained Official History calls 'superhuman dash and valour'. With Ras Zouai in the hands of the Gurkhas, the men of 1st Royal Sussex struck out northwards and then eastwards and those of 4/16th Punjabis southwards to clear most of the Djebel Fatnassa by about 0400 on the 6th.

Two hours earlier, 5th Indian Brigade, led by 1/9th Gurkhas, had also headed into the hills. 1/4th Essex then moved round the flank of the anti-tank ditch between Fatnassa and the Djebel Roumana, capturing large numbers of Italian prisoners in the process, and quickly got to work preparing a crossing over the ditch.

Meanwhile at 0330, supported by a tremendous artillery barrage from some 450 guns, the main attacks had begun. 152nd Brigade broke through the forward defences, gaining the crest of the Djebel Roumana by 0615, and Point 112 at its north-eastern end by 0700. Further east, 154th Brigade thrust across the anti-tank ditch facing it and captured 2,000 Italians.

69th Brigade fared less well. Its attacking battalions, 5th East Yorkshires and 7th Green Howards, overran the enemy outposts, then passed through the minefields under cover of a bombardment provided by the New Zealand artillery. When the anti-tank ditch was reached, however, the brigade came under heavy fire from both flanks and was brought to a halt. Lieutenant Colonel Seagrim, the Mareth Line VC, was mortally wounded at the head of the Green Howards, while 5th East Yorkshires won a new VC, sadly a posthumous one, thanks to the heroism of Private Eric Anderson, a stretcher bearer who three times brought back wounded comrades under intense fire before being killed in an attempt to rescue a fourth. Not until 0935, when pressure from 4th Indian Division was beginning to tell, could 69th Brigade make further progress, but then its reserve battalion, 6th Green Howards, got over the ditch, taking 400 Italian prisoners.

Earlier at 0845, a jubilant Tuker had told Horrocks that the way was clear for X Corps to break through the enemy lines to Sfax, that there was nothing to stop it and that the end of the war in Tunisia was in sight. Horrocks notified Montgomery who gave permission for X Corps to advance at once and sent off a triumphant signal to Alexander.

Unhappily Tuker's prediction was not to be fulfilled and, in very human fashion, he would later complain bitterly that Horrocks and Briggs had missed their opportunity. Yet the character of these officers, to say nothing of their recent achievements at Tebaga, must surely give pause for consideration. In reality Tuker's hopes would be dashed because both the premises on which he had founded them were mistaken. It was not correct that the way was clear for X Corps to break out. Beyond the crossing won by 1/4th Essex was another line of hills, the Oudane el Hachana, and it was not until 0935 that this could be attacked by 4/6th Rajputana Rifles. That attack took 1,000 Italian captives, relieved much of the pressure on the suffering 69th Brigade, and won a DSO for the battalion commander, Lieutenant Colonel Robert Scott. But it achieved success too late to prevent Horrocks from feeling – rightly – that Tuker's optimism had been premature, and, no doubt for that reason, there was then a further delay while X Corps waited for the situation to become more clear.

Then when 1st Armoured Division did move up to join the advanced elements of 4th Indian at about noon, it was quickly discovered that there were in fact obstacles to its progress. These were 88mm anti-tank guns, backed by a number of field guns sited in protected positions north of the Djebel Roumana – which were still killing some of Tuker's men four hours later – and they were soon to be supported by some tanks from 15th Panzer. It may be argued that 1st Armoured should have rushed the anti-tank guns, but this was not a practice which was recommended by the lessons of the past, and in any event the situation of the Allied infantry was by this time rapidly changing for the worse.

Because by late morning, the Axis reserves, in particular the main part of 90th Light, had begun a series of counter-attacks which, it may be noted, fell mainly on the unlucky 51st Highland Division. 152nd Brigade was forced off the crest of the Djebel Roumana; captured it again; was driven off it again; and once more regained it. Wimberley sent 5th Battalion, the Black Watch from 153rd Brigade to assist, and the key localities remained in the Highlanders' hands. Across the anti-tank ditch to the east, the fighting was, if possible, still more desperate, for here 15th Panzer as well as 90th Light was taking part in the battle. All afternoon and into the evening, 154th Brigade held the enemy back, its efforts being crowned and symbolized by the

Victoria Cross awarded to Lieutenant Colonel Lorne Campbell, the CO of 7th Battalion, Argyll and Sutherland Highlanders.

That a Victoria Cross was gained by each of the three Infantry Divisions most involved provides the final proof that the Battle of Wadi Akarit was won not by any particular formation but by Eighth Army as a whole. It had lost some 600 men killed and perhaps 2,000 wounded, and 32 tanks had been destroyed or damaged. It had taken 7,000 prisoners, though almost all were Italians, had temporarily destroyed the Trieste and La Spezia Divisions as effective fighting units and had exhausted even the dauntless 90th Light. On the night of 6th/7th April, First Italian Army withdrew, though Eighth Army did not realize this until next morning since Messe had cleverly covered his retreat with local thrusts, chiefly against 69th Brigade. The Allied airmen, however, harassed the enemy throughout the hours of darkness, with Wellingtons and the flare-dropping Albacores again seeking out targets, and Flying Officer Henderson of No. 73 Squadron shooting down a Junkers Ju 88.

On the 7th, the Desert Air Force once more saw combat, though the anti-tank Hurricanes of No. 6 Squadron suffered severely. This was the last appearance of this unit in the campaign and it may be worthwhile to summarize its achievements. In the course of the fighting in Tunisia the squadron had claimed the destruction of forty-six tanks as well as many other vehicles, but attacking as it did at very low level it inevitably attracted every kind of anti-aircraft fire and during this same period the squadron lost twenty-five machines. Mercifully, and astonishingly, only four pilots died, but this loss-rate provides a true measure of the dangers which they had to face and gladly did face in support of Eighth Army.

The soldiers of Eighth Army were also in action on the 7th, as they moved triumphantly out of the Gabes Gap, 51st Highland Division taking the coast road, 1st Armoured and 2nd New Zealand Divisions guarding the inland flank, and 7th Armoured Division advancing in the centre. There were a number of clashes with enemy rearguards, the wretched Pistoia Division incurring very heavy losses, but in the main the Axis forces were intent only on retreat. The garrisons in the Eastern Dorsale fell back with them and on 7 April, the 12th Lancers made contact with Patton's II US Corps. Thereafter Eighth Army was handicapped mainly by the almost embarrassing numbers of prisoners it was taking – they were coming in at the rate of 1,000 every day.

On 9 April, 7th Armoured Division caught up with and mauled 15th Panzer at Agareb to the west of Sfax. Next day, Sfax fell and Montgomery claimed his Flying Fortress. The day following, Eighth Army overran some twenty Axis landing grounds and linked up with IX Corps from First Army at Kairouan south-west of Sousse. On the 12th, it captured Sousse, and by the evening of the 13th, after covering 150 miles, it had completed its conquest of the central plain and, as even the ever-optimistic Kesselring accepted, 'the end of the Tunisian campaign was in sight.' The remaining bridgehead, he tells us, had 'insufficient depth' and could be subjected to 'concentrated air and sea attacks on ports and airfields' under which 'our supply lines and accordingly whole resistance would break down within a few days.'

This indeed was the exact position. The capture of the ports of Sfax and Sousse not only provided advanced bases for the light craft of the Royal Navy and the transports that were supplying Eighth Army but robbed the Axis powers of their use. Their convoys were therefore restricted to a narrow funnel leading to Tunis and Bizerta and this quickly became a hunting-ground for the submarines from Malta and the bombers from North Africa, increasingly large numbers of which came from the United States Army Air Force.

The consequences were inevitable. In November 1942, the Italian Navy and merchant marine had delivered 90,000 tons of food, fuel, tanks and guns to Tunisia without loss. Thereafter casualties had mounted but the Italian seamen with praiseworthy fortitude had continued their efforts and for the next three months the tonnage received had varied between 60,000 and 75,000. Even in March 1943, 43,000 tons had come in by sea. But in April, over half the vessels making for Tunisia were sunk and only some 27,000 tons of supplies and 2,500 troops reached their destination, while in the first few days of May, some three-quarters of the cargoes sent went to the bottom and only 2,000 tons passed safely over what had become known as 'the death route'.

In an attempt to compensate for the crippling of their seaborne traffic, the Axis leaders turned to their transport aircraft, but their efforts were thwarted almost before they had begun. The capture of their landing grounds in central Tunisia meant that the Axis warplanes had to be grouped together on their few remaining airfields. Here they were exceptionally vulnerable to Allied air raids which were made more effective by the use of the recently developed small fragmentation bomb. As a result the enemy air forces were rapidly brought to the point where they could not possibly mount a challenge to the Allied attacks on 'thin-skinned' vehicles, on supply-dumps – and on the Axis aerial transports.

Already on 5 April, a major attempt to interrupt the Axis airborne supply-line had commenced. Code-named Operation FLAX, it had achieved useful results even before Eighth Army overran the central Tunisian airfields, but thereafter its successes were spectacular. The Junkers Ju 52s had managed to deliver 8,000 tons of supplies during March. They still managed to deliver 5,000 tons during April as well as a fair number of troops, but at the cost of losses so heavy as to deal, in the words of the RAF Official History, 'a grievous blow' not merely to the Axis powers' 'hopes in Tunisia but to their whole future prospects of success elsewhere'; reducing their transport fleets, 'so potent an asset at the beginning of the war', to a factor 'of little account'.

The destruction, caused mainly by the Kittyhawk and Warhawk squadrons of the Desert Air Force, reached its culmination in the 'Palm Sunday massacre' of 18 April. On that day, four American units, the 64th, 65th, 66th and 314th Squadrons, shot down twenty-four Junkers Ju 52s, besides causing thirty-five more to crash-land on the coast – five of these were later finished off by the Hurricanes of No. 73 Squadron. Next day, the Kittyhawks of Nos. 2 and 5 Squadrons SAAF destroyed eight Italian transport aircraft and badly damaged four more. Finally on the 22nd, the Kittyhawks of Nos. 4 and 5 Squadrons SAAF sighted some twenty Messerschmitt Me 323s, huge, six-engined transports, each carrying ten tons of petrol, sent sixteen of them blazing into the sea and for all practical purposes ended the Axis attempts to replenish their forces in Tunisia by air.

For the men of Army Group Afrika the future was now only too clear. The decimation of the Junkers Ju 52s and the dominance of the Allied Navies and Air Forces over the waters around Tunisia meant that almost certainly they could not be evacuated even had Hitler altered his fixed refusal to permit this course of action. They had therefore to fight or to surrender, and if they fought they would face a situation far worse than any they had previously experienced. Their ammunition was dangerously low, their fuel was so restricted that they could carry out only limited manoeuvres, they were almost without protection from the air, and von Arnim would later tell Paul Carell that: 'Even without the Allied offensive I should have had to capitulate by the 1st of June at the latest because we had no more to eat.' Such were the consequences of Eighth Army's campaign in central Tunisia.

On 7 April that campaign, de Guingand tells us, had 'cost me and many others, a very dear friend'. Brigadier Frederick Kisch, Eighth Army's brilliant, inventive and much-loved Jewish Chief Engineer, who had served in the Desert from the start of the fighting there, was killed by a mine while examining the defences of the Wadi Akarit. In war, even more than other human activities, no success is ever achieved without sacrifice.

Notes

1   The alternative plans and Montgomery's signal can be found in the Official History.

2   Liddell Hart does rebuke Montgomery for his original attempt to break through near the coast and for 'disclosing' his 'desert manoeuvre', the flanking attack, prematurely. In reality the 'desert manoeuvre' was not disclosed prematurely as it was already known to the enemy. Certainly the coastal thrust had not been well

planned – mainly because of the misleading information given by 'Ultra' – but this in no way qualifies the praise due to Montgomery for his subsequent flexibility.

3 A Subedar was a senior 'Viceroy's Commissioned Officer'. These men, all Indians or Gurkhas, were roughly akin to the warrant officers of the British Army but enjoyed the additional privilege of being saluted by their soldiers, though not by the British troops.

Chapter 13

THE FINAL CONQUESTS

It was just eight months since Montgomery had taken charge of Eighth Army. During that time his soldiers had first defeated their enemy's last and best chance of reaching the Nile while Malta was still unconquered, at Alam Halfa; then ensured that Malta never would be conquered, at El Alamein. Then they had 'swept across the breadth of Africa'. In a week they had reconquered Egypt. In three months they had conquered Libya. In two-and-a-half months more they had conquered a good three-quarters of Tunisia and had doomed two Axis armies. And in the immediate future some of Eighth Army's units under one of Eighth Army's leading commanders would strike the final blow that ended the North African campaign. The days of the 'Djebel Stakes' and the 'nonsenses of July' must have seemed a world away.

During that time also, the soldiers of Eighth Army had won seven battles, two on the defensive, four on the offensive, and the most famous on what can only be called the defensive offensive since they had gained their victory not by their own attacks but by their successful repulse of enemy counter-attacks. It seems sad therefore that all except Alamein have tended to be forgotten all, even Alamein, have tended to be belittled. The fashionable appears to be that it was easy for Eighth Army to achieve its conquest it now had the superior numbers and the superior equipment cessors had lacked.

Such suggestions are grossly unjust. In sheer numbers did have the advantage throughout the period of its done throughout the period of its ordeals. Indeed on which all else depended, 'the strength of th even balance than it was either before or l increased the number of his German div independent parachute brigade; who ha

Italian divisions, the Folgore; who had doubled the number of his flak regiments with their 88mms; who had at last received the 'murderous Mark IV Specials'; whose Mark III Specials had more than doubled in number from those available in June, more than quadrupled in number from those available in July. No wonder he was confident that Alam Halfa would be his 'decisive battle'. And even in later encounters, Eighth Army would never have the overwhelming weight of numbers in its favour that it had done under Auchinleck in July.

Nor did Eighth Army enjoy a qualitative superiority of weapons during the period of its conquests. On the contrary, while the Allies had had the better tanks throughout the whole of Auchinleck's rule as C-in-C, Middle East, in August 1942, the arrival on the battlefield of the Mark IV Specials gave the Germans a tank which was superior to all on the Allied side and would remain so despite the later advent of the best of the Allied tanks, the Shermans. Eighth Army's disadvantage was again of course at its greatest at Alam Halfa when the Shermans had not yet reached the front line.

The German 88mm anti-tank guns had been superior to any that the British could find throughout the days of Eighth Army's ordeals – and they remained superior until the first few 'Pheasants' arrived at the time of Medenine. The only difference was that at Alam Halfa, Alamein and the Mareth Line, the Axis commanders had more than, and at Wadi Akarit almost, twice the number of 88mms that had been present during CRUSADER, three times the number that had been present at 'First Alamein'.

It should also be emphasized that throughout its conquest of North Africa, Eighth Army had had to overcome problems not experienced by its predecessors. Its supply-line had to stretch further than ever before at the time of its victory at El Agheila, and even further still at the time of its final thrust to Tripoli. At Medenine also, Eighth Army's supply-line was far from adequate, a fact which makes the admirable defensive preparations it carried out in an astonishingly short space of time all the more remarkable.

In addition, when Auchinleck had launched his attacks in July 1942, the ʾemy had had no opportunity to prepare adequate defences, while during ᵁSADER he could outflank the defences altogether through the open ᵜ For that matter Rommel had enjoyed the same advantage during his -offensive after CRUSADER and at Gazala.

ʾrast when Eighth Army took the offensive at Alamein in October ᵡis position could not be by-passed and was protected by half-a- and all the hideous devices of the 'Devil's Gardens'. At El ᵗssible to avoid the defences but only by crossing terrain worse ᵗ Eighth Army or *Panzerarmee Afrika* had yet encountered. ʾine could be outflanked without too much difficulty, but ᵗ later left even the tough, experienced New Zealanders 'speechless'; while the Homs–Tarhuna escarpment was only mastered because Eighth Army moved too quickly for Rommel to offer adequate resistance there. At Mareth, Eighth Army was opposed by long-prepared fixed defences, the only way round which led to a 'bottleneck' so dangerous that it was feared an attack through it would be 'a second Balaclava'. And finally in the Gabes Gap Eighth Army faced a formidable natural barrier which it had to assault head-on. Only superb troops could have surmounted such a series of difficulties.

But then the men of Eighth Army had always been superb troops. All they had lacked had been 'a clearly defined purpose and a leader'. They 'got both in Montgomery'. His critics have referred to him slightingly as 'a superlative actor' or 'a great showman', and certainly some aspects of his attempts to restore morale when he arrived in the Desert are open to such complaints. These were, however, unimportant, in fact largely irrelevant, compared with the actions which really did restore morale: first, his cancellation of all previous plans for withdrawals to reserve positions, whether within the Alamein defences or outside the combat-zone altogether; next, his victory at Alam Halfa, won in just the way he had foretold and as a result of precisely those alterations which he had made to the previous plans.

Moreover Montgomery made other contributions to success at least as significant as his restoration of morale, vital though that was. He welded the different branches of Eighth Army into one integrated whole, and added to it the close co-operation of 'his' Air Force. He displayed great strategical insight as demonstrated by his ability to think 'one battle ahead'. Most of all perhaps, in his seven victories he justified the opinion of Brooke that he was 'without question the best tactical commander in the [British] Army'.[1]

It might indeed be queried whether any mere actor or showman would have proved capable in just over a fortnight of transforming a plan which 'might almost have been written for Rommel's express benefit' into one which provided the basis for the victory of Alam Halfa. Or of devising those 'crumbling' operations against the enemy infantry at Alamein which compelled the enemy armour to risk crippling losses in counter-attacks and at the same time made the enemy anti-tank guns less effective. Or of showing that combination of ruthless resolution and flexibility of mind which then saw Alamein through to its successful conclusion. Or of making the imaginative move of 'grounding' one corps and using it to provide supplies to the front for the advance on Tripoli. Or of thrusting past the Homs–Tarhuna defences before these could be organized properly. Or of winning the flawless defensive battle of Medenine. Or of executing the 'Left Hook' which so brilliantly redeemed the initial failure at Mareth. Or of overcoming the positions in the Gabes Gap – according to Rommel the most formidable natural obstacle in North Africa – in less than twenty-four hours.

Brigadier Sir Edgar Williams certainly thinks otherwise. Williams is frequently reported as hating the Army and although this was not the case he had no intention of making it his career and he was very far from being respectful of its senior officers. He was also well aware of the advantages and deficiencies of 'Ultra'. His judgement: 'Montgomery was the best British field-commander since Wellington.'

Alexander also has often received less credit than he deserves. Despite his great charm, he too was a forceful personality and it is interesting to note that when he arrived in Algiers in February 1943, to find a dangerous situation awaiting him, he took charge of Eighteenth Army Group prematurely, exactly as Montgomery had done with Eighth Army – perhaps on reflection Alexander felt that he had been over-obliging on that earlier occasion. It was Alexander who directed the strategy of the Tunisian campaign, and if he did not attempt to control Eighth Army's strategy during his term as C-in-C, Middle East – or its tactics in Tunisia – there was a good reason for this. He believed, states the Official History, that Montgomery was undoubtedly 'better qualified' to lead Eighth Army 'than any other British officer of his acquaintance . . . In the operations which began with El Alamein he never had cause to override his Army Commander.' This though is no criticism of Alexander; rather it is a compliment. There had been far too many attempts to control Eighth Army from Middle East Headquarters in the past.

Not that Alexander's assistance was of a purely passive kind. Montgomery, adds the Official History, 'was fortunate in having a Commander-in-Chief who understood him so well, had confidence in him and was determined to help him in every possible way'. 'My great supporter throughout,' Montgomery confirms in his *Memoirs*, 'was Alexander. He never bothered me, never fussed me, never suggested what I ought to do, and gave me at once everything I asked for – having listened patiently to my explanation of why I wanted it. But he was too big to require explanations; he gave me his trust.'

The men of Eighth Army displayed a similar trust in their leader. By the end of the North African campaign, his 'personal popularity,' says Alan Moorehead, had 'gone to fantastic lengths'. Still more important, there was also 'an almost passionate belief in him. The whole army identified itself with the general.' 'I believe they would have done anything I asked,' declares Montgomery proudly. 'They gave me their complete confidence. What more can any commander want?'

So great was this trust that the sick rate, already low enough in all conscience,[2] dropped still further when a battle was imminent. Horrocks declares that no one wanted 'to be left out' and 'on many occasions NCOs and men who had recovered from their wounds and had been sent to some reinforcement unit in the Delta escaped and thumbed lifts for over a thousand miles to rejoin their units at the front'.

In return Montgomery showed an intense loyalty towards, sympathy with and interest in those under his command, particularly if they had suffered for his sake. When de Guingand broke down after Alamein, Montgomery came to see him, encouraged his intention to marry, urged him to have a quiet honeymoon in Jerusalem and 'not rush about to parties etc.' and then, but only then, 'come back to me' – which de Guingand did just prior to Montgomery's final thrust on Tripoli. When Harding, whom Montgomery called 'that little tiger', was injured during the same thrust, Montgomery visited him in hospital and, says Harding, 'spent an hour or more telling me all that had happened since I was wounded, particularly the exploits of my old division, and of his plans for my future'. At that time it was believed that Harding had no chance 'of further active duty and Monty knew it. I shall always remember with deep gratitude,' Harding concludes, 'that act of kindness and compassion.'[3]

Nor did Montgomery show this attitude only towards trusted officers. He came to treat his army, Alan Moorehead relates, 'as a kind of family. He delighted in being with the soldiers, and he drove among them for hours every day.' He might be ungracious or ungenerous to his equals or his superiors but never to the men under his command. 'The soldiery gave of their best,' he reports. His 'only fear' was that he personally 'might fail these magnificent men'.

Yet in two instances it might be said that Montgomery did fail them. At the beginning of 1944, it was decreed that the men of Eighth Army could wear an Arabic '8' on the ribbon of the Africa Star, but this privilege was restricted to those who had fought at or after Montgomery's victory at El Alamein. It was not Montgomery's decision, but he was well aware that when he reached the Desert he took command of 'truly magnificent material' and that it was no fault of the soldiers that lasting success had previously eluded them. Moreover the decision slighted those who had won Alam Halfa, his most commendable triumph and one which, as he personally complains in *El Alamein to the River Sangro*, 'has never received the interest or attention it deserves'. At the time Montgomery had many other matters on his mind since he had just begun planning for the great invasion of Normandy. Even so it seems a pity that he should not have protested against such an invidious distinction.

And right at the end of the North African campaign, Montgomery appears to have allowed his ambition for himself and for his army to blur his normally very clear military vision. On 10 April 1943, he had signalled to Alexander suggesting that either First or Eighth Army should deliver the 'final assaults on the enemy's last positions' while the other should 'sit tight and merely exert pressure' but 'on no account must we split our effort and launch two or more thrusts none of which can be sustained.' He was probably not pleased when his superior replied on the 11th: 'Main effort in next phase will be by First Army. Preparations already well advanced.'

Alexander's decision was undoubtedly correct. First Army had an easier line of attack through country more suited to the employment of armour. Moreover Eisenhower had made it clear that for political reasons it was essential that II US Corps, which was now entrusted to Major General Omar Bradley, should take part in the culmination to the campaign. Bradley therefore skilfully transferred his corps to the northern flank of First Army, his objective being the capture of Bizerta.

Eighth Army's task was limited by Alexander to putting 'maximum pressure against Enfidaville position' to draw enemy reserves away from the First Army area. In addition having already had a number of valuable officers – Roberts for instance – sent to First Army, Montgomery now lost Briggs and his First Armoured Division plus the armoured cars of the 1st King's Dragoon Guards; they left for the northern front on 18 April. Nonetheless Montgomery still hoped that Eighth Army might do more than exert pressure; that it might be able to break through the Enfidaville position altogether and so have the honour of capturing Tunis.

The defences at Enfidaville bore a considerable resemblance to those in the Gabes Gap. There was no wadi on the eastern sector but the village of Enfidaville, about 5 miles inland, was protected by an anti-tank ditch, while beyond it the coastal strip narrowed still more to form a 'bottleneck' between the sea and another confusingly named Djebel Tebaga; this was blocked by wire, mines and a further anti-tank ditch. To the west of the coastal area was a line of hills culminating in the 1,000 foot high Djebel Garci, the equivalent of the Djebel Fatnassa at Gabes. Between the Djebel Garci and Enfidaville was the equivalent of the Djebel Roumana, the steep-sided crag of Takrouna, topped by a rocky pinnacle on which stood a few stone buildings. But the great difference between the defences at Enfidaville and those in the Gabes Gap was that behind the former was no wide fertile plain but a series of hills which ran almost all the way to Tunis. And the determination of Messe's defenders, both German and Italian, was stiffened by the knowledge that this time they would be fighting in the 'last ditch'.

Probing operations quickly showed that there was no possibility of the enemy retiring without a fight, so Montgomery delivered a full-scale attack, supported as usual by aircraft and artillery, on the night of 19th/20th April. While 7th Armoured demonstrated on the left flank and 50th Division made a subsidiary move along the coast to pin down the Young Fascists and 90th Light, 2nd New Zealand Division attacked Takrouna and 4th Indian Division attempted to seize the Djebel Garci, after which it was optimistically intended that it should strike north-eastward through the hills to take the 'bottleneck' from the rear.

These initial actions were not unreasonable – 'worth the attempt' is the way General Jackson expresses it. Unfortunately Messe was not to be caught by surprise a second time. In the face of savage resistance 4th Indian Division captured part, though not all, of the Djebel Garci, Havildar-Major Chhelu Ram of 4/6th Rajputana Rifles winning a Victoria Cross and Jemadar Dewan Singh of 1/9th Gurkhas an Indian Order of Merit.[4] 5th New Zealand Brigade took Takrouna despite heavy casualties which included every company commander of 28th Maori Battalion. The final pinnacle was captured by a Maori force of two NCOs and seven 'other ranks' 'led,' reports Horrocks, 'by a most gallant sergeant called Manahi'. 'The enemy casualties,' he adds, 'were 150 prisoners and forty to fifty killed, all by this handful of men' – of whom only four were left standing. Horrocks considers that this was 'the most gallant feat of arms I witnessed in the course of the war, and I was bitterly disappointed when Sergeant Manahi, whom we had recommended for a VC, only received a DCM'.

The valour of Eighth Army's soldiers had remained exceptional until the end. During 20 and 21 April, 50th Division captured Enfidaville and advanced a further three miles beyond it, all enemy counter-attacks were repulsed with heavy losses and the number of Axis prisoners taken rose to about 800. Yet the New Zealanders had suffered 500 casualties by this time, the Indians 550, and it seemed obvious that further progress would be both difficult and costly.

It was at this point that Montgomery's vision appears to have failed him, though in fairness it should be pointed out that he could not possibly have exercised his normal tight control over events as he had to be in Cairo from 23 to 26 April, engaged yet again in planning 'one battle ahead' – for the invasion of Sicily. In addition he was far from well and on the 27th he retired to bed with a high temperature, suffering from influenza and tonsilitis.

Probably for these reasons, Montgomery showed none of his customary flexibility but insisted that Eighth Army should continue its attempt to break through the Enfidaville position by delivering a further assault in the coastal area. To provide fresh troops for this he sent 56th (British) Division into action on the night of the 28th/29th – but only to afford one more proof that 'reinforcements, whether of men or material' could never be 'guarantors of victory'. 56th Division had come forward all the way from Iraq, one of its brigades only arriving on the 28th, and it was completely inexperienced. On the 29th, an Axis counter-attack, supported by heavy artillery fire, threw it back in disorder.

Montgomery's vision now cleared again. On his return from Cairo, Horrocks had warned him: 'Of course we can break through, but there won't be much left of your fine Eighth Army when we have done it.' Montgomery had 'merely grunted', but Horrocks had made the one point most likely to make Montgomery pause. On the 29th, all Eighth Army attacks were cancelled and Montgomery, who was still too ill to travel, asked Alexander to visit him.

On 22 April, Alexander's own main thrust in the north had begun. It was delivered on a wide front, had petered out by the 28th, and was rudely called a 'partridge drive' by Montgomery. Yet it had in fact prepared the way for the final triumph. Green, Bald and Longstop Hills were at last in Allied hands. The German tanks had been reduced to some sixty in number, almost all with 15th Panzer; while the half-dozen or so remaining with 10th or 21st Panzer were out of fuel and would in due course have to be destroyed by their own men. Ammunition was also desperately low and most of the remaining Axis warplanes were being withdrawn to Sicily.

Alexander was confident therefore that one more assault could end the campaign and there seems no doubt that when he saw Montgomery on 30 April, he intended to order a further transfer of Eighth Army personnel to the north. Yet the order never needed to be given, for Montgomery, again demonstrating the mutual understanding that existed between these two very different but very fine soldiers, offered the reinforcements unasked. The units selected, 7th Armoured Division, 4th Indian Division and 201st Guards Brigade, set out before dark that same day, the tanks being carried on transporters. They had some 300 miles to cover but with typical Eighth Army efficiency the move was completed in only two days.

Montgomery had again recovered brilliantly from a set-back. As at Mareth he proposed to set in train a 'Left Hook' and it is clear from the account of Air Vice-Marshal Broadhurst, who was present at the meeting between Alexander and Montgomery, that the Eighth Army Commander had decided exactly what was to be done. Nigel Hamilton quotes Broadhurst as revealing that Alexander had intended another attack on a broad front, but Montgomery retorted that this would suit the Germans, since they had 'no transport, no petrol'. He urged instead that Alexander 'pick the best place and then overwhelm it . . . you'll be through in 48 hours.'

Alexander, to his credit, appreciated the advice. Without even consulting Eisenhower, he made prompt preparations for an assault in the 'best place' – the Medjerda valley. The Eighth Army units were added to the British 6th Armoured and 4th Infantry Divisions in IX Corps to which Alexander proposed to entrust the main blow. Its commander was also supplied by Eighth Army, for Lieutenant General Crocker had been injured during a weapons demonstration and Montgomery, rejecting Alexander's suggestion that Freyberg be appointed, had recommended Horrocks for the task in the belief that his experiences in the Tebaga Gap would prove invaluable. It is worth noting incidentally that Montgomery clearly bore no resentment towards Horrocks over the latter's forthright criticism of the Enfidaville operation.

So at 0300 on 6 May, it was Horrocks who watched with satisfaction as a tremendous artillery bombardment fell on the enemy defences in the Medjerda area, almost annihilating 15th Panzer's 115th Motorized Infantry Regiment. 'I never felt so confident about any battle before or after,' he relates; adding that he was 'fortunate to be in command of a battle in which victory was a foregone conclusion'. The 4th (British) Division did experience some difficulties but 4th Indian, at a cost of only some 100 casualties, had broken through the Axis positions by 0730; a series of heavy air attacks starting at dawn helped to paralyse the defenders; and by 1000, 7th Armoured was already thrusting out beyond the ground gained by the infantry. By noon, 6th Armoured had also broken through and, says Horrocks, 'the tanks were grinding their way forward down the valley towards Tunis.'

Even now the Axis soldiers showed their mettle. 15th Panzer temporarily checked the advance around the village of Massicault – but the odds were too great and by evening the last of the German armour had been wiped out. Nonetheless the British tank commanders decided to halt for the night while the supporting infantry joined them. Next day they moved on, only to be held up again near St Cyprien by those old adversaries, the German anti-tank guns. But by the afternoon the last obstacles had been overcome and at about 1545 on 7 May, the leading British armoured cars entered Tunis.

Which armoured cars has remained a matter of dispute. Horrocks tactfully states that the 11th Hussars from 7th Armoured and the Derbyshire Yeomanry from 6th Armoured 'entered Tunis by different routes at exactly the same moment'. Liddell Hart says they 'entered almost simultaneously' but gives the prize to the 11th Hussars. De Guingand thinks that the 11th Hussars was 'probably' the first unit in, while Montgomery, always loyal to his Eighth Army, has no doubt of it. Nor, it should be said, has Paul Carell who may be regarded as reasonably impartial. Incidentally, he refers to 'Montgomery's 11th Hussars' and Major General Erskine the Commander of 7th Armoured would write to the Eighth Army Commander next day, telling him that 'we are all very proud to have been your representative here to finish the job'.

The men of Eighth Army, even if temporarily under First Army command, had deserved this honour. Over the next few days they and their erstwhile comrades still under Eighth Army's control gained the reward for their months of toil. 7th Armoured, swinging north from Tunis, attacked the remnants of von Vaerst's Fifth Panzer Army which had evacuated Bizerta on 7 May. During the 8th, 11th Hussars took 10,000 prisoners. In the early morning of the 9th, it took 9,000 more and von Vaerst was reporting to von

Arnim that he was 'without ammunition and fuel'. Though he added 'we shall fight to the last', not even the Germans could fight with no ammunition and by midday his remaining men had capitulated.

South of Tunis, 6th Armoured Division cut across the base of the Cape Bon Penninsula to prevent any retirement there by the surviving Axis soldiers – though their shortage of fuel would probably have prevented this in any case. On 12 May, 4th Indian Division claimed the capture of von Arnim who surrendered to Lieutenant Colonel Glennie, CO of 1st Royal Sussex. At Enfidaville on the two previous days, Freyberg had demanded the surrender of 90th Light but Graf von Sponeck, though repeatedly attacked by the Desert Air Force's light bombers, had refused to comply.

At midday on the 13th, however, Messe, who had just been made a Field Marshal – a promotion well earned by his earlier stubborn resistance, if scarcely appropriate in its timing – ordered his First Italian Army to give up the fight. Then he personally hurried south to ensure that his own capitulation should be received by the renowned Eighth Army, not by the forces closing in from the rear. Like von Thoma before him, he dined with Montgomery and 'we discussed various aspects of the battles we had fought against each other'. Ronald Lewin watched 90th Light surrender, seeing 'the white flags go up: first in small clusters, turning into larger groups as platoons merged with companies. White everywhere as if butterflies were dancing over the hills. It had been a long haul from Alamein, and exhilaration predominated. But there was a sense of compassion too: this had been a good enemy.'

Estimates of the final total of prisoners vary widely. Eisenhower and Alexander were both to give it as 250,000 but it seems their claims were somewhat exaggerated. The number of men in prisoner-of-war camps was later stated at over 238,000 but this no doubt included many who had been taken earlier. Liddell Hart reports that the Axis powers assessed their own strength in early May at between 170,000 and 180,000 men but their records may well have become incomplete in the prevailing confusion. General Fraser believes that 'over 100,000 German soldiers passed into Allied captivity – a greater number than taken at Stalingrad a few months before – and nearly 90,000 Italian.'

In any case it mattered little. The main point was that Alexander could signal to Churchill: 'All enemy resistance has ceased. We are masters of the North African shores.' Even after Stalingrad the Germans could and did hit back in Russia. From this defeat there could be and was no recovery. Never again would the Allies be threatened in North Africa. Instead from North Africa the Allies could threaten the Axis powers with fresh assaults. 'In the six months since the break-out at Alamein,' declares General Fraser, 'the British Army had ridden a turning tide of war. Norway, Dunkirk, Gazala and

Singapore could be put aside as nightmares. Ahead, in the new dawn, lay the coasts of Europe.'

And in Eighth Army, 'the soldiers,' says Alan Moorehead, 'stripped off their uniforms, washed and fell asleep in the sunshine.'

Notes

1   Quoted in General Fraser's biography *Alanbrooke*.
2   By the time Tripoli was captured the sick rate in Eighth Army had fallen to one man in every thousand. By the time the central Tunisian plain was reached it was only a fraction more than one man in every two thousand.
3   Harding was speaking on the occasion of the unveiling of a memorial window to Montgomery in Sandhurst Chapel on 30 October 1977. The full text of his address can be found in *Monty at Close Quarters: Recollections of the Man*.
4   A havildar-major was a sergeant-major; a jamadar, a junior Viceroy's Commissioned Officer.

BIBLIOGRAPHY

ALEXANDER, Field Marshal the Earl, 'The African Campaign from El Alamein to Tunis', London Gazette Supplement, 1948.

ALEXANDER, Field Marshal the Earl, *The Alexander Memoirs*, Cassell, 1962.

ARNOLD-FORSTER, Mark, *The World at War*, Collins, 1973.

AUCHINLECK, Field Marshal Sir Claude, 'Operations in Middle East 1.11.41 to 15.8.42', London Gazette Supplement, 1948.

BEHRENDT, Hans-Otto, *Rommel's Intelligence in the Desert Campaign*, Kimber, 1985.

BRYANT, Sir Arthur, *The Turn of the Tide 1939–1943*, Collins, 1959.

CARELL, Paul, *The Foxes of the Desert: The Story of the Afrika Korps*, Macdonalds, 1960.

CARVER, Field Marshal Lord, *Dilemmas of the Desert War: A New Look at the Libyan Campaign 1940–1942*, Batsford, 1986.

CARVER, Field Marshal Lord, *El Alamein*, Batsford, 1962.

CARVER, Field Marshal Lord, *Out of Step (Memoirs)*, Hutchinson, 1989.

CARVER, Field Marshal Lord, *Tobruk*, Batsford, 1964.

CHURCHILL, Sir Winston, *The Second World War*, Volume IV: *The Hinge of Fate*, Cassell, 1951.

CONNELL, John, *Auchinleck*, Cassell, 1959.

COWLES, Virginia, *The Phantom Major: The Story of David Stirling and the SAS Regiment*, Collins, 1958.

DE GUINGAND, Major General Sir Francis, *Generals at War*, Hodder & Stoughton, 1964.

DE GUINGAND, Major General Sir Francis, *Operation Victory*, Hodder & Stoughton, 1947.

FRASER, General Sir David, *Alanbrooke*, Collins, 1982.

FRASER, General Sir David, *And We Shall Shock Them: The British Army in the Second World War*, Hodder & Stoughton, 1983.

FULLER, Major General J.F.C., *The Decisive Battles of the Western World*, Volume III, Eyre & Spottiswoode, 1957.

FULLER, Major General J.F.C., *The Second World War 1939–1945*, Eyre & Spottiswoode, 1948 (Revised Edition 1954).

HAMILTON, Nigel, *Monty: The Battles of Field Marshal Bernard Law Montgomery*, Hodder & Stoughton, 1994.

HAMILTON, Nigel, *Monty: The Making of a General 1887–1942*, Hamish Hamilton, 1981.

HAMILTON, Nigel, *Monty: Master of the Battlefield 1942–1944*, Hamish Hamilton, 1983.

HINSLEY, F.H. with THOMAS, E.E., RANSOM, C.F.G. and KNIGHT, R.C., *British Intelligence in the Second World War: Its Influence on Strategy and Operations*, Volume II, HMSO, 1981.

HORROCKS, Lieutenant General Sir Brian, *A Full Life*, Collins, 1960.

HOWARTH, T.E.B. (Edited), *Monty at Close Quarters: Recollections of the Man*. Articles by: HARDING, Field Marshal Lord: 'In Memoriam'; WILLIAMS, Brigadier Sir Edgar: 'Gee One Eye, Sir', Leo Cooper, 1985.

JACKSON, General Sir William, *The North African Campaign 1940–43*, Batsford, 1975.

KESSELRING, Field Marshal Albert, *Memoirs*, Kimber, 1963.

KIPPENBERGER, Major General Sir Howard, *Infantry Brigadier*, Oxford University Press, 1949.

LEWIN, Ronald, *The Life and Death of the Afrika Korps*, Batsford, 1977.

LEWIN, Ronald, *Montgomery as Military Commander*, Batsford, 1971.

LEWIN, Ronald, *Rommel as Military Commander*, Batsford, 1968.

LEWIN, Ronald, *Ultra Goes to War: The Secret Story*, Hutchinson, 1978.

LIDDELL HART, Captain B.H., *History of the Second World War*, Cassell, 1970.

LIDDELL HART, Captain B.H., *The Tanks: The History of the Royal Tank Regiment and its Predecessors*, Cassell, 1959.

LLEWELLYN, Harry, *Passports to Life: Journeys into Many Worlds*, Hutchinson, 1980.

LUCAS PHILLIPS, Brigadier, C.E., *Alamein*, Heinemann, 1962.

MACINTYRE, Captain Donald, *The Battle for the Mediterranean*, Batsford, 1964.

MAJDALANY, Fred, *The Battle of El Alamein*, Weidenfeld & Nicolson, 1965.

MASTERS, David, *With Pennants Flying: The Immortal Deeds of the Royal Armoured Corps*, Eyre & Spottiswoode, 1943.

MELLENTHIN, Major General F.W. von, *Panzer Battles*, Cassell, 1955.

MONTGOMERY, Field Marshal the Viscount, *El Alamein to the River Sangro*, Hutchinson, 1948.

MONTGOMERY, Field Marshal the Viscount, *Memoirs*, Collins, 1958.

MOOREHEAD, Alan, *The Desert War: The North African Campaign 1940–1943*, Hamish Hamilton, 1965.

NICOLSON, Nigel, *Alex: The Life of Field Marshal Earl Alexander of Tunis*, Weidenfeld & Nicolson, 1973.

OWEN, Roderic, *The Desert Air Force*, Hutchinson, 1948.

PENIAKOFF, Lieutenant Colonel Vladimir, *Popski's Private Army*, Jonathan Cape, 1950.

PLAYFAIR, Major General I.S.O. with FLYNN, Captain F.C., MOLONY,

Brigadier C.J.C. and GLEAVE, Group Captain T.P., *The Mediterranean and Middle East*, Volume III: *British Fortunes Reach their Lowest Ebb*, HMSO, 1960.

PLAYFAIR, Major General I.S.O. and MOLONY, Brigadier C.J.C. with FLYNN, Captain F.C. and GLEAVE, Group Captain T.P., *The Mediterranean and Middle East*, Volume IV: *The Destruction of the Axis Forces in Africa*, HMSO, 1966.

RICHARDS, Denis and SAUNDERS, Hilary St G., *Royal Air Force 1939–1945*, Volume II: *The Fight Avails*, HMSO, 1954.

RICHARDSON, General Sir Charles, *Flashback: A Soldier's Story*, Kimber, 1985.

RICHARDSON, General Sir Charles, *From Churchill's Secret Circle to the BBC: The Biography of Lieutenant General Sir Ian Jacob*, Brasseys (UK), 1991.

RICHARDSON, General Sir Charles, *Send for Freddie: The Story of Montgomery's Chief of Staff, Major General Sir Francis de Guingand*, Kimber, 1987.

ROBERTS, Major General G.P.B., *From the Desert to the Baltic*, Kimber, 1987.

ROMMEL, Field Marshal Erwin (Edited by LIDDELL HART, Captain B.H.), *The Rommel Papers*, Collins, 1953.

ROSKILL, Captain S.W., *The War at Sea 1939–1945*, Volume II: *The Period of Balance*, HMSO, 1956.

RYDER, Rowland, *Oliver Leese*, Hamish Hamilton, 1987.

SHORES, Christopher and RING, Hans, *Fighters over the Desert: The Air Battles in the Western Desert June 1940–December 1942*, Neville Spearman, 1969.

SHORES, Christopher, RING, Hans, and HESS, William N., *Fighters over Tunisia*, Neville Spearman, 1975.

SMITH, Peter C., *Pedestal: The Malta Convoy of August 1942*, Kimber, 1970.

STEWART, Adrian, *Hurricane: The War Exploits of the Fighter Aircraft*, Kimber, 1982.

STRAWSON, Major General Sir John, *The Battle for North Africa*, Batsford, 1969.

War Diaries of GHQ Middle East, Eighth Army, X Corps, XIII Corps, XXX Corps and individual divisions and brigades in Eighth Army, Public Record Office, Kew.

INDEX OF EIGHTH ARMY
FORMATIONS AND UNITS

GENERAL INDEX